Religious Freedom in Israel and the Occupied Palestinian Territory: Selected Issues

A Report to the United States Commission on International Religious Freedom

Palestine Works

Editors
Omar Yousef Shehabi
Dr. Sara Husseini
Hady Matar
Emma Borden

Contributors
Jessica Boulet
Dario D'Ambrosio
Lojain al-Mouallimi
John Pino
Helena van Roosbroeck
Andrew Udelsman

ISBN: 0692688242
ISBN-13: 978-0692688243

Published by Palestine Works Inc.
1875 Connecticut Avenue NW, 10th Floor
Washington, District of Columbia 20009
United States of America

PALESTINE WORKS

Palestine Works is a U.S.-based §501(c)(3) nonprofit organization founded in 2012 to promote Palestinian human rights and human development. Our vision is a Palestinian society that can enjoy the improved prospects and economic, social and political benefits of a strong economy, one powered by the development and deployment of Palestinian human capital. Our mission is to help realize this vision by engaging, developing and harnessing the expertise of young professionals through the creation of high-impact knowledge exchange opportunities, including internships, legal advocacy projects, conferences, publications and networking.

CONTENTS

DETAILED TABLE OF CONTENTS

1
INTRODUCTION

This report addresses the state of religious freedom in Israel and the occupied Palestinian territory (oPt). Its aim is to inform the United States Commission on International Religious Freedom (USCIRF or Commission) of select religious freedom violations committed in the territory under Israeli control. This report is not a comprehensive review of religious freedom in Israel and the oPt. Rather, it analyzes certain religious freedom practices in accordance with the Commission's precedent and accepted standards of freedom of thought, conscience, religion or belief, as defined in international human right instruments.

USCIRF staff visited Israel in preparation of the first Annual Report on International Religious Freedom in 1999, yet the Commission, in its 15-year history, has not issued any report, brief, or press release referencing the State of Israel or its responsibilities to uphold religious freedom. [1]

In May 2014, on the occasion of Pope Francis' visit to Israel and the oPt, the Commission issued a press release condemning and urging accountability for so-called 'price tag' attacks by Israeli-Jewish extremists against Palestinian individuals, homes, property, and religious institutions.[2] Such attacks are widespread: the Israeli NGO Yesh Din documented 1,104 such cases between 2005 and 2015, consisting of 580 suspected property offenses (including attacks on holy places[3]), 380 suspected acts of physical violence by Israeli civilians towards Palestinians, and 160 seizures or attempts to seize Palestinian-owned land.[4] Of these cases, 940 investigation files (91.6%) were closed without an indictment being issued against the suspects.[5]

Yet the Commission's press release on price tag attacks failed to identity the perpetrators, the victims, the responsible state or its religious freedom obligations. The Commission thus broke from its practice of urging the state to undertake an investigation in cases of violence by private actors against religious minorities, as it did in similar cases with Egypt and Pakistan.[6] Conversely, the Commission's press release condemning the November 2014 armed attack at a West Jerusalem synagogue identified the perpetrators as Palestinians.[7]

The USCIRF met with the Latin Patriarch of Jerusalem, His Beatitude Fouad Twal, on July 22, 2014. The Latin Patriarch is the Roman Catholic Archbishop of Jerusalem, whose jurisdiction covers Palestine, Israel, Jordan, and Cyprus, with a total congregation of over 160,000 Roman Catholics. His Beatitude addressed the Commission during Israel's "Operation Protection Edge" in Gaza, which claimed over 2,200 Palestinian lives, including at least 1,483 civilians and 521 children; and 71 Israeli lives, including four civilians.[8] His Beatitude expressed grave concern over the vast number of casualties and the allegations of excessive force in the ongoing hostilities. He also expressed concern over various forms of Israeli interference with the religious freedom of his congregation, including:

- construction of the Separation Wall in the Cremisan Valley and its impact on the ministry of the local Salesian Order, which operates a monastery, convent, and elementary school in Cremisan;

- restrictions on freedom of movement for clergy between Israel, the oPt, and Jordan;

- initiatives to introduce 'Christian' as a 'nationality' on the Israeli national ID and to enlist Christian Palestinians in military and national service; and

- continued failure to implement the Israel-Vatican Fundamental Agreement, including the failure to conclude an agreement on Church property rights and taxation.[9]

His Beatitude invited the Commission to Jerusalem as his guests.[10] The Commission wrote privately to thank His Beatitude and promised to consider "the challenges faced by the Christian community in the Holy Land" in its future sessions. Yet the Commission issued no public communications regarding the meeting, nor visited Israel and the oPt to investigate the issues raised therein.

CONTEXT

The contested territory of Israel/Palestine is inhabited by Jewish Israelis and Palestinians. The Palestinian population is comprised of Christian and Muslims and includes both Palestinian citizens of Israel and non-citizen residents of the oPt. Jewish Israelis and Palestinians constitute distinct ethnoreligious communities for purposes of international human rights law and the IRFA, as explored in chapter 2, *infra*.

Jews are unquestionably an ethnoreligious group based on descent, ethnic or national origin, and religion. Whether Jewish identity should be premised on its national dimension or its religious dimension is a longstanding, unresolved tension in Israeli society and law.

Palestinian identity is based principally on national origin – familial roots in historic Palestine – and is distinguished from the wider Arab "nation" to which they belong through that connection to the homeland. While religion is not the defining feature of Palestinian identity, Israeli state discrimination against Palestinians, including Palestinian citizens of Israel, is based on their non-Jewish identity and is therefore a clear religious freedom issue. To suggest that such discrimination is based on citizenship rather than religion or national origin is tautological because, if Palestinians were Jews, they would be entitled to Israeli citizenship as a matter of right under the Law of Return (discussed in chapter 2, *infra*).

Accordingly, as used in this report, "Palestinians" refer to Palestinian Muslims and Christians, whether citizens or non-citizens of the State of Israel. "Jewish Israelis" refer to Israeli citizens who are considered members of the Jewish "nationality" (Hebrew: *le'om*), including persons who are not considered Jews by rabbinical tradition (i.e. matrilineal descent). "Israelis" refer to all persons with Israeli citizenship, including both Jewish Israelis and Palestinian citizens of Israel.

ISSUES SELECTED AND ANALYZED

This report examines selected religious freedom violations occurring in the territory under Israeli control. As argued herein, these violations are not isolated, but are structural features of the Israeli ethnocracy, a regime which "promotes the expansion of the dominant group in contested territories and its domination of power structures while maintaining a democratic facade."[11]

These religious freedom violations are arranged and analyzed herein as follows:

- Privileging Jewish Israeli citizens and Jewish national, religious and territorial claims by:

    o Denying citizenship to Palestinians in the 1967 occupied territory.

    o Denying Jewish national rights to Palestinian citizens of Israel, including access to land and certain public benefits.

    o Promoting maximalist Jewish claims to the Al-Aqsa Mosque Compound/Temple Mount.

    o Discriminating against non-Jewish communities in the protection and administration of holy places.

    o Imposing arbitrary or discriminatory restrictions on visas for clergy and lay religious workers.

- Preserving this system of ethnoreligious control by:

    o Facilitating religious discrimination in public and private affairs through national IDs that disclose religious affiliation.

    o Insisting upon the unity of Jewish identity by: refusing to recognize a secular Israeli nationality; preserving Orthodox control over personal status matters of non-Orthodox Jews, including marriage, child registration, and religious conversion; and discouraging proselytism and tolerating harassment and incitement against evangelical faiths by anti-assimilation and anti-miscegenation groups.

- Promoting the fragmentation of Arab Palestinian identity by:

  o Recognizing an Aramean national minority that objectively does not exist as a way to distinguish and divide Palestinian Christian citizens of Israel from the larger Palestinian nation.

  o Denying Arab Palestinian Druze citizens of Israel the right to conscientiously object to serving against fellow Arab Palestinians.

STANDING

Palestine Works is a U.S.-based nongovernmental organization that is active in the field of human rights in Israel and the oPt through partnerships with various Palestinian and Israeli human rights organizations. Section 102(c)(2) of the International Religious Freedom Act of 1998 (IRFA) provides that:

> [i]n compiling data and assessing the respect of the right to religious freedom for the Human Rights Reports, the Annual Report on International Religious Freedom, and the Executive Summary, United States mission personnel shall, as appropriate, seek out and maintain contacts with religious and human rights nongovernment organizations, with the consent of these organizations, including receiving reports and updates from these organizations and, when appropriate, investigating such reports.[12]

Concurrently with the submission of this report, Palestine Works has requested a meeting with the Commission to discuss the issues raised herein.

SCOPE OF REPORT

The subject of this report is Israel's compliance with its international human rights and religious freedom obligations in all territory, and vis-à-vis all populations, under its control. The compliance of the Palestinian Authority and the *de facto* authorities (the Hamas government) in Gaza are outside the Commission's mandate and beyond the scope of this report. Additionally, this report breaks from the State Department's practice of disaggregating Israel's practices within its recognized borders from its practices as an occupying power in the oPt. As discussed herein, the more relevant distinction for purposes of religious freedom is drawn between Jews and non-Jews, and specifically between Jewish Israelis and Muslim and

Christian Palestinians, regardless of their citizenship or place of residence.

Scope of Israeli Responsibility

Under international law, Israel is responsible for upholding religious freedom in all territory under its control, including the oPt.

Israel's obligations as an occupying power under international humanitarian law (IHL) towards the civilian Palestinian population of the oPt are absolute, non-derogable and non-delegable.[13] These obligations include respecting the religious convictions and practices of the civilian population and maintaining, unless absolutely prevented, the laws, institutions, infrastructure, and physical character of the occupied territory. The Oslo Accords, which established the PA in 1994, delegated certain responsibilities for civil affairs and internal security over limited parts of the oPt from the Israeli military government to the PA. However, the Accords did not alter Israel's status as an occupying power; all powers and responsibilities not expressly delegated to the PA were retained by the Israeli military government.[14] The protections afforded by IHL to the civilian population of the occupied territory cannot be delegated, derogated from, or waived by agreement between the occupying power and the authorities of the occupied territory.[15] Thus, the Accords did not, and lawfully could not have, delegated or waived Israel's IHL obligations.

Further, Israel's obligations under international human rights law extend to all territory and persons under its effective control, including Palestinians in areas living under PA jurisdiction. The principal organs of the United Nations have consistently reaffirmed these principles.[16]

The Commission's precedent is consistent with these principles. The USCIRF has consistently held Turkey responsible for violations in areas of the Republic of Cyprus under the control of Turkish military forces and administered by Turkish Cypriot authorities. Relying on European Court of Human Rights precedent, the Commission determined that whatever "degree of autonomy" the local Turkish Cypriot authorities (i.e. the government of the self-declared "Turkish Republic of Northern Cyprus") possessed vis-à-vis Turkey, it remained that "Turkey as an occupying power is responsible for its actions and those of its 'subordinate local administration' in the northern part of Cyprus."[17]

Similarly, the Commission holds Russia accountable for violations of religious freedom in occupied Crimea and regions of eastern Ukraine controlled by Russian-supported separatists. In declaring Russia an occupying power in Crimea and holding it responsible for Crimea's deteriorating religious freedom, the Commission ignored the unilateral declaration of independence of the "Republic of Crimea" and subsequent referendum on annexation by Russia. Thus, the Commission considered Russia's annexation of Crimea to have no legal effect, describing the situation as an "illegal military occupation."[18] In a 2015 op-ed, Commissioners Rev. Thomas Reese and Dr. Daniel Mark asserted that "there is no question that Russia bears the responsibility" for religious freedom violations in occupied Crimea.[19] On that basis, the Commission's 2015 Report condemned the extension of Russian law in a variety of areas that affect religious freedom, including more onerous clergy visa restrictions and registration requirements for religious communities.[20]

Following this precedent, the Commission must recognize that Israel's administration of the oPt, including East Jerusalem, is governed by the law of belligerent occupation. As discussed in chapter 3, *infra*, Israel's changes since 1967 to status, character, and landscape of the oPt, particularly East Jerusalem and its Holy Places, far exceed the limits set by the law of occupation, with significant consequences for the religious freedom of non-Jewish religious communities. Accordingly, consistent with the Commission's precedent, this report considers Israel's religious freedom record with respect to all territory and all populations under its control.

Palestinian Duty-Bearers

The Palestinian Authority and the Hamas government in Gaza unquestionably bear a duty to uphold religious freedom within the territory and competences that they control. Here it should be noted that many of the sensitive religious sites in the oPt are not under PA control, including all of the holy sites in the Old City of Jerusalem, the Ibrahimi Mosque (Tomb of the Patriarchs) in Hebron, and Rachel's Tomb in Bethlehem. Indeed, in April 2014, the State of Palestine acceded without reservations to the core UN human rights treaties, including the ICCPR.[21]

However, because the United States does not recognize a Palestinian state, the religious freedom records of the PLO/PA and the Hamas government in Gaza are outside the Commission's mandate under the IRFA and thus beyond the scope of this report. The U.S. Government denies that Palestine fulfills the requirements of statehood, and opposes any acts that imply recognition of a Palestinian state.[22] The IRFA mandates the Commission to "consider and recommend options for policies of the United States Government with respect to each *foreign country* the government of which has engaged in or tolerated violations of religious freedom...."[23] U.S. federal courts have repeatedly held that in deference to the Government's position, Palestine cannot be considered a foreign state for purposes of the Foreign Sovereign Immunities Act.[24] Thus, the PLO/PA and the Hamas government in Gaza do not come within the Commission's mandate or the scope of this report.

METHODOLOGY

Because Israel is responsible for guaranteeing religious freedom in all territory and vis-à-vis all populations under its control, this report, unlike the State Department's human rights ("HR report") and international religious freedom ("IRF report") reports, does not consider Israel's practices within its recognized borders separately from its practices as an occupying power in the occupied Palestinian territories (oPt).

The State Department's practice of considering the oPt separately from Israel is not a principled distinction, but reflects the division of labor between the U.S. Embassy in Tel Aviv, which prepares the Israel sections, and the U.S. Consulate-Jerusalem, which prepares the "Occupied Territories" section.[25] As a consequence of this artificial distinction, the State Department's Israel reports virtually ignore Israel's treatment of the Palestinian population in the oPt, which is outside of the Embassy's jurisdiction. The Occupied Territories sections intermingle violations committed by Israel, the PA, and the Hamas government in Gaza, without reference to Israel's status as an occupying power, or to the PA's status as a representative of the occupied population, operating under a limited delegation of authority by the occupying power.[26]

Indeed, while the State Department identifies the oPt as the "Occupied Territories," neither the 2013 Religious Freedom Report nor the 2014 Human Rights Report makes reference to the occupation, Israel's obligations as an occupying power under international humanitarian law, or the illegality of settlements under international law. The 2013 Religious Freedom Report states that "Israel exercises varying degrees of legal, military, and economic control in the Occupied Territories," while the 2014 Human Rights Report observes that "[t]he PA exercised varying degrees of authority in restricted areas of the West Bank due to the Israel Defense Forces' (IDF) *continuing presence*, and none over Arab residents of East Jerusalem *due to Israel's extension of Israeli law and authority to East Jerusalem in 1967.*"[27] Furthermore, the 2013 Religious Freedom Report observes that "[t]he PA does not provide financial support to Jewish institutions in the West Bank,"[28] a curious statement given that the Jewish population of the West Bank is comprised almost exclusively of Israeli settlers whose residence in the oPt is illegal under international law and "illegitimate" as a matter of United States policy.[29] Today, the settler population is estimated at 547,000, representing nearly nine percent of Israel's Jewish population, is growing at a rate two and a half times faster than that of the overall population in Israel, and integrated legally and physically into Israel's recognized territory.[30] The Green Line, as a political boundary, now serves only to differentiate citizen and noncitizen Palestinians within the Israeli control system.

Differentiating Israel's practices within its recognized borders from its practices in the oPt is untenable because Israel does not uphold such a distinction in its laws, policies, and practices. Israel has legislatively granted itself the right to extend Israeli law, jurisdiction, and administration to "any area of *Eretz Israel* [Mandatory Palestine] designated by the Government by order."[31] It has exercised that authority in East Jerusalem and the Golan Heights, and reserves the right to exercise such authority over the entirety of the oPt, at its sole discretion. Indeed, in the 2004 cabinet resolution authorizing the Gaza "disengagement," the Israeli government declared its intention to annex further parts of the West Bank, including existing settlements, security areas, and "other places of special interest to Israel."[32] Further, Israel has extended its domestic law to various activities in the oPt through its exercise of personal jurisdiction over Israeli settlers,[33] effectively establishing separate legal systems for Israeli Jews and Palestinians within a single territory,[34] an arrangement increasingly identified as apartheid.[35]

Applicable Law

International Religious Freedom Act of 1998 (IRFA)

The International Religious Freedom Act of 1998 (IRFA) defines "violations of religious freedom" as "violations of the internationally recognized right to freedom of religion and religious belief and practice, as set forth in" the international human rights instruments identified in the Act and "as described in" Article 18 ICCPR.[36] Some of these human rights instruments are legally binding treaties, including the UN Charter, ICCPR, and European Convention on Human Rights. The other instruments are non-binding declarations, including the UDHR, UN General Assembly Declaration on the Elimination of All Forms of Intolerance and of Discrimination Based on Religion or Belief ("1981 UN Declaration"), and Helsinki Accords. By including non-binding instruments, "the Act adopts an expansive view of freedom of religion and belief, encompassing both settled conventional and customary international law and extending even further to include *lex ferenda* and non-binding political commitments."[37] The Commission may thus consider political commitments made by Israel and the PLO in the Oslo Accords, including the commitments to respect the status of the West Bank and Gaza as a single territorial unit and to abstain from measures during the Oslo-governed interim period that would prejudice final status negotiations[38]; as well as additional commitments made during the U.S.-sponsored peace process, including the commitment to facilitate the normal functioning of Palestinian institutions in East Jerusalem.[39]

The human rights instruments that define "violations of religious freedom" under the IRFA establish four basic religious freedom norms:

- right to freedom of thought, conscience and religion;

- right to equal protection of the law, including prohibition of discrimination based on religion;

- right of persons belonging to religious minorities to profess and practice their religion;

- right to protection from incitement to discrimination, hostility or violence based on religion.[40]

The IRFA further includes, as violations of religious freedom, other violations of human rights law if motivated by religious animus.[41]

International Law

The ICJ's 2004 advisory opinion on the *Legal Consequences of the Construction of a Wall in the Occupied Palestinian Territory* represents a definitive pronouncement of the legal framework governing Israel's administration of the oPt, including East Jerusalem. This law is outlined briefly below.

International Humanitarian Law (IHL)

The ICJ ruled that, in addition to the 1907 Hague Regulations,[42] which Israel recognizes as binding as a matter of customary international law, its occupation of the oPt, in its entirety, is governed by Geneva Convention (IV), which Israel ratified in 1951.[43] The Court thereby rejected conclusively Israel's arguments denying the applicability of Geneva Convention (IV) to the West Bank, including East Jerusalem, and affirmed numerous UNSC resolutions asserting its applicability.[44]

Under IHL, Israel, as the occupying power, has the following obligations to the Palestinian population of the oPt that relate to religious freedom:

- ensure respect for "religious convictions and practices" [Hague art. 46/GC IV art. 27];

- allowing individuals "to practise their religion and to receive spiritual assistance from ministers of their faith" [GC (IV) art. 38];

- "permit ministers of religion to give spiritual assistance to the members of their religious communities" [GC (IV) art. 58];

- refrain from denying protected persons of these and other rights protected under Geneva Convention (IV) "by any change

introduced, as the result of the occupation of a territory, into the institutions or government of the said territory, nor by any agreement concluded between the authorities of the occupied territories and the Occupying Power, nor by any annexation by the latter of the whole or part of the occupied territory"
[GC (IV) art. 47].

Human Rights Law

The ICJ ruled that Israel's obligations under the international human rights treaties it has ratified, including the ICCPR, extend to all persons and territory under its jurisdiction, including Palestinian residents of the oPt.[45] The Court further reiterated the complementarity between IHL and human rights law.[46] The European Court of Human Rights has recognized this complementarity in ruling that movement restrictions on Greek Cypriots in northern Cyprus imposed by Turkish occupying forces, which limited access to places of worship and participation in other aspects of religious life, violated their freedom of thought, conscience, and religion under art. 9 ECHR.[47] Thus, in addition to IHL, Israel's administration of the oPt must be evaluated according to the complete set of human rights norms embodied in the IRFA.

Peremptory Norms (Jus Cogens)

Peremptory norms are the core prevailing norms of customary international law upon which the international system is premised.[48] They are recognized as absolutely binding by the international community, and no derogation from these norms is permitted. Among the *jus cogens* norms relevant to Israel's administration of the oPt are the obligation to respect the right of self-determination;[49] the corresponding prohibitions on the acquisition of territory, and the establishment and maintenance of colonial domination, by force;[50] and the prohibition on institutionalized and systematic racial segregation and apartheid.[51]

The ICJ held in its 2004 advisory opinion that by constructing the Wall, Israel breached its obligation to respect the Palestinian people's right of self-determination in the entirety of the 1967 occupied territory. Subsequently, two UN Special Rapporteurs on the situation of human rights in the oPt, John Dugard and Richard Falk, called (in their official capacities) for a referral to the ICJ for an advisory opinion on the question of whether "elements of the [Israeli] occupation constitute forms of colonialism and apartheid."[52] Falk analyzed that question at length in his 2014 final report, which concluded that the systemic human rights violations engendered by Israel's occupation of the oPt seek to maintain domination over the Palestinian population, and thus meet the legal definition of the crime of apartheid:

> None of the human rights violations discussed in the context of possibly constituting "inhuman acts" for the purpose of the [Apartheid Convention] or the Rome Statute [of the International Criminal Court] can be said to be isolated events. Rather, their commission reflects systematic and discriminatory Israeli policies, laws and practices, which determine where in the occupied land Palestinians may or may not travel, live and work. Laws and policies have also institutionalized just how lightly a civilian Palestinian life may be weighed, when placed on the scales against claims of overarching security concerns, contrasting with the legal protection of the Israeli constitutional system given to unlawful Israeli settlers. The combined effect of the measures designed to ensure security for Israeli citizens, to facilitate and expand settlements, and, it would appear, to annex land, is *hafrada* [separation], discrimination and systematic oppression of, and domination over, the Palestinian people.

> Through prolonged occupation, with practices and policies which appear to constitute apartheid and segregation, ongoing expansion of settlements, and continual construction of the wall arguably amounting to de facto annexation of parts of the occupied Palestinian territory, the denial by Israel of the right to self-determination of the Palestinian people is evident.[53]

Israeli Law

Freedom of religion in Mandatory Palestine was guaranteed by a 1922 law, which remains in effect in Israel and which provided in part:

> All persons in Palestine shall enjoy full liberty of conscience, and the free exercise of their forms of worship subject only to the maintenance of public order and morals.[54]

From Israel's establishment in 1948 through the start of its "constitutional revolution" in 1992, most basic human rights, including freedom of religion, were considered part of Israeli common law and developed by means of judicial rulings.[55] This arrangement was described by Justice

Aharon Barak in a 1984 Supreme Court decision:

> Every person in Israel enjoys freedom of conscience, of belief, of religion, and of worship. This freedom is guaranteed to every person in every enlightened democratic regime, and therefore it is guaranteed to every person in Israel. It is one of the fundamental principles upon which the State of Israel is based .... This freedom is partly based on Article 83 of the Palestine Order in Council of 1922, and partly it is one of those fundamental rights which are not written in the book but derive directly from the nature of our State as a peace-loving democratic State .... On the basis of these rules – and in accordance with the Declaration of Independence – every law and every power will be interpreted as recognizing freedom of conscience, of belief, of religion and of worship....[56]

The Basic Law: Human Dignity and Liberty and the Basic Law: Freedom of Occupation, enacted in 1992, codified the quasi-constitutional status of certain human rights. A more comprehensive Basic Law: Human Rights was never enacted due to the opposition of certain religious parties to provisions regarding gender equality and religious pluralism. As a result, these Basic Laws do not specifically protect freedom of religion.[57] The Basic Law: Human Dignity and Liberty provides that "there shall be no violation of the life, body or dignity of any person as such"[58] and that "all persons are entitled to protection of their life, body and dignity."[59] A 1994 amendment to this Basic Law provides that these rights shall be "upheld in the spirit of the principles" set forth in Israel's Declaration of Establishment, which includes a guarantee of freedom of religion.[60] Special provisions of the Penal Law make it unlawful to outrage religious sentiments, disturb worship, or desecrate places of worship.[61]

PART ONE

EXTENDING ETHNORELIGIOUS CONTROL OVER MANDATORY PALESTINE

2
ETHNORELIGIOUS CITIZENSHIP IN THE ISRAELI CONTROL SYSTEM

Unlike the United States and many Western democracies, Israel maintains a crucial distinction in its laws and policies between citizenship (*ezrahut*) and nationality (*le'om*). This distinction reflects the Zionist vision that Israel be not merely a state in which Jews constitute a majority of citizens, but a "national home for the Jewish people," including the Jewish diaspora. Since 1977, Israeli politics have been dominated by right-wing parties that descend from Revisionist Zionism, the faction within the Zionist movement which sought to establish a Jewish state over all of Mandatory Palestine (as well as present-day Jordan), and are faithful to its maximalist territorial aspirations. That vision remains the animating force behind Israeli law and policy, which seek to establish Jewish control over the entirety of Mandatory Palestine, but which are inescapably at odds with democratic governance. Many Israeli and Palestinian scholars thus characterize the state as an ethnocracy, defined as "a non-democratic regime which attempts to extend or preserve ethnic control over a contested multi-ethnic territory."[62]

Although Israel is widely considered a Western democracy, this categorization is only accurate if one overlooks the Palestinian population, both citizens and noncitizens, living under its control. Only Jewish Israelis, living on either side of the Green Line, enjoy the full complement of Israeli citizenship rights and Jewish national rights. Palestinian citizens of Israel have citizenship rights, but they are not granted Jewish national rights, nor

16

are they allowed to exercise collective rights commensurate with their status as a native national community. Palestinians in the 1967 occupied territory are denied both citizenship and nationality rights.

Through its laws and policies, the Israeli state also seeks to maximize and consolidate Jewish territorial control over Mandatory Palestine – inside Israel's recognized borders and in the oPt. Israel not only expropriated the property of Palestinian refugees and internally-displaced persons (IDPs) from the 1948 War, but it also ensured that the land could never return to Palestinian ownership. Israel designated the Palestinian refugee land that it confiscated as a joint holding of the state and the entire Jewish people. The new state transferred much of this land to the Jewish National Fund, a Zionist institution which, along with the World Zionist Organization/Jewish Agency, were absorbed into the state structure and which exercise sovereign functions of land ownership, development, and settlement exclusively for the Jewish people, as distinct from the citizens of Israel. Consequently, Palestinian citizens of Israel, 20 percent of Israel's population, own less than four percent of the state's land.[63] Jewish localities control and administer 83 percent of the state's territory while Palestinian localities control only three percent.[64]

Israel applies the same law and policies to East Jerusalem, over which it has extended its law, jurisdiction, and administration. In the West Bank, Israel has consolidated its territorial control through continued settlement activity, construction of the wall, de facto annexation of West Bank territory (including in East Jerusalem) to the west of the Wall, and legally-dubious declarations of "state land" and closed military zones. In the Gaza Strip, which constitutes one percent of Mandatory Palestine, Israel abandoned its territorial ambitions in 2005 and has, since 2007, confined Gaza's 1.8 million Palestinian residents by means of a land, air and sea blockade.

In sum, Israel lacks the *demos* required of any democracy: a defined territory (whether its pre-1967 borders or Mandatory Palestine in its entirety) within which the entire population enjoys equal rights (first-class citizenship). Therefore, Israel should be regarded as an ethnocracy rather than a democracy.[65] Understood in this context, the second-class citizenship of its Palestinian citizens is not merely the product of discriminatory legislation, nor is its denial of citizenship to Palestinians in the 1967 occupied territory an unfortunate consequence of the occupation. Rather, the subordination of the Palestinian population is a structural feature of the Israeli ethnocracy.

This system of ethnoreligious citizenship and Jewish control is reinforced by measures such as a law banning Palestinians citizen of Israel from living in Israel with their spouses from the oPt, which has clear demographic motivations; and by linking certain state benefits and employment privileges to military service, from which the vast majority of Palestinian citizens of Israel are exempted. These measures will be explored in more detail below.

LEGAL STANDARD

Human Rights Law

The international human rights instruments, which the IRFA incorporates by reference, establish that any degradation in the rights of citizenship, or the outright exclusion from citizenship, on the basis of religious affiliation constitutes a violation of religious freedom. article 2 ICCPR prohibits discrimination on the basis of race, religion, and national or social origin in the protection of Covenant rights, including the right to marry freely and have a family (art. 23), certain citizenship rights (art. 25), and equal protection of the law (art. 26). The ECHR's nondiscrimination principle, article 14, further prohibits discrimination on the basis of "association with a national minority," including minority groups defined directly or indirectly by religion. Article VII of the Helsinki Declaration obligates states to "respect the right of persons belonging to [national] minorities to equality before the law" and to "afford them the full opportunity for the actual enjoyment of human rights and fundamental freedoms." Discrimination, as defined in and prohibited by article 2 of the 1981 UN Declaration, covers "any distinction, exclusion, restriction or preference based on religion or belief and having as its purpose or as its effect nullification or impairment of the recognition, enjoyment or exercise of human rights and fundamental freedoms on an equal basis."

Other human rights instruments prohibit any such degradation or denial of citizenship on the basis of race, ethnicity, national origin, or association with a national minority. For example, article 5 CERD guarantees equality before the law, without distinction as to race, color, or national or ethnic origin, with respect to civil and political rights including the right to marriage and choice of spouse and the right to nationality. Similarly, article 9 of the 1961 Convention on the Reduction of Statelessness, to which Israel is a party, provides that "a Contracting State may not deprive any person or group of persons of their nationality on racial, ethnic, religious or political grounds."

States are also prohibited from discrimination in their treatment of non-citizen residents. In *Kurić v. Slovenia*, the European Court of Human Rights (ECtHR) found that Slovenia had, in the course of its independence from Yugoslavia, engaged in unlawful discrimination by withdrawing permanent residency from 25,000 former Yugoslav citizens of other Yugoslav republics, but not permanent residents from non-Yugoslav states.[66] Against the backdrop of nationalist sentiment unleashed by Yugoslvia's dissolution, as manifested in an unsuccessful 1994 Slovene parliament request for a referendum on withdrawing Slovene citizenship previously granted to former Yugoslav citizens, the Court rejected Slovenia's argument that the withdrawal of residency was necessary to rapidly form a corpus of Slovene citizens before the country's first parliamentary elections, with concurring judges calling it "a legalistic means of ethnic cleansing."[67]

<u>USCIRF precedent</u>

Accordingly, in Iraq and especially in Burma, the Commission has found that the systematic denial or revocation of citizenship, or a degradation in the rights associated with citizenship, to members of an ethnoreligious group constitutes a violation of religious freedom. These states are designated or recommended as CPCs. Without suggesting that Israeli citizenship practices towards the Palestinians under its control approach the same level of severity, they nevertheless constitute severe violations of religious freedom according to the principles elaborated by the Commission in these cases.

Burma: Rohingya stateless Muslim minority[68]

The Rohingya are an ethnoreligious minority in Rakhine State in Burma, which has been designated a CPC since 1999. They are defined by a common language (Rohingya) and religion (Islam). Rohingyas assert that they are indigenous to Rakhine, while the Burmese government claims they migrated from Bengal during British rule in Burma (1824-1948) and subsequently. Consequently, they are not among Burma's 135 state-recognized ethnic groups and the Burmese government characterizes them as illegal "Bengali" immigrants who should be deported.

Rohingyas are denied citizenship under the tiered citizenship system introduced by the Burmese military junta in 1982, under which full citizenship is reserved for descendants of recognized residents of Burma prior to British rule. Even associate or naturalized citizenship requires "conclusive evidence" of family residence in Burma prior to 1948, a standard that virtually no Rohingya can meet given that the state presumes they are illegal immigrants. Indeed, as the Commission's 2015 Report notes, they are denied the right to self-identify as Rohingya because they must declare themselves Bengali to even apply for the lower tiers of citizenship.[69] Lacking citizenship, they are classified as "resident foreigners" and denied an array of state benefits. An estimated 140,000 Rohingya Muslims have been forced into internal displacement camps[70] and over 100,000 have fled Burma since 2012.[71]

The Commission has recommended that the United States enter into a binding agreement with Burma pursuant to section 405(c) of the IRFA, which would require Burma, as a condition of eventually lifting its CPC designation, to undertake "crucial legal and legislative reform that strengthens protections for *religious and ethnic minorities*, including citizenship for the Rohingya population through the review, amendment, or repeal the 1982 Citizenship Law or some other means."[72] Further, the Commission urged that such an agreement obligate the Burmese government to "[u]se the term Rohingya, both publicly and privately, in respect for the Rohingya Muslim community's right to identify as they choose."

Iraq: Jews prohibited from regaining Iraqi citizenship[73]

The 2005 Iraqi constitution provides that the citizenship of Iraqi nationals by birth cannot be revoked and that any such person whose citizenship was previously revoked may reclaim it.[74] Accordingly, a 2006 citizenship law establishes a procedure for persons whose citizenship was revoked on political, religious, racial or sectarian reasons to regain it. However, the 2006 law excludes persons whose citizenship was cancelled upon a voluntary request to leave Iraq, the procedure required of Jews who left Iraq (mainly to Israel) in the 1950s. The Commission recommended in 2015 that Iraq be designated a CPC, as it had been each year since 2008.

ANALYSIS

Jewish Israelis, Arab Palestinians, and Religious Identity

The formation and evolution of Jewish and Palestinian identities is a complex topic that need not be explored in detail here.[75] For present purposes, it suffices to establish that Jewish Israelis and Arab Palestinians (both Christians and Muslims) constitute distinct ethnoreligious communities for purposes of the international human rights instruments on which the IRFA relies, and between which discrimination in the protection of human rights, whether individual or systematic, is prohibited.

Jews are unquestionably an ethnoreligious group based on descent, ethnic or national origin, and religion. According to religious law (*halacha*) and social norms, Jewish identity is descent-based, conveyed from mother to child. In Israel's early years, this conception of Jewish identity and nationality was challenged by a secular conception based on "self-identification and choices expressed through the person's actions," including residence in Israel and participation in its civic life.[76] In its 1968 *Shalit* decision, the Israeli Supreme Court adopted this secular understanding of Jewish nationality, ruling that, for purposes of the Law of Return and the population registry, the government had no authority to determine a person's national or religious affiliation and was obligated to accept as conclusive a person's bona fide statement of such affiliation.[77] The Knesset overruled the Supreme Court with a 1970 amendment to the Law of Return which codified a "semi-*halachic*" definition of Jewish identity: "for the purposes of this Law, 'Jew' means a person who was born of a Jewish mother or has become converted to Judaism and who is not a member of another religion."[78] This definition is consistent with an Orthodox interpretation of *halacha*. In Reform Judaism, by contrast, a person is also a Jew if born to a Jewish father, raised exclusively as a Jew and whose Jewish status is "established through appropriate and timely public and formal acts of identification with the Jewish faith and people."[79]

The growing numbers and political influence of the Orthodox and the settler population are strengthening the *halachic* religious understanding of Jewish identity and weakening the concept of national Israeli identity grounded in citizenship.[80] While the Zionist movement, which was founded and led in its early years by secular Jews, has "traditionally framed Jews and Jewish interests in Palestine in ethno-racial terms,"[81] Orthodox and ultra-Orthodox Jews believe this ethno-racial understanding is inseparable from observance of the Jewish faith.

Palestinian identity is based principally on national origin – familial roots in historic Palestine – and Palestinians are distinguished from the wider Arab "nation" through that connection to the homeland.[82] The 1968 Palestinian National Charter states that "Palestine is the homeland of the Arab Palestinian people; it is an indivisible part of the Arab homeland, and the Palestinian people are an integral part of the Arab nation."[83] The Charter defines the Palestinians in terms of national origin as "the Arab citizens who were living permanently in Palestine until 1947 and their patrilineal descendants," including "Jews who had normally resided in Palestine" before the start of Zionist immigration.[84]

The Christian Palestinian population of Israel and the oPt is currently estimated at 213,000, of whom 161,000 are Palestinian citizens of Israel (roughly 10% of Israel's Palestinian population) and 52,000 are non-citizen residents of the West Bank and Gaza (roughly 1.4% of the Palestinian population of the oPt). However, Christians comprised roughly 10 percent of the Arab inhabitants of Mandatory Palestine before the 1948 War and roughly 8 percent of the Palestinian population following the Palestinian exodus (*nakba*) before, during and after the War.

Because of their higher rates of emigration since the *nakba*, Christians are proportionately overrepresented in the Palestinian diaspora. For example, Christians make up 80 to 85 percent of the estimated 500,000 Palestinians in Central and South America. Further, Christians continue to play an oversized role in Arab Palestinian society relative to their current numbers. For example, a 2012 study by the Palestinian Christian consortium *Diyar* found that 45% of civil society institutions in the West Bank were founded as Christian institutions or are owned, managed or funded by Christian institutions.[85]

As observed by John Dugard, former UN Special Rapporteur on the situation of human rights in the Palestinian territories occupied since 1967, while "religion itself is not a defining feature of Palestinian identity ... it does impact directly upon identity politics in the region insofar as Israel excludes and discriminates against Palestinians on the basis of a constructed 'non-Jewish' identity."[86] Dugard thus concludes that Jewish Israelis and Palestinians are distinguished on several bases protected by human rights law, including religion:

> Jewish and Palestinian identities, while not typically seen as 'races' in the old (discredited) sense of biological or skin colour categories, are constructed as groups distinguished by ancestry or descent as well as ethnicity, nationality, *and religion*. As such they are distinguished from each other in a number of forms within the parameters of racial discrimination under international human rights law.[87]

Thus, Israel has an obligation of nondiscrimination in citizenship and citizenship rights towards the non-Jewish Palestinian population under its control, irrespective of whether Jewish identity is conceived in ethnic/national terms, as it is understood by secular Jews, including the founders and original leaders of the Zionist movement, or in religious terms, as is it understood by Orthodox Jews. The discrimination based on religious affiliation that Palestinians endure is generally not based on the particular religious identification of individual Palestinians, but on the fact that the Palestinians, individually and collectively, are *not* Jewish.

Citizenship and Nationality in Israel

Israel's Declaration of Establishment appealed to the state's "Arab inhabitants" to participate in the construction of the state and in its institutions "on the basis of full and equal citizenship."[88] However, this promise of equality of citizenship conflicts with, and is invariably subordinated to, rights and privileges reserved for the Jewish people – both Jewish Israeli citizens and a Jewish diaspora that is unaccountable to the State.

Citizenship and Nationality in Contemporary State Practice

In the contemporary practice of states, citizenship and nationality are used synonymously to refer to the legal relationship between an individual and the state, wherein the state recognizes and guarantees the individual's rights.[89] Neither term refers to the individual's ethnic origin. As defined by the International Court of Justice in the *Nottebohm* case, "nationality is a legal bond having as its basis a social fact of attachment, a genuine connection of existence, interests and sentiments, together with the existence of reciprocal rights and duties."[90] As a matter of public international law, each state is broadly free to determine who it will recognize as its citizens and nationals. However, *Nottebohm* held, and subsequent treaty law has recognized, that a state's nationality law need only be accepted by other states "in so far as it is consistent with applicable international conventions, customary international law and the principles of law generally recognised with regard to nationality."[91] The full complement of citizenship rights vary between states, but generally include the right to permanent residence within the state, freedom of movement within the state, the right to vote and be elected or appointed to public office, the right to public services, and the state's diplomatic protection when abroad.[92]

Israeli Citizenship Rights and Jewish National Rights

Israel does not abide by this contemporary state practice. It assigns special status and state functions to Zionist organizations that represent the Jewish people, including the diaspora, and that serve only Israeli citizens with Jewish nationality. Maintaining these parastatal institutions and preserving the rights and privileges reserved for Israelis with Jewish nationality has compelled the Israeli government to refuse to recognize an Israeli nationality. While Palestinian citizens of Israel experience institutionalized discrimination that is based in law, they are, broadly speaking, allowed to exercise *citizenship* rights. However, they are not granted nationality rights, which the State recognizes only for the Jewish people. This Palestinian minority demands recognition as the native national community in Israel and internal self-determination consistent with that status.[93]

The State's response, which reflects the rightward drift of the Israeli Jewish polity, has been a series of laws promoting the Jewish character of the state at the expense of its democratic character. In late 2014, the Knesset introduced the Basic Law: Israel as the Nation-State of the Jewish People. The Basic Law would elevate the distinction between citizenship and nationality rights, which is already anchored in law through various pieces of legislation, to constitutional status. All versions of the proposed Basic Law, including the version introduced by Prime Minister Netanyahu in November 2014 and the more moderate version introduced in the Knesset in July 2015, declare that "the right of national self-determination in the State of Israel is unique to the Jewish People," thereby denying the right of the native Palestinian minority to internal self-determination.[94] The day after Prime Minister Netanyahu introduced his version of the Basic Law, the State Department warned that the United States "expect[s] Israel to stick to its democratic principles."[95] Nevertheless, the coalition agreement of the current Israeli government, which was formed in May 2015, stipulates the passage of the Basic Law.[96]

Segregated Citizenship Regimes for Jews and non-Jews

Acquisition of citizenship in Israel is governed by separate regimes for Jews and non-Jews. For Jews and others deemed to have Jewish nationality (particularly immigrants from the former Soviet Union), citizenship in Israel is acquired as a matter of right under the 1950 Law of Return, with immediate effect upon arrival and without having to renounce one's previous citizenship. Any child born in Israel to an Israeli mother or father is automatically granted Israeli citizenship, as is the first generation of children born outside the state to an Israeli parent. Palestinians and other residents of Mandatory Palestine who could prove that they remained continuously present in, or "lawfully" returned to, the new State of Israel received citizenship by residence under the 1952 Citizenship Law. Under the 1952 law, citizenship for non-Jews is conferred at the discretion of the Minister of Interior following a lengthy and intrusive naturalization process, and requires the renouncement of one's previous citizenship.[97]

1950 Law of Return: Birthright Citizenship for Jews

The Law of Return gives every Jew the right to immigrate to Israel, and to apply for and receive Israeli citizenship. The State Department's 2007 Religious Freedom report outlined its provisions:

> Under the Law of Return, the Government grants immigration and

residence rights to individuals who meet established criteria defining Jewish identity. Included in this definition is a child or grandchild of a Jew, the spouse of a Jew, the spouse of a child of a Jew, and the spouse of a grandchild of a Jew. ... The Law of Return generally does not apply to non-Jews or to persons of Jewish descent who have converted to another faith. Approximately 36 percent of the country's Jewish population was born outside of the country.[98]

As noted by Israeli legal scholar Ayelet Shachar, "the Law of Return views every Jew and his or her family members as *in potentia* citizens of the State of Israel, thus establishing a formal, legal link between the State of Israel and the community of world Jewry."[99] That link finds expression in subsequent legislation, including the 1952 World Zionist Organization – Jewish Agency (Status) Law, which declares the responsibilities of diaspora Jews towards the state and deputizes the WZO/JA as the state's agent in ensuring the fulfillment of those responsibilities:

> The mission of gathering in the exiles, which is the central task of the State of Israel and the Zionist Movement in our days, requires constant efforts by the Jewish people in the Diaspora; the State of Israel, therefore, expects the cooperation of all Jews, as individuals and groups, in building up the State and assisting the immigration to it of the masses of the people, and regards the unity of all sections of Jewry as necessary for this purpose.[100]

The 1950 Law of Return "thus reflects a perception of membership in the state which is not territorially bound or defined, but rather is based on a *preexisting* affiliation with the Jewish people, in its perception of that people as a 'nation.'"[101] Consistent with this perception of *a priori* belonging, Israel is "exceptionally lenient" in permitting new Jewish citizens to maintain dual citizenship.[102] Already sharing in the Jewish national collective, Jews immigrating to Israel under the Law of Return are not subject to a naturalization process; their citizenship is effective "from the day of [their] *aliyah* [return]."[103]

The UN Committee on Economic, Social and Cultural Rights has repeatedly expressed concern with the concept of a "Jewish nationality" manifested in the Law of Return:

> The Committee is particularly concerned about the status of "Jewish

26

nationality", which is a ground for exclusive preferential treatment for persons of Jewish nationality under the Israeli Law of Return, granting them automatic citizenship and financial government benefits, thus resulting in practice in discriminatory treatment against non-Jews, in particular Palestinian refugees.[104]

1952 Citizenship Law: Citizenship Denied to Arab Palestinian Refugees

The 1952 Citizenship Law granted citizenship to roughly 150,000 Palestinians who remained in or "lawfully" returned to the new State of Israel and were registered in the 1951 population registry. The Law also granted birthright citizenship to their children. However, by requiring an uninterrupted presence in Israel from its establishment in 1948 through 1951 (or, in rare cases, lawful departure and return with official permission), the Law denied Israeli citizenship to an estimated 750,000–1,000,000 Palestinians who became refugees as a result of the 1948 War. These refugees and their descendants now number six million, roughly five million of whom are registered with and assisted by the UN Relief and Works Agency for Palestine Refugees in the Near East (UNRWA). A 1980 amendment retroactively extended citizenship to former citizens of mandatory Palestine residing in Israel who could not prove uninterrupted residence or lawful return under the 1952 Law, and thus were neither citizens nor lawful permanent residents.[105]

Thus, while Israeli citizenship is not territorially defined for persons of Jewish nationality, who acquire citizenship by *ius sangunis*, citizenship is limited territorially and temporally for persons of Palestinian nationality. Only Palestinians who managed, between 1948 and 1952, to remain in parts of Mandatory Palestine that became Israel, acquired citizenship by residence.

The 1952 Citizenship Law also governs citizenship through naturalization. Beyond residency requirements, an applicant for citizenship by naturalization must have basic knowledge of Hebrew, take a loyalty oath to the state, and have renounced, or prove willingness to renounce, his or her prior citizenship. This final requirement, according to Shachar, reflects "the deeply entrenched ethnocultural conception of Israeli citizenship," wherein "those who are not by religion, ancestry or family affinity related to the Jewish people, must assert their loyalty to the Israeli state by severing their citizenship ties to a former political community."[106]

Denial of Citizenship to Palestinians in the 1967 Occupied Territory

Palestinians in the West Bank (except East Jerusalem) and in the Gaza Strip are under Israeli military jurisdiction. They are considered permanent residents of the West Bank or the Gaza Strip, rather than residents of the oPt as a whole, and have neither citizenship nor residency rights in Israel. As a result of Israel's de facto annexation of East Jerusalem in 1967, Palestinians in East Jerusalem are granted revocable permanent residency status in Israel.

The 1967 War displaced an estimated 270,000–390,000 Palestinians from the West Bank and Gaza, including 240,000 who became refugees.[107] Approximately 193,500 Palestinian refugees from the 1948 War were displaced for a second time in 1967.[108] Upon occupying the West Bank and Gaza, the Israeli military authorities declared the territories to be "closed areas" and required Palestinian residents to obtain permits from the military authorities in order to enter or leave. Tens of thousands of West Bank and Gaza residents who happened to be outside the territory for work, education, or other reasons at the time of the War were thus prevented from returning home. In August and September 1967, the Israeli military conducted a census that became the basis for the Israeli registry of the Palestinian population, which is maintained by the Ministry of Defense.[109] The new refugees and other residents stranded outside the territory were not counted in the census and subsequently lost their right to residency in the oPt. The 1967 refugees and their descendants now number over one million.[110] Between 1967 and 1994, Israel revoked the residency of an additional 140,000 Palestinians in the West Bank and Gaza.[111]

Despite the Oslo Accords, Israel continues to control the Palestinian population registry and frequently refuses to register new permanent residents of the West Bank and Gaza, including in cases of family unification. The 1995 Interim Agreement purported to transfer responsibility for the registry to the Palestinian Authority: the PA would track the number of existing residents and, with prior Israeli approval, would grant permanent residency to the spouses and children of Palestinian residents, to foreign investors, and to other persons based on family unification or humanitarian considerations.[112] In practice, Israel retained control over the population registry in that the Israeli authorities, including the security forces and border authorities who control movement to, from and within the oPt, continued to treat the Israeli version of the population registry as authoritative.[113] New residency registrations were processed sporadically between 1994 and 2000 due to disputes regarding Israel's unilaterally-imposed annual quota system.[114] Since September 2000, Israel has refused to record changes in the population registry, except when registering children of existing residents.[115]

Israel's prolonged occupation of the West Bank and the Gaza Strip, and its *de facto* annexation of parts of that territory, is recognized by the UN Special Rapporteur on the situation of human rights in the Palestinian territories occupied since 1967 as a denial of the Palestinian people's right to self-determination.[116] The occupation also perpetuates the widespread statelessness of Palestinians inside and outside the oPt: more than half of all Palestinians around the world are considered to be *de jure* stateless persons, making Palestinians the largest stateless population in the world.[117] The UN General Assembly's recognition of the State of Palestine on the 1967 occupied territory has, to date, not led to the practical realization of Palestinian citizenship. This is for reasons both related to the occupation (such as the need for continued correspondence between Palestinian identity/travel documents with the Israeli-controlled population registry) and unrelated to the occupation (such as an unwillingness or inability to assert diplomatic protection of Palestinians abroad).[118]

According to international law, a stateless person is one who is not considered a national by any state under the operation of its law.[119] All Arab and Jewish residents of Mandatory Palestine became Palestinian citizens under the 1925 Palestine Citizenship Order. According to Israeli law, Palestinian citizenship was voided with Israel's establishment, and Arab citizens of Mandatory Palestine who did not obtain Israeli citizenship under the 1952 Citizenship Law were effectively denationalized.[120]

Jordan purported to annex the West Bank through a 1950 act of union. Palestinian residents of the West Bank, including refugees, were granted Jordanian citizenship by the 1952 Jordanian Constitution and the 1954 Citizenship Law.[121] However, Jordan severed its legal and administrative links with the West Bank with a 1988 royal directive, which declared that West Bank residents were now "Palestinian citizens." The directive stripped nearly one million West Bank Palestinians of their Jordanian citizenship and rendered them stateless.[122] The Gaza Strip came under Egyptian control in 1948, and its Palestinian population, including refugees, remained *de jure* "Palestinian" but *de facto* stateless, as they are today. While the Palestinian Authority currently issues travel documents to West Bank and Gaza Palestinians, these documents are not evidence of citizenship. The documents use ID numbers from the Israeli-controlled population registry, reaffirming the PA's dependence on Israeli institutions and its inability to grant explicitly Palestinian citizenship.[123] Palestinians living in territory occupied in 1967 remain stateless insofar as persons whose status is recognized only by a non-state entity like the PA are, by definition, stateless.[124]

Family Reunification Ban: Reinforcing Ethnoreligious Citizenship

Since 2002, Israel has prohibited its Palestinian citizens and permanent residents from living in Israel with spouses who are residents of the West Bank or the Gaza Strip. For purposes of the present report, this ban is notable in two respects. First, it demonstrates that Palestinian residents of the oPt are considered enemy aliens in Israeli law, notwithstanding Israel's international law status as an occupying power and Israel's incorporation of the oPt into its territory with respect to settlements and settlers. Second, it represents an infringement on the citizenship rights of Palestinian citizens, which are guaranteed under human rights law, in the interest of preserving the state's Jewish demographic majority.

Israeli Government Decision No. 1813 of May 12, 2002 placed a moratorium on applications for family reunification between Israeli citizens or permanent residents and their Palestinian spouses who are residents of the oPt. On July 21, 2003, the Knesset enacted the Citizenship and Entry into Israel Law (Temporary Order), turning the government decision into legislation for a renewable one-year period.[125] The Law has been renewed annually ever since, most recently in June 2015.[126] It prohibits the Minister of Interior from granting Israeli citizenship or issuing an Israeli residency permit to a Palestinian resident of the oPt who is married to an Israeli citizen, with various exceptions (including the discretion to grant residency to Palestinians who collaborate with the Israeli security services).[127] The Law was amended in 2005 to give the Minister of Interior discretion to allow temporary residence (but not permanent residence or citizenship) to men aged 35 or older and women aged 25 or older who are married to Israeli citizens or permanent residents. In May 2006, the Israel Supreme Court upheld the Law.[128]

A 2007 amendment expanded the Law's application to residents of "enemy states": Lebanon, Syria, Iraq, and Iran. The amendment also created a committee that could recommend granting temporary or permanent residence in exceptional humanitarian cases. This committee suffers from serious due process shortcomings, including the lack of a definition of, or criteria for assessing, "humanitarian" considerations, a lack of transparency (including no hearings with the applicant and his/her counsel and no public record of its meetings, decisions, or rationale), and the discretion of the Minister of Interior to set an annual cap on the number of applications that the committee may approve.[129] According to the Israeli human rights NGO HaMoked, which frequently represents applicants for family reunification, most applications approved by the humanitarian committee were approved only after the applicant had initiated court proceedings.[130] As of March 2010, the committee had approved one percent of applications received.[131]

The Law's implementation and impact were documented in the State Department's 2013 Human Rights report:

> The Law of Citizenship and Entry in Israel, renewed in April, prohibits Palestinians from the West Bank or Gaza, including those who are spouses of Israeli residents or citizens, from obtaining resident status in East Jerusalem or Israel on security grounds. The law provides for exceptions in special cases. NGOs argued that the government rarely granted exceptions and that the law prevented some families from living together unless the citizen or resident family member chose to relocate to the West Bank or Gaza Strip. Authorities required East Jerusalem residents who relocated to forfeit their Jerusalem identification cards.[132]

The UN human rights treaty bodies have consistently declared the Law a violation of Israel's human rights obligations. By essentially banning Palestinian citizens of Israel and Palestinian permanent residents of East Jerusalem from living in their place of residence with the spouses of their choice, the law disregards Israel's commitments under several human rights treaties. These include the ICCPR, which protects the family and the home from outside interference and which gives the State the responsibility of protecting the family;[133] the CERD, which protects "the right to marriage and choice of spouse;"[134] and the ICESCR, which requires that the "widest possible protection and assistance should be accorded to the family, which is the natural and fundamental group unit of society."[135] Furthermore, Israel's law disregards a fundamental component of these treaties: that the protection of the rights articulated in the treaties be provided without discrimination.

Palestinian Residents of the 1967 Occupied Territory as "Enemy Aliens"

In the Explanatory Notes to the Law preventing family reunification, the Israeli government characterized its relationship with Palestinians in the 1967 occupied territory, or at least those living in territory under the jurisdiction of the Palestinian Authority (Areas A and B of the West Bank), as one of armed conflict.[136] The notion that Israel is engaged in an armed conflict with the West Bank and the Gaza Strip is fundamentally inconsistent with its responsibility, as an occupying power under IHL, to maintain law and order in the oPt.[137] It also violates Israel's human rights obligations to all persons under its effective control, which include Palestinians living in territory occupied in 1967.

In June 2005, the Israeli cabinet appointed an Advisory Committee for the Examination of an Immigration Policy for the State of Israel (the Rubinstein Committee), which was charged with laying the groundwork for permanent legislation to replace the current "temporary" Law. The Committee studied "immigration from countries deemed hostile." These countries were separated into three categories: (1) "states and regions at risk," notwithstanding formal peace with Israel (e.g. Jordan, Egypt), immigrants from which are presumed disloyal to Israel and who must prove otherwise; (2) "enemy states and conflict regions" (e.g. Iran, Syria), immigrants from which could, in addition to having to rebut the presumption of disloyalty, be limited by quota; and (3) "combat areas" – the West Bank and the Gaza Strip – immigrants from which could remain banned completely.[138]

The Israeli government adopted the Committee's position regarding "immigration" from the oPt in its arguments before the Supreme Court in the *Adalah v. Minister of Interior* case (2006). The Court's majority adopted the government's position, as expressed by Justice Cheshin:

> Israel finds itself in a difficult armed conflict with the Palestinians. An authority against a state. One collective against another. And this armed conflict has become like a war. ... And a state that finds itself in a state of war with another state usually prohibits – and is entitled to prohibit – the entry of the residents of the enemy state into its territory. This is also the case here.[139]

In subsequent cases, the Court similarly characterized Israel as being in a constant state of armed conflict vis-à-vis the 1967 occupied territory, particularly the Gaza Strip.[140] Thus, as Israeli political scientist Yoav Peled argues, the 2003 Law and the Supreme Court's decision to uphold it rely on the fiction that oPt Palestinians are "enemy aliens" to whom Israel owes no right of citizenship, nor the right to exercise self-determination within the 1967 occupied territory.[141]

Demographic Motivations of the Family Reunification Ban and Immigration Policy

The Government Decision and subsequent Law were adopted during the second intifada, in which approximately 700 Israeli civilians were killed. Understandably, security measures were intensified during this period. However, the Knesset has renewed the Law every year, most recently in June 2015, despite the fact that the State never established a correlation between family reunification and security offenses.

The June 2005 cabinet resolution declared that Israel's immigration policy "will be based not only on security considerations, but ... will also guarantee the existence of Israel as a Jewish and democratic state."[142] The Rubinstein Committee, which worked under the auspices of Israel's National Security Council, revealed that Israel had not evaluated the security risk posed by family reunification and could not evaluate it because there was no reliable information on the number of Palestinians from the oPt who had been granted some form of residency in Israel prior to the Law's enactment.[143] The Committee estimated the number to be between 5,400 and 21,300 for the period 1993 to 2003, whereas Israel's attorney general and population administration (PIBA), in representations to the Supreme Court, estimated the number to be around 130,000 for the period 1994 to 2005.[144] From this total, the State identified 68 oPt Palestinians who had acquired residency in Israel through marriage and were subsequently suspected of involvement in security offenses: one suicide bomber, 25 persons who were suspected but never charged, and 42 persons whose naturalization process was suspended on such suspicions.[145]

Several of the Supreme Court judges who dissented in the 2006 ruling that upheld the Law acknowledged its demographic purpose. Justice Esther Hayut concluded that "it emerges from the data presented by the state that the scope of the involvement in hostile activities of Palestinian spouses of Arab citizens of Israel who had gained permission for family unification was miniscule, if at all."[146] Justice Ayala Procaccia observed that "the demographic issue hovered over the legislative processes" which produced the Law, noting that the legislative record included statements by several Knesset members, both supporters and opponents of the Law, who "believed that the demographic aspect was the main justification for the legislative arrangement that was adopted."[147] Peled notes that while the Court's majority denied that the Law was motivated by anything other than security considerations, its opinions are "rife with demographic allusions." As Judge Cheshin concluded in joining with the Court's majority:

> the strong and decisive interest of the state in *protecting the identity of society in Israel* is capable of overriding ... the strength of the right to family life in so far as the immigration of a foreign spouse into Israel is concerned.[148]

The ban on family reunification, with its clear demographic motivations, reflects the prioritization of Israel's Jewish demographic majority and character over the citizenship rights of its Palestinian population.

Dispossession of Palestinian Land through Jewish Parastatal Organizations

The World Zionist Organization (WZO), Jewish Agency (JA), and Jewish

National Fund (JNF) were key Zionist institutions in the pre-state period, with operations in Mandatory Palestine and around the world. After Israel's establishment, they were anchored in Israeli law as quasi-governmental or parastatal institutions, despite the fact that, by charter, they serve only the Jewish people in Israel and the diaspora.

The UN human rights treaty bodies have long expressed concern with the role and activities of the WZO/JA and JNF. In 1998, the Committee on Economic, Social and Cultural Rights found that these organizations contributed to Israel's violations of the right to nondiscrimination in the provision of housing, as guaranteed by articles 2 and 11 ICESCR:

> The Committee takes the view that large-scale and systematic confiscation of Palestinian land and property by the State and the transfer of that property to these agencies constitute an institutionalized form of discrimination because these agencies by definition would deny the use of these properties to non-Jews. Thus, these practices constitute a breach of Israel's obligations under the Covenant.[149]

The discrimination engendered by their operations of the parastatal organizations illustrates the distinction in Israeli law and policy between citizenship rights and nationality rights, the latter of which exist only for Jewish Israelis.

World Zionist Organization/Jewish Agency

The WZO was founded at the first World Zionist Congress in 1897 and served as an umbrella organization for the Zionist movement. The JA was founded in 1908 as the WZO's Palestine Office, and in 1929 was designed as the "Jewish agency" recognized in the Mandate for Palestine.[150] The WZO/JA was crucial to the establishment of Israel. It represented the interests of the Zionist movement before the Palestine (Mandate) Administration and helped to build state-like institutions long before Israel's establishment. After the State's establishment, the WZO/JA was anchored in Israeli law through the World Zionist Organization – Jewish Agency for Israel (Status) Law (1952) and its Amendment (1975), in which the state recognized the WZO/JA as "the authorized agency" for the "development and settlement of the country, the absorption of immigrants from the Diaspora and the coordination of the activities in Israel of Jewish institutions and organizations active in those fields."[151] This authority was confirmed in a 1954 covenant between Israel and the Zionist Executive, representing the WZO/JA. Two new covenants in 1979 established the current division of labor, wherein the WZO is responsible for work in the diaspora and on diaspora issues, while the JA is responsible for the initial absorption of the immigrants in Israel, including educational activities and employment programs, immigrant absorption in rural settlements, immigrant housing, and welfare services.

In addition, the WZO performs the core state function of land registration in West Bank settlements. The WZO's Settlement Division has exclusive control over the registration of property rights and titles in nearly all West Bank settlements, where Israel's official Land Registry does not operate, and is considered the legal equivalent in the settlements of the Land Registry inside Israel.[152]

Jewish National Fund

The JNF, also known by its Hebrew name *Keren Keyemeth LeIsrael* (KKL), was founded at the fifth World Zionist Congress in 1901 to purchase land in Ottoman Palestine for the Jewish people.[153] The organization was registered in Britain in 1907. The Congress resolved that "the fund shall be the property of the Jewish people as a whole."[154] The 1920 Zionist Congress established the JNF as "the instrument of Jewish land policy in town and country" and clearly redefined its objective: "to use the voluntary contributions received from the Jewish People in making the land of Palestine the common property of the Jewish People; [and] to lease the land exclusively on hereditary leasehold and on hereditary building right...."[155] By 1943, total Jewish land ownership reached 1,514,247 dunums, corresponding to 5.8 percent of mandatory Palestine, of which the JNF owned 43 percent (660,100 dunums) in whole or in common with other landowners.[156]

After the 1948 War, the State utilized the JNF in an attempt to foreclose Palestinian refugees from returning to their homes and reclaiming their property. On December 11, 1948, the UN General Assembly adopted

Resolution 194 (III), which resolved that "the refugees wishing to return to their homes and live at peace with their neighbours should be permitted to do so at the earliest practicable date," and instructed the UN Conciliation Commission for Palestine (UNCCP), established by the resolution, to "facilitate the repatriation, resettlement and economic and social rehabilitation of the refugees and the payment of compensation...."[157]

By the time Resolution 194 (III) was adopted, the new State of Israel controlled 3.5 million dunums of land privately owned by Palestinian refugees and "present absentees" (Palestinians internally displaced within the new State of Israel, who would become Israeli citizens in 1952), corresponding to one-sixth of Israel's territory in its pre-1967 borders. Fearing international condemnation should the State appropriate that land, Israeli Prime Minister David Ben-Gurion sought to quickly transfer the land to private Jewish ownership. At his initiative, Israel sold the JNF 2,373,677 dunums of Palestinian refugee land in two sales, finalized in January 1949 and October 1950 (the so-called "first million" and "second million" sales).[158] These two sales tripled the JNF's holdings; the Fund owned 17 percent of Israeli territory, of which 68 percent was Palestinian refugee property.[159]

The JNF's parastatal role was ensured by a series of laws passed after the State's establishment. Legal sanction for the "first million" and "second million" sales was provided by the 1950 Absentees' Property Law, which vested the state with title to the property of "absent" Palestinian refugees. The remainder of Palestinian refugee land was transferred to the Custodian of Absentee Property, which under the 1950 Abesentees' Property Law cannot sell the land to any entity other than a Development Authority, which was duly established.[160]

In 1953, the Knesset passed the 1953 *Keren Keyemeth LeIsrael* Law, which established the JNF as an Israeli company and arranged the transfer of all Israeli land holdings of the British-registered JNF to the new entity.[161] The Israeli JNF was given the status of a local authority for purposes of the Mandatory law governing the expropriation of private property for public use, which was incorporated into Israeli law.[162] The Law thus gives the JNF the same status as a municipal corporation or local council, thereby making it a lawful beneficiary of private property expropriated by the state for public use.[163] This parastatal status was confirmed in the 1954 Covenant, wherein the State vested the JNF with exclusive responsibility for rural land development in Israel, including land reclamation and afforestation.[164]

In 1960, the Knesset adopted the Basic Law: Israel Lands, which states that "the ownership of Israel lands, which are lands in Israel belonging to the State, the Development Authority or the Jewish National Fund, shall not be transferred, whether by sale or by another manner."[165] In the JNF's words, this Basic Law "rests on KKL-JNF's principle of national land ownership and the biblical perception whereby the land is owned by the Jewish People and may not be sold, but only leased for renewable jubilee periods of 49 years."[166] The "biblical perception" is drawn from Leviticus 25:23 – "the land must not be sold permanently, because the land is mine and you reside in my land as foreigners and strangers" – which some rabbinical authorities, but not Israel's Chief Rabbinate, interpret as prohibiting Jews from selling land in the Land of Israel to non-Jews.[167] That same year, the JNF transferred administration of its non-forested lands to the newly-established Israel Land Administration (now known as the Israeli Land Authority). The ILA also assumed the management of land owned by the state and its Development Authority. In exchange, the JNF-KKL received the right to nominate 10 of the ILA's 22 directors, giving it significant leverage over the development and settlement of all ILA-managed lands, which total 93 percent of pre-1967 Israeli territory.

The Parastatal Institutions and Israel's Segregated Land Regime

The WZO/JA and JNF are tasked in Israeli law with carrying out the core state functions of land development, settlement, and registration. Yet they are chartered to operate for the exclusive benefit of the Jewish people, in Israel and the diaspora, and as such they do not serve Israel's native Palestinian minority. The right to benefit from their operations derives from Jewish nationality rather than Israeli citizenship. Although Israel officially regards these institutions as private organizations, they are anchored in Israeli law, perform public functions pursuant to covenants with the State, and are guaranteed a host of exemptions and waivers on fees and taxes for transactions undertaken for Jewish nationals. These institutions are thus parastatal organizations, and their operations implicate, and violate, Israel's obligation under human rights law to uphold equality and nondiscrimination in protecting fundamental rights.

These parastatal organizations most visibly discriminate against Israel's Palestinian citizens with regard to land access, as illustrated by the Kaadan family's struggle to move into the Israeli "community settlement" of Katzir and the legislative response.

Case Study: Katzir and the Kaadan family

Katzir is located in Wadi Ara, also called the Triangle, an elongated region running along the northwestern edge of the Green Line. The region is mainly populated by Palestinians: as of 1998, the region had a population of approximately 170,000 Palestinian citizens of Israel and 43,000 Israeli Jews.[168] Jewish settlement in Wadi Ara has long been a state priority. Israel regularly designates Jewish population centers in Wadi Ara and other areas outside the country's central region as National Priority Areas (NPAs), a classification which gives these villages access to a variety of benefits, including grants financed by public funds. Although socioeconomic conditions are generally worse in Palestinian population centers than in Jewish Israeli ones, as of 2011 only four of 553 towns and villages designated as NPAs had a Palestinian majority population.[169] Jewish settlement in Wadi Ara is also a priority of the Jewish Agency, which "has set itself the goal to settle Jews all over the country in general, and in border areas and areas with sparse Jewish population in particular" – that is, areas with a Palestinian majority population.[170] Accordingly, the ILA allocated state-owned land in Wadi Ara to the Jewish Agency, which in turn established Katzir in 1982 as a Jewish cooperative settlement.

In 1995, the Kaadans, a Palestinian family from the Wadi Ara city of Baka al-Gharbiya, applied to buy a home in Katzir. The Katzir cooperative society rejected their application on the basis that the community accepted only Jews as residents, in accordance with Jewish Agency regulations. The Kaadans filed suit, arguing that the ILA, as a public body, could not legally allocate land to a third party – the Jewish Agency – that explicitly discriminates against the Palestinian minority. The Supreme Court of Israel ruled in 2000 that notwithstanding the "the Jewish Agency's unique status in the State of Israel" and "its role in realizing the Jewish facets of our Jewish and democratic state," the ILA "was not permitted, by law, to allocate state land to the Jewish Agency, for the purpose of establishing the communal settlement of Katzir on the basis of discrimination between Jews and non-Jews."[171]

However, the Court was unwilling to order the Katzir cooperative society to approve the Kaadan's application. Instead, it sought to "reach an appropriate balance" between the principle of equality and the "serious difficulties" that the Court's order posed to the Jewish Agency, the cooperative society, and Katzir residents, "not only from a social perspective, but also from a legal perspective."[172] The Court thus let the State decide "whether it [could] enable the petitioners, within the framework of the law, to build a house for themselves within the bounds of the Katzir communal settlement."[173] The state took no action, pending legislation that would overrule the Court's decision. Such a bill was approved by the Israeli Cabinet in 2002 but did not pass the Knesset. In May 2004, after the Kaadans initiated contempt proceedings, the ILA sold them a plot of land in Katzir.[174]

The Knesset did eventually adopt laws that nullify the Court's decision in the *Kaadan* case and further facilitate discrimination in land access. The 2009 Israel Land Administration Law (Amendment No. 7) authorizes land exchanges between the State and the JNF, through which the State may acquire JNF land in Jewish-populated urban areas that it can privatize, while the JNF may receive state land in the Galilee and the Naqab (Negev), both areas with substantial Palestinian populations, where it can continue to promote Jewish settlement.[175] The law also consolidates the dispossession of Palestinian refugee property in the 1948 War by authorizing the transfer of title of absentee property to its current lessors.

The 2011 Cooperative Societies Ordinance (Amendment No. 8) legalized admission committees, like the one that rejected the Kaadan's application, in hundreds of small community towns built on state land in the Naqab (Negev) and the Galilee.[176] When adopted, the law applied to 695 communities in Israel, comprising 68 percent of all communities in the state and 85 percent of its rural communities.[177] It vests the Committee with near-total discretion to reject candidates on the basis that they are "not suitable for the social life in the community" or lack "compatibility with the social-cultural fabric of the community town."[178] Under the law, a representative of the WZO/JA sits on each of these committees. Since these officials represent institutions whose explicit goal is to promote Jewish interests, they reinforce discriminatory practices restricting Palestinian citizens' access to land. In September 2014, the Israeli Supreme Court dismissed a petition challenging the law, claiming it could not yet ascertain whether application of the law violated fundamental rights.[179]

Today, in nearly 700 small communities in Israel, admission committees that include representatives of the WZO/JA (that is, representatives of the Jewish people worldwide, including the diaspora) can exclude Palestinian citizens on the basis of their social suitability or their compatibility with the "fabric" of the community. The JNF, while in theory barred from discriminating against non-Jews in its development and administration of state land, does so in practice by means of these admissions committees. Thus, the WZO/JA and JNF continue to restrict Palestinian access to land and contribute to systematic discrimination in citizenship rights based on religious affiliation.

Discrimination Against Palestinian Citizens through the Proxy of Military Service

The majority of Israel's Palestinian citizens are, by administrative practice, exempt from military service. (Male members of the Druze and Bedouin communities are conscripted and recruited, respectively, under agreements between the State and their community leaders reached in the 1950s; *see* discussion of Druze conscription in chapter 10, *infra*.) Citizens who have completed their military service receive additional state benefits, including supplementary child allowances, tax credits, and mortgage subsidies.[180] Further, a variety of proposed laws would gives preferences in public employment to persons who have completed military service.[181] By using military service as a criterion for employment opportunities and other benefits, the state perpetuates discrimination against its Palestinian citizens.[182]

Shachar argues that military service is the cornerstone of Israel's "republican conception of citizenship," wherein "a connection is made between the commitment to make sacrifices for the nation and the right to fair share in governing."[183] However, she concedes that Palestinian citizens and Orthodox Jewish citizens are generally exempted from military service "with very different consequences." For Orthodox Jews, as members of the "dominant Jewish community, their full membership in the nation is hardly ever challenged, even if they refrain from some of its crucial civil expressions." They receive stipends for full-time Torah study and disproportionately draw from other welfare programs, including married student subsidies, income support, and child allowances.[184] Palestinian citizens, in contrast, are subject to "various overt and covert discriminatory government polices" that "serve as a constant reminder that while [they] are full members in the state, they are not fully included in the nation."[185] Shachar acknowledges that linking state benefits to military service, in the context of Israel's prolonged occupation of Palestinian and other Arab territory, "has the divisive effect of creating stratification between 'first class' and 'second class' Israeli citizens."[186]

CONCLUSION

Within the Israeli system, Jewish Israelis residing on either side of the Green Line enjoy both Israeli citizenship rights and Jewish national rights. Palestinian citizens of Israel have citizenship rights but are excluded from Jewish national rights and, at the same time, denied recognition as a native national minority with its own collective rights. Palestinian residents of the oPt are denied Israeli citizenship and are denied the exercise of national self-determination in an independent Palestinian state. Thus, Israel denies oPt Palestinians of both citizenship rights and nationality rights. These disparities in the conferral of citizenship and the rights of citizenship are undeniably based on religious affiliation: if Palestinians were Jews, they would hold Israeli citizenship as a matter of right and would share in Jewish national rights. Accordingly, this system of ethnoreligious citizenship, which is increasingly recognized as a system of apartheid, reflects a most fundamental violation of religious freedom.

3
MAXIMALIST JEWISH CLAIMS TO AL-AQSA MOSQUE COMPOUND/TEMPLE MOUNT

The Al-Aqsa Mosque is the third holiest site in Islam, after the Sacred Mosque in Mecca and the Mosque of the Prophet in Medina. It stands within a 144-dunum (approximately 35.5-acre) walled compound, which is also known as the Noble Sanctuary (*Haram al-Sharif*). In addition to the Mosque itself, the compound also contains the iconic golden-colored Dome of the Rock (*Qubbat al-Sakhra*), an ablution fountain (*al-Kas*), an Islamic museum, a *shari'a* court, and other structures which are all holy to Muslims.[187] The same area is known to Jews as the Temple Mount (*Har HaBayit*) and is the holiest site in Judaism. The Western Wall is located at the base of the western side of the site. The Wall is revered by Jews as a partial remnant of the ancient Jewish Temple. Throughout this section, the site will be referred to as the "Al-Aqsa Mosque Compound" ("Compound"), with the understanding that it refers to the Mosque/Noble Sanctuary/Temple Mount in its entirety.

The Compound has been under continuous Muslim administration since Jerusalem was liberated from Crusader rule in the 12th century, including throughout British and Jordanian rule. Today, administration of the Compound is vested in the Jerusalem Islamic *waqf* ("Waqf"),[188]which operates under the custodianship of the Hashemite Kingdom of Jordan. In

1930, the British government, with the endorsement of the League of Nations, established an international commission of inquiry to determine rights at the Western Wall in response to 1929 riots between Jews and Muslims sparked by a dispute at the site. The commission recognized Muslim Waqf ownership of the entire Compound, including the Western Wall (as the Compound's western edge), while recognizing that Jews had the right to free access to the Western Wall for prayer at all times. Thus, a new status quo developed wherein the Compound's esplanade was reserved for Muslim prayer and the Western Wall was reserved for Jewish prayer.

In the early years of its occupation of East Jerusalem, Israel generally respected the administration of the Waqf and preserved this status quo. The Israeli leadership at the time recognized that maintaining the status quo was in the national interest; the United States agreed, and since 1967 it has insisted that Israel maintain the status quo.

In recent years, however, the Israeli government has begun to change the status quo. Since 2003, Israel has encroached on Muslim self-governance of the Compound by ending coordination with Jordan and denying the Waqf its historic right to regulate the entry of non-Muslim visitors to the Compound. As a result, visits to the site by activists from "Temple movements" seeking to assert Israeli sovereignty and Jewish national rights over the Compound have increased in frequency, size, and prominence. These activists are not ordinary visitors; they promote Jewish Israeli access to the Compound as a means to change the status quo. Temple movement activists seek varying degrees of change, from recognizing a right to Jewish prayer at the site to construction of a new Jewish Temple on the ruins of the Muslim shrines. With several forms of state support, these Temple movements have succeeded in bringing the once-fringe idea of Jewish prayer on the Compound into Israel's mainstream political discourse. Government ministers and Knesset members now speak openly about abrogating the status quo entirely and "asserting Israeli sovereignty" over the Compound. Emboldened by shifting public opinion and state support, elements within these Temple movements, including Knesset members, call for and portray the destruction of the Compound's Muslim shrines. These representations constitute incitement to sectarian violence which Israel has a responsibility to end.

The violations of religious freedom at issue here are:

- Israel's encroachment into Muslim self-governance at the Compound, in violation of the status quo and international humanitarian law (IHL), by denying the Waqf its historic right and responsibility to regulate and supervise all entry to the Compound.

- As a consequence of the Waqf's current inability to regulate the entry of non-Muslim visitors, the increase in the number, size, and visibility of Jewish Israeli activists who explicitly desire to change the status quo in ways that would further marginalize or eliminate Muslim self-governance at the Compound and provoke sectarian strife. The changes sought range from recognition of a Jewish right of collective worship at the Compound, to its temporal or physical partition, to the destruction of its Muslim shrines and the construction of a new Temple.

- State support for organizations that incite sectarian strife by calling for the destruction of the Muslim shrines at the Compound and their replacement by a new Jewish Temple.

The harm caused by these acts go beyond violations of religious freedom. The fate of the Al-Aqsa Mosque Compound is a deeply sensitive issue. Not only is the preservation of the status quo a national issue for Palestinians, and part of a broader question of sovereignty over East Jerusalem, but also an explicitly religious one, which has, on more than one occasion, given rise to violent clashes.[189] Given drastic Israeli changes to the status and character of East Jerusalem, preserving the status quo at the Compound is vital to preserving a two-state solution with Jerusalem as a shared capital, as prescribed by U.S. policy.

To be clear, persons of all faiths and nationalities, including Jewish Israelis, should be allowed to visit the Compound, subject to time, place, and manner restrictions set by the Waqf, as its lawful and recognized administrator. Indeed, until the Compound was temporarily closed to non-Muslims by agreement between Israel and Jordan in 2000, persons of all faiths and nationalities, including Jewish Israelis, visited the site under the Waqf's regulation and supervision.

LEGAL STANDARD

As noted in chapter 1, *supra*, Israel's administration of East Jerusalem, like all parts of the oPt, is governed by IHL, in addition to human rights law and the preemptory norms of international law. Additionally, the status quo is itself an autonomous legal regime that the Israeli government, like the Mandatory and Jordanian authorities before it, has pledged to uphold.

International Humanitarian Law

Article 27 of Geneva Convention (IV) requires an occupying power to "show respect" for the occupied population, including "their religious convictions and practices, and their manners and customs." The ICRC Commentaries to the Conventions elaborate that "customs" as used in article 27 refer to:

> the body of rules hallowed by usage which man observes in his relations with his fellow men. Custom draws its authority from its tacit acceptance by the whole body of citizens. Such ancient and general customs taken as a whole constitute part of the law of each country.[190]

The status quo is the "body of rules hallowed by usage" governing rights and responsibilities at the Jerusalem Holy Places, including the Compound. The contemporary status quo, which derives from Ottoman *firmans* (edicts) of 1757 and 1852 codifying the status quo at the Christian Holy Places, has been recognized at the Compound since the early Mandatory period. Indeed, the status quo has been recognized as an autonomous legal order, which, as the *lex specialis* governing the Holy Places, generally prevails over local law.[191] It thus constitutes part of the law of the occupied territory that, under IHL, Israel is obligated to respect and maintain unless absolutely prevented by the demands of public order and civil life.[192]

The United States recognizes that Israel, as an occupying power, is obligated to preserve existing religious practices, including maintenance of the status quo. This policy was clearly stated in response to a May 1975 incident in which Israeli conscripts affiliated with the *Beitar* youth organization entered the Compound and removed their street clothes to reveal their military uniforms. Defying police orders, they conducted a prayer service and chanted nationalist songs. Several of the individuals were charged with provoking a breach of the peace. A magistrate dismissed the charges, asserting that the police had, in fact, violated the conscripts' right to prayer under the 1967 Holy Places Law (discussed *infra*).[193]

At a special session of the Security Council convened to discuss the incident, the U.S. Ambassador to the United Nations, William Scranton, voiced concern that the magistrate court's ruling "would have the effect of altering the status at *Al-Haram*."[194] In that regard, Ambassador Scranton stated the view of the U.S. government:

> It is our view that Israel's responsibilities to preserve religious practices as they were at the time the occupation began ... cannot be changed by the ruling of an Israeli court.[195]

Status quo legal principles

The status quo may even be considered an autonomous legal regime, with both procedural and substantive norms, which Israel is bound to follow, independently of its IHL obligation to respect the law of the occupied territory. This legal regime has been endorsed by the international community and confirmed by the state practice of successive powers in Jerusalem, such that it is now accepted to "bind any local authority in charge of the Jerusalem administration and especially the walled city."[196] Acts relating to the Compound must be evaluated against Israel's binding unilateral commitment to uphold the status quo regime.

Molinaro identifies three main procedural principles characterizing the status quo legal regime:

> 1. The recognized communities must consent to any change in the Status Quo, either in its procedural or material aspect.
>
> 2. A distinction among the different rights of access, possession and worship is possible, since each corresponding right potentially belongs to a different recognized community.
>
> 3. Controversies over the Status Quo between the communities are currently immune from ordinary judicial jurisdiction.[197]

While there is no single, authoritative statement of the substantive rights protected by this regime, Adv. Shmuel Berkowitz has identified eight core principles of consensus to the interested parties:

1. Protection of the Holy Places

2. Respect for their dignity and sanctity

3. Freedom of worship

4. Freedom of access and exit

5. Proper maintenance

6. Exemption from taxation

7. Observance of the 'status quo' in its broad [cultural-religious, as opposed to legal] sense.

8. Precedence of the public interest in matters such as safety, health and proper conduct, over the above principles.[198]

Within this legal regime, a religious community that tolerates encroachments on its recognized right risks losing that right, as the Western Wall Commission recognized in its 1930 report:

> In the whole system of status quo, "tolerance" plays an important role for deciding what, at any given time, may be considered to have grown into an "existing right." Why should there be this scrupulous application of a fixed status quo, and why should there be this fear of the prejudice that is assumed to follow as an inevitable consequence of any act or omission that alters the actual existing state of things, if "tolerance" was not regarded as a possible basis for an altered legal position?

Disputes regarding changes to the status quo are resolved by executive rather than judicial authorities. The 1924 Order-in-Council (Holy Places) Act removed from judicial jurisdiction any "cause or matter in connection with the Holy Places or religious buildings or sites in Palestine or the rights and claims relating to different religious communities in Palestine." Authority to resolve such disputes was vested in the British High Commissioner for Palestine. That law remains in effect under Israeli rule, with the authority to resolve such disputes vested with the government.[199]

This regime has been repeatedly confirmed by the international community, including in Security Council Resolution S/801 of May 1948, which established a four-week ceasefire and urged "the protection of the Holy Places of the City of Jerusalem, including access to all shrines and sanctuaries for the purpose of worship *by those who have an established right to visit and worship at them*;"[200] and in General Assembly Resolution 194, which "resolves that the Holy Places – including Nazareth – religious and sites in Palestine should be protected and free access to them assured, *in accordance with existing rights and historical practice*."[201] Against the backdrop of this international consensus that the status quo be maintained and the prospects of Jerusalem placed under UN administration, Israel declared its commitment to upholding the status quo regime in December 1949, when Prime Minister David Ben-Gurion reaffirmed, and the first Knesset unanimously endorsed, the commitments made by the Israeli delegation to the UN Conciliation Commission for Palestine, including the undertaking "to respect all existing rights regarding the Holy Places and religious buildings in Jerusalem."[202] Under customary international law governing unilateral declarations, Israel thus made a binding commitment to the international community to respect the settled principles that has governed the Compound across successive regimes.[203]

Human Rights Law

It has been argued that the exclusive rights of religious communities recognized in the status quo are inconsistent with the principle of non-discrimination in the exercise of the right to religious worship and observance, embodied in the ICCPR and other human rights instruments. This argument was considered and rejected by the 1930 Western Wall Commission:

> As regards the terms of the Mandate it is true that in Articles 13, 15 and 16 the principle of religious liberty is proclaimed and that Article 13 especially provides for "free exercise of worship" for all concerned. But from this general rule the conclusion cannot reasonably be drawn that the partisans of any special confession should have the right to exercise their worship in all places without any consideration to the rights of others. If that were so then the whole structure of the status quo in the Holy Places and other religious sites would break down.[204]

Beyond the political and sectarian chaos resulting from its breakdown, there is a clear legal reason why the principle of nondiscrimination in religious worship cannot be used to justify changes to the status quo. International humanitarian law, as the *lex specialis* governing belligerent occupation, prevails over human rights law, as *lex generalis*, to the extent their norms cannot be reconciled.[205] As applied here, IHL protects the local population's religious practices and customs, and limits the occupying power's authority to change the laws and institutions of the occupied territory. More broadly, IHL protects the interest of the occupied population in preserving the laws and institutions of its territory, such as the Waqf, until its sovereignty is restored, a concept known as the conservationist principle. Application of the human rights principle of non-discrimination in religious worship and observance is thus limited by these IHL safeguards. Accordingly, that principle cannot be invoked to justify changes that exceed IHL's limits on an occupying power's authority, in accordance with the conservationist principle.

ANALYSIS

<u>Israeli violations and threats against the status quo</u>

Israel has changed or has threatened to change the status quo in several key respects. Further, it furnishes state support to the Temple movements that advocate for these unilateral changes and has failed to take action against religious incitement in the form of encouraging or graphically depicting the destruction of the Muslim shrines at the Temple and the construction of a new Jewish Temple in their place.

"Asserting Israeli Sovereignty" over the Compound

Upon occupying East Jerusalem in 1967, Israel broadly complied with its IHL obligation not to disturb the laws and institutions of the occupied territory with respect to the Compound, which remains under Waqf administration and Jordanian custodianship. However, pressure from Israeli lawmakers to abrogate this arrangement is growing. On February 25, 2014, the Knesset held its first-ever plenum hearing on Israeli sovereignty over the Compound.[206]

Israel affirmed its commitment in 1967 to maintaining Muslim administration of the Compound as Waqf property, as has existed continuously since the 12th century. During the Mandate, the Waqf was administered by the Jerusalem-based Supreme Muslim Council. Under Jordanian rule, administration passed to the Jordanian Ministry of Awqaf and Islamic Affairs, which continues to fund and supervise the operations of the current Jerusalem Islamic Waqf. On June 17, 1967, Israel confirmed that the Waqf would continue to administer the Compound while the Israeli Security Forces (ISF) would be responsible for its external security.[207] Jordan's custodial role was confirmed in the 1994 Israel-Jordan Peace Treaty, wherein Israel recognized "the present special role of the Hashemite Kingdom of Jordan in Muslim Holy shrines in Jerusalem" and pledged to give "high priority to the Jordanian historic role in these shrines" in final-status negotiations.[208]

The Palestinian leadership today accepts this status quo. The Palestinian Authority challenged Jordan's control of the Waqf upon its founding in 1994, reconstituted the Supreme Muslim Council, and by 1997 had largely gained control of the Waqf.[209] However, Israel's crackdown on PA/PLO activity in Jerusalem since the start of the second intifada allowed Jordan to reassert its control over the Waqf and recognize Jordanian custodianship of the Compound. In 2013, King Abdullah II of Jordan and Palestinian President Mahmoud Abbas signed an agreement that recognized the King's custodianship of the Jerusalem Holy Places, including the Compound in its entirety, within the context of Palestinian sovereignty over East Jerusalem.[210] The agreement charges Jordan with representing the interests of the Holy Places in relevant international forums and organizations, and overseeing the Waqf in accordance with Jordanian law.[211]

On February 26, 2014, the Knesset held a plenum debate regarding Israeli sovereignty at the Compound. The debate was held on the motion of MK Moshe Feiglin, which decried "the conduct of the Israeli government, which allows the government of Jordan and the Muslim world to illegally control the rock of our existence," and urged the government to "realize the State of Israel's full sovereignty in all of the Temple Mount."[212] MKs from the Likud, Jewish Home, and Yisrael Beitenu parties – all members of Israel's current coalition government – spoke in favor of abrogating Waqf administration and Jordanian custodianship of the Compound. In response, Jordan's parliament unanimously adopted a non-binding resolution calling upon the government to end diplomatic relations with Israel.[213]

As used in this discourse, "sovereignty" means the full panoply of rights that a state may exercise within the limits set by international law.[214] These rights of a sovereign within its recognized borders far exceed the authority of an occupying power, which by definition is nonsovereign, as set by international humanitarian law.[215] Any expression of Israeli sovereignty over the Compound, such as purporting to abrogate the Waqf's administration or Jordan's custodianship in favor of direct Israeli administration, would presuppose that Israel has annexed East Jerusalem, which Israel has never officially declared.[216] It would confirm that Israel has violated the prohibition on the acquisition of territory by force, and thereby further suppressed the Palestinian people's right of self-determination in the 1967 occupied territory in its entirety.[217]

Encroachments on the Waqf's responsibility to regulate access and preserve dignity at the Compound

Under the status quo, the Compound is reserved for Muslim prayer while the Western Wall is reserved for Jewish prayer. After 1967, Israel restored the Jewish rights of access and prayer at the Western Wall while upholding the prohibition on demonstrative prayer by non-Muslims at the Compound. However, under pressure from Temple movements and other nationalist elements, the Israeli government has stripped the Waqf of its historic right to regulate the entry of non-Muslim visitors. This infringement on the status quo has led to an upsurge in visits by Jewish Israeli activists who demand that Israel, at a minimum, unilaterally establish Jewish prayer rights at the Compound, thereby abrogating the status quo and risking sectarian strife.

Palestine passed from the Ottoman Empire to Great Britain at the end of the First World War, first as enemy territory governed by a military administration and, after 1923, under a Mandate for Palestine conferred by the League of Nations. The Mandate charged Britain with "preserving existing rights and ... securing free access to the Holy Places."[218] The British government in Palestine affirmed the Ottoman status quo in 1923 and expanded its scope in 1929 to cover additional holy places, including the Western Wall.[219] Following its policy of noninterference with the Waqf's operations, the Mandatory government did not extend the status quo to the Compound.[220] The Compound was first opened to non-Muslim visitors in the mid-19th century, although non-Muslim prayer remained prohibited.[221]

Under Jordanian rule, Jews could access the Western Wall only through a "cumbersome, rarely-used" coordination system.[222] Israel asserts that Jordan thereby violated the 1949 Jordan-Israel Armistice Agreement, which provided for free access to the Holy Places. Jordan asserts that, according to the Armistice, Jewish Israeli access to the Jerusalem Holy Places was conditioned upon the establishment of a special committee to facilitate the following: access to the Holy Places, the normal functioning of Jewish institutions on Mount Scopus, the normal functioning of the Jerusalem-Bethlehem road, and the restoration of water and electricity to the Old City. Such a committee was never convened.[223]

On June 7, 1967, the day Israel took East Jerusalem, the Israeli Minister of Religious Affairs stated that "arrangements at the Western Wall shall be determined by the Chief Rabbis of Israel."[224] With regard to the Compound, however, Israel abided by its obligation not to disturb the Waqf's administration of the Compound though coordination with Jordan. The Waqf was, and remains, responsible for operating and maintaining the Compound's structures, regulating Muslim worship, managing opening hours and the dress code, and administering rules for non-Muslim visitors.

In August 1967, the Israeli government issued a provisional order instructing the ISF to direct Jewish worshippers seeking access to the Compound to the Western Wall instead.[225] This decision was made on political and security grounds and, according to Temple activists, was not intended to be a permanent, principled decision.[226] Nevertheless, it was consistent with the longstanding (and current) position of the Chief Rabbinate of Israel that Jews are strictly prohibited from entering or praying at the Compound because of its holiness.[227] To that end, Israel cooperated with the Waqf in preventing non-Muslim prayer at the Compound, facilitating the entry of non-Muslim tourists, and banning certain religious Jews who were deemed to be provocateurs.[228]

The Supreme Court of Israel initially upheld the prohibition on Jewish prayer at the site in light of this rabbinical authority, reasoning that "it would be absolutely absurd to grant a person freedom of prayer into a place which God, to whom he prays, forbids him even to enter."[229] Over time, the Court came to recognize the right of individual Jews to pray at the Compound under the Holy Places Law also passed in the days after the 1967 War, which guarantees freedom of access for all faiths to their holy places.[230] The Court's contemporary jurisprudence holds that the right of individualized prayer is inherent in the right of access to the holy places, and thus that individual Jews have the right under the 1967 law to engage in private, non-demonstrative prayer on the Compound without religious paraphernalia.[231] Despite this jurisprudence, the ISF continues to prohibit Jewish Israelis from engaging in any manifestation of prayer at the Compound in the interest of preserving public order.[232]

However, by usurping the Waqf's right to regulate non-Muslim entry to the Compound since 2003, Israel has encroached on the status quo, which ensures Muslim self-governance of the Compound, and has strengthened elements within Israeli society who use such visitations as a step towards more drastic changes to the status quo. Following the outbreak of the second intifada, Israel and Jordan agreed to suspend non-Muslim visitation to the Compound. In August 2003, Israel lifted this ban without the agreement of Jordan and without restoring coordination with the Waqf and the Jordanian authorities. That coordination and the Waqf's regulation of non-Muslim entry through the Mughrabi Gate have never been restored. Thus, since 2003, Israel has usurped the Waqf's historic right and responsibility to regulate the entry of non-Muslim visitors entering the Compound, including by limiting the size of groups, excluding known provocateurs, and preventing Jewish Israelis from entering the Compound in military uniforms.

Consequently, the size, frequency, and prominence of visits by Temple activists have increased. Whereas the Waqf required Jewish Israeli visitors to enter the Compound in groups of five or less, the ISF allows Jewish groups of up to 50 persons to enter, which exceed the Waqf's capacity to effectively supervise. This usurpation of authority violates the Waqf's procedural right to control access as well as its substantive responsibility to ensure respect for the dignity and sanctity of the Compound.

Case Study: Visits by Israeli and American Politicians

Israel's encroachment on the Waqf's right to regulate access to the Compound is exacerbated by visits from Israeli and American politicians, which are often organized in conjunction with Temple movements.

The danger inherent in politicians entering the Compound to brandish their right-wing credentials is well-known. Ariel Sharon's September 28, 2000 visit to the Compound, undertaken in the midst of his successful campaign for prime minister, is regarded as the catalyst that sparked the second intifada.[233] Accordingly, the government has previously banned ministers from visiting the Compound,[234] and in November 2014, Israel's chief of police called on the attorney-general to reinstitute that ban.[235] Instead, Prime Minister Netanyahu called upon Knesset members to "show responsibility and restraint" by not entering the Compound.

The next day, MK Moshe Feiglin defied the prime minister (and his party leader) by entering the Compound. Feiglin campaigned on a platform of advancing the Temple movement. After a strong showing in Likud's 2013 primary effectively confirmed his place in the Knesset, he told his supporters, "this is not the end. It is just the beginning, until we build the Temple at the top of the Temple Mount and fulfill our destiny in this country."[236]

Feiglin is one of several right-wing Jewish members of the Knesset to enter the Compound in recent years. Others include Danny Danon (now Israel's ambassador to the United Nations), Uri Ariel (Minister of Housing and Construction from 2013-2015 and current Minister of Agriculture), Ze'ev Elkin (current Minister of Immigrant Absorption and Minister of Jerusalem Affairs), Yariv Levin (current Minister of Tourism), Otniel Schneller, Shulamit Mualem-Rafaeli, and Michael Ben-Ari.[237]

Several members of the U.S. House of Representatives have also visited the Compound in recent years, often as part of junkets funded by right-wing pro-Israel groups. Rep. Keith Rothfus (R-Pa.), Rep. Evan Jenkins, (R-W.Va.), Rep. Andy Harris (R-Md.), Rep. Bill Johnson (R-Ohio) and David McKinley (R-W.Va.) have all participated in such visits.[238] These tours were led by the Israel Allies Foundation, which began organizing Congressional delegations in early 2014 in conjunction with two far-right organizations: Yes to a Strong Israel, a project of the Israeli consultancy Jaffe Strategies, and Proclaiming Justice to the Nations, a Christian Zionist organization.[239] Notably, the American Israel Education Foundation (AIEF), the educational arm of the American Israel Public Affairs Committee (AIPAC) and the largest provider of Israel tours for members of Congress and their staffs, does not include visits to the Compound as part of its congressional delegations.

At least one such visit to the Compound, which included Rep. Andy Harris, was led by Rabbi Chaim Richman of the Temple Institute, which promotes the construction of a new Temple on the site of the Dome of the Rock. When asked in a 2013 interview whether the Institute's plans for a new Temple involve destroying the Muslim shrines, Richman responded, "I don't like to speculate about highly sensitive matters ... [b]ut there is only one place where the temple will be built, and it is where the Dome of the Rock and the Al-Aqsa mosque are currently standing."[240]

A bill introduced in the Knesset in May 2014, sponsored by members of the right-wing Likud and center-left Labor Party, would give Jews the right to engage in demonstrative prayer and use religious paraphernalia at the Compound.[241] Under pressure from Jordan and the international community, the bill was not brought to a vote. Similar legislation is likely to be introduced in the current Knesset because, as noted by International Crisis Group, "the March 2015 elections brought the champions of Temple activism into the coalition as ministers."[242]

State Support of Temple Movements

The presence of Temple activists in key government positions has translated into increasing government support for "Temple movements," broadly defined as organizations focused on "shaping public opinion to embrace a change in worship arrangements on the [Temple] Mount and ultimately to advance the construction of the Third Temple."[243]

Over the past 30 years, and particularly since the Oslo Accords, these Temple movements have succeeded in building support for their goals among the political and rabbinical leadership of the national-religious movement, thereby rendering proposals for new arrangements at the Compound (which would be unilaterally set by Israel) as a "legitimate subject of public discourse."[244] The national-religious movement, also called Religious Zionism, is an ideology that combines Zionism and Judaism. It recasts Zionism, originally a political movement initiated by secular Jews, as an expression of divine will and a religious obligation.[245] Most adherents of the national-religious movement embrace right-wing politics and are represented in the Knesset by the Likud, Jewish Home, and smaller far-right parties.

Virtually all of the Temple movements call on their followers to visit the Compound. Accordingly, visits by Jewish Israelis to the Compound, who by policy are always escorted by armed ISF personnel, have increased sharply in recent years.[246] On certain Jewish holidays, including Sukkot, and at times of heightened tensions, such as the summer of 2014 (including Ramadan), the ISF closes the Compound to Muslim worshippers during visitation periods designated for Jews. On October 30, 2014, Israel imposed its first complete closure of the Compound since the start of second intifada in 2000.[247] As the number and visibility of Jewish Israeli visits to the Compound increases, so does the Palestinian resistance to the changing status quo. That resistance, in turn, prompts new ISF access restrictions on Palestinians and other Muslim worshippers during Jewish visits, bringing the situation at the Compound closer to the model of the Ibrahimi Mosque (Tomb of the Patriarchs) in Hebron. Indeed, right-wing Israeli politicians advocating for new arrangements at the Compound identify the Ibrahimi Mosque as the model.

It is important to note that, while all Temple movements advocate the construction of the Third temple, not all argue that this construction should take place on the Dome of the Rock. Some of the Temple movements, however, do advocate constructing a new Temple on the approximate location of the biblical Temples, where the Dome of the Rock stands today. Groups which advocate "capturing the Temple Mount from 'enemy hands'" or "Judaizing the Temple Mount" include 'Temple Mount is Ours' and the 'Headquarters for the Rescue of the Nation and the Temple'. These initiatives presuppose destroying the Muslim shrines at the Compound. Groups advocating for reconstruction of the Temple (without expressly calling for the destruction of the Muslim Holy Places) include the 'Temple Institute', the 'Movement for Temple Renewal', the 'Temple Treasury Trust', and 'Women for the Temple'.[248]

Rhetoric advocating and depictions of the destruction of the Al-Aqsa Mosque and the Dome of the Rock provoke outrage among Muslims worldwide and Palestinians of all faiths, for whom the sites are symbols of national identity.[249] The following cases serve as examples of the use of this dangerous rhetoric and imagery:

- Former MK Aryeh Eldad was quoted as saying in 2012, while serving in the Knesset, that "when the time comes to build the Temple, and it will come soon, we will saw down the building standing there today [the Dome of the Rock]. We will saw it and they can take it wherever they want, because that is where the third Temple should stand."[250]

- A video posted to the Haredi (ultra-Orthodox) website Kikar Hashabat and other outlets since 2012 depicts the Dome of the Rock being destroyed by airstrikes and replaced by the third Temple.[251]

- The announcement of a 2011 demonstration at the Compound by Temple Mount Faithful declared that participants will "swear allegiance to building the Temple on the ruins of the temporary mosques standing on Temple Mount, in the life of this generation."[252]

Given the inflammatory objectives and rhetoric of these groups, some of which originated in the underground movements of the 1970s and 1980s that plotted attacks on Muslim Holy Places,[253] the Israeli security establishment assesses a greater risk of Jewish extremists harming the Muslim Holy Places at the Compound when the government acts against settlement activity or pursues negotiations that could lead to Israel ending its occupation of East Jerusalem. For example, the thwarted plot by the Jewish Underground organization to blow up the Dome of the Rock in the early 1980s was motivated by the Camp David Accords and Israel's withdrawal from the Sinai, including the evacuation of Yamit settlement. Recognizing this link, the Knesset held a special hearing on the "security establishment assessment of risk of attack on the Temple Mount and assassination attempt on public figures" prior to Israel's 2005 "disengagement" from Gaza.[254] At the hearing, Avi Dichter, former director of the General Security Service (Shin Bet), testified to a "direct link" between government tolerance or endorsement of such nationalist rhetoric, a popular "atmosphere of legitimacy" towards such violence, and the commission of political violence.

But while many Israeli intelligence and security officials are weary of the Temple movements and their potential for creating national and sectarian strife, these movements nevertheless receive financial, security, and ideological support from the Israeli government. This support reflects the success of the Temple movements, once disreputable fringe organizations, in making new worship arrangements at the Compound a mainstream political issue and construction of a new Temple where the Muslim Holy Places today stand a legitimate political objective., In 1971, Israel's attorney-general blocked the establishment of an "Association for the Construction of the Temple in Jerusalem" based on the "insult of the subject" and the "exploitation" inherent in the group's efforts to "raise funds for an activity they are neither authorized nor capable of carrying out."[255] Today, there are at least 19 registered associations and one public trust (which by law requires a legitimate public purpose, in this case construction of a third Temple) with Temple-related missions.[256]

Several of these organizations receive public funding.[257] One such movement, the Temple Institute, received an annual average of NIS 412,000 ($106,000) between 2008 and 2011 from the Ministry of Culture, Science and Sports and the Ministry of Education. The religious youth movement Ariel, which operates mainly in West Bank settlements and seeks to "strengthen Temple awareness and spiritual and practical action to hasten its rebuilding," received an annual average of NIS 8 million ($2.05 million) in public funding. These movements are also represented in the educational curriculum, without being challenged by competing Jewish, Muslim, and secular perspectives on the Compound's religious, historical, and political significance. The Temple Institute's educational arm, Midrasha, is registered with the Ministry of Education as an educational body and gives Temple presentations annually to tens of thousands of students, faculty, and administrators.

CONCLUSION

Israel is obligated under IHL and the status quo legal regime that governs the Jerusalem Holy Places to respect and maintain the established rights of the religious communities, including Muslim self-governance/Waqf administration at the Compound. Increasingly strident pronouncements by Israeli government officials about "realizing Israeli sovereignty" over the Compound are contributing to greater sectarian strife.[258] Any expression of Israeli sovereignty over the site would confirm that Israel has illegally annexed East Jerusalem and would effectively abrogate Jordan's custodianship of the Compound, which Israel has already compromised by encroaching on the Waqf's authority to regulate entry. The rise of the Temple movements and the support for their initiatives at the highest levels of the current Israeli government foreshadow stronger popular and legislative efforts to assert Israeli sovereignty and Jewish national rights at the Compound. These actions not only threaten the delicate relationship between religious communities in Jerusalem; they threaten to disrupt Israel's relationship with the Palestinians, Jordan, and the wider Islamic world, and thus pose a threat to regional security and U.S. policy.

4

DISCRIMINATORY AND INADEQUATE
PROTECTION OF NON-JEWISH HOLY PLACES

Israeli laws and practices regarding the registration, administration, and funding of holy places are characterized by an institutionalized preference for Jewish holy places and a refusal to register or provide adequate protection to non-Jewish holy places. This applies particularly to Muslim places of worship, often leading to their destruction or their conversion for purposes of commercial exploitation.[259] These laws and policies persist despite repeated legal challenges by representatives of the Palestinian minority to ensure respect for non-Jewish holy places.

LEGAL STANDARD

Human Rights Law

Human rights law requires states to uphold the principle of nondiscrimination in regulating the right of members of religious groups to practice their religion, "either individually or in community with others and in public or private."[260] This principle, as it applies to minority religious communities, is established by articles 2, 18 and 27 ICCPR.[261] Limitations on this right are extremely restricted and only permitted when prescribed by law and necessary for public safety, order, health, morals, or the protection of others' rights.

The concept of equality in the public practice and worship of religion includes equality in access and protection of the holy places and sites of worship. This view is supported by the State Department and the USCIRF, which has expressed concern in other situations in which national governments have infringed on religious practice by limiting physical access to holy places. The Commission has pointed to discriminatory issuance of building and repair permits for places of worship and at deliberately complex methods of registering and practicing in places of worship.

Various ECtHR cases have held that the right to freedom of religion under article 9 ECHR encompasses the right to operate houses of worship and to associate freely at them. Furthermore, under ECtHR case law, violations of religious freedom extend to discriminatory permit and registration regimes that restrict meaningful access to places of worship.[262] The ECtHR precedent is particularly strong where minor or insignificant violations of laws have been used as a pretext to restrict religious freedom, and the USCIRF has noted this. The Court has established that violations of administrative procedures—including the lack of a necessary permit—may not be used as a pretext to shut down religious institutions in a discriminatory manner. Rather, the government's response to religious organizations' violations of neutral administrative and licensing regulations should be proportionate to the legitimate aim pursued.[263] Disproportionate penalties imposed for violations of administrative procedures that have the effect of inhibiting religious groups' access to places of worship constitute a violation of the freedom of religion and association clauses of articles 9 and 11 ECHR.

In *Biblical Centre of the Chuvash Republic v. Russia,* the local government of Russia's Chuvash Republic shut down a Pentecostal Church and its educational center for failing to obtain the registration license required under Russian law.[264] In effect, this law only applied to non-Orthodox religious groups, as Russia acknowledged that many Russian Orthodox institutions lacked licenses but were permitted to operate under the "standard Orthodox statute."[265] The Court held that the State's response must be "proportionate to the legitimate aims pursued,"[266] such that there is "no other means of achieving the same end that would interfere less seriously with the fundamental right concerned."[267] The total closure of a religious institution can be justified only for the most serious violations of the law, given its grave and immediate consequences for members of the religious community. Applying this standard, the Court ruled that Russia's practice of dissolving religious organizations that failed to comply with the discriminatory licensing requirement under Russian law violated the ECHR.

In its twin case released during the same period, *Krupko and Others v. Russia*, the State shut down a religious gathering of the Jehovah's Witnesses under the pretext that it was forbidden under the Public Gatherings Act. The ECtHR held that when the government chose to forcibly disrupt the religious peaceful assembly when such a disruption was not "necessary"—notwithstanding that it may have been a technical violation of the law—the disruption and restriction on access to place of worship constituted a violation of Article 9 of the ECHR.[268]

USCIRF Precedent

Russia

In its 2015 report, the USCIRF criticized Russia's practices as exposed in the *Biblical Centre of the Chuvash Republic v. Russia* ECtHR ruling. As the Commission succinctly stated, "the lack of registration status should not result in the banning of a religious group."[269]

Belarus

In Belarus, the government often refuses to allow religious groups to register properties as religious houses of worship. In several instances, the Belarusian government has prevented the creation of new holy places by requiring that the religious group be registered before being able to convert properties to religious use.[270]

Sudan

The Commission has criticized the Sudanese government's restrictions on Sudan's Christian community's access to houses of worship. As of July 2014, the government of Sudan no longer issues permits for the construction of new churches. This building freeze is compounded by the government's active and passive facilitation of the destruction of over 11 churches in the last few years.[271]

Tajikistan

The situation in the forcibly secular former Soviet republic of Tajikistan mirrors that in Russia to a large extent; the government places strict limits on the number of mosques permitted to operate. In addition, in the last seven years hundreds of unregistered mosques built in excess of the strict number of mosques permitted to operate under Tajik law have been closed by the government. And although the Jewish population is a small minority, in 2008 the central government demolished the country's only synagogue.[272]

ANALYSIS

Protection and Registration of Jewish and Non-Jewish Holy Places under the Protection of Holy Places Law, 1967

Holy places in Israel and occupied East Jerusalem are protected by the 1967 Protection of Holy Places Law, which states that holy places are protected from desecration, violation, and "anything likely to violate the freedom of access of the members of the different religions to the places sacred to them."[273] The law imposes stiff penalties of seven and five years imprisonment for desecration and violating freedom of access, respectively, and it holds the Minister of Religious Affairs responsible for implementing the law.[274]

While the Law directs the Minister of Religious Affairs to promulgate implementing regulations, nearly 50 years later, the Israeli government has adopted regulations for the protection for Jewish holy sites only. Consequently, as of the State Department's last count in 2008, there were 137 designated Jewish holy sites and no officially designated Christian or Muslim holy sites. The Jewish holy sites thus receive formal legal protection under Israeli law while non-Jewish holy sites are often "neglected, inaccessible, or threatened by property developers and municipalities."[275]

In 2004, Adalah: The Legal Center for Arab Minority Rights in Israel petitioned Israel's Supreme Court for an order directing the Minister of Religious Affairs to issue regulations for the protection of non-Jewish holy sites. As Adalah set forth, the law requires the Minister of Religious Affairs to regulate on a non-discriminatory basis.[276] Adalah provided ample evidence and documentation of non-Jewish holy sites, especially Muslim sites, which did not receive protection under the law and were in need of protection. The evidence included a report from an Israeli government-created Special Committee established in February 2000 to investigate the condition of non-Jewish holy sites. The report found an extensive list of Muslim holy sites and cemeteries that were in immediate need of repair, but the Minister of Religious Affairs failed to implement the Committee's recommendations. Nevertheless, the Supreme Court rejected Adalah's petition in 2009, reasoning that the designation of religious sites was a "sensitive matter" involving questions of fact, degree, and value that could not be adequately addressed by the judiciary. The Court's decision gives the Minister of Religious Affairs complete discretion to refuse to designate sites as holy and in need of protection, without judicial review.

Lack of Legal Recognition of non-Jewish Holy Places Permits the Destruction of Muslim Holy Places

In Israel, the lack of legal recognition and protection of non-Jewish holy places leaves these religious sites vulnerable to destructive social and economic forces. Existing Muslim religious sites are especially vulnerable, and often suffer from the lack of protection against general municipal planning schemes or general exploitation by investors.

Mosques Slated for Demolition in Unrecognized Bedouin Villages

In the Naqab (Negev), tens of thousands of Bedouins live in "unrecognized villages" that pre-date the establishment of the State of Israel but are not formally included within the State's planning schemes.[277] Mosques in these villages and communities are neither recognized as holy places or houses of worship under the Holy Places Law, or even as valid structures generally subject to protections within the municipal planning schemes. Rather, they are considered illegal structures subject to demolition, which often occurs.

In a particularly egregious episode that garnered international attention, Israeli forces demolished a mosque in the Bedouin town of Rahat because it was built without a permit.[278] The construction permit system is discriminatory against non-Jews and especially against Bedouins living in unrecognized villages. The villages are not recognized as communal areas and often appear empty on official maps. The government's reaction to the construction of a house of worship, albeit without a permit, is disproportionate, as understood within ECtHR case law. The USCIRF has used such case law, including *The Case of Biblical Centre of the Chuvash Republic v. Russia*, to criticize the Russian government's destruction and prohibition on religious activity within houses of worship due to registration and permit requirements.

Conversion from Houses of Worship

Non-Jewish holy places and places of worship lack special protections under Israeli law, are consequently vulnerable to economic exploitation, and are often repurposed for secular use. For example, in Beer el-Sabe (Be'er Sheva) the municipality sought to reopen the city's old mosque, which was shut down in 1948, as a museum. The State Department's 2011 IRF report noted the conversion and local residents' campaign to have it restored as a place of worship.[279] Adalah unsuccessfully petitioned the Supreme Court to halt the renovation, arguing that it was the only mosque in the city to serve the city's 5,000 Muslim residents, whereas the city had one synagogue for every 700 Jewish residents.[280]

CONCLUSION

While Israeli law would seem to provide protection for the holy places of all faiths, the Israel government has refused since 1967 to register non-Jewish holy places, leaving these sites vulnerable to neglect, destruction or conversion for purposes of commercial exploitation. Legal challenges to this discriminatory policy by the Palestinian minority have failed to achieve equal treatment for Jewish and non-Jewish holy sites. Further, places of worship in unrecognized Bedouin communities in the Naqab (Negev) are threatened with demolition as part of the Israeli government's plan to consolidate Palestinian Bedouin communities into urbanized townships, so as to facilitate the establishment of new Jewish communities. These policies and practices are inconsistent with Israel's obligation to uphold equality and nondiscrimination between faiths in the protection of holy places and places of worship.

5
RESTRICTIONS ON CLERGY VISAS

Israel/Palestine is the birthplace of the three major monotheist religions, home to communities of numerous denominations, and a source of history, meaning, and inspiration to believers worldwide. Its universal religious significance is such that the UN General Assembly, in its 1947 Partition Plan and in Resolution 194 of 1948, called for Jerusalem to be placed under international sovereignty:

> in view of its association with three world religions, the Jerusalem area, including the present municipality of Jerusalem plus the surrounding villages and towns ... should be accorded special and separate treatment from the rest of Palestine and should be placed under effective United Nations control.[281]

Religious institutions in Israel and the oPt are responsible not only for spiritual life of their communities, but, as part of their ministry, also provide education, health, and social services to the wider community. Given the significance of these religious institutions, it is especially problematic that Israel's laws, policies, and practices governing visas for clergy and religious workers fall short of the international religious freedom standards set by the Commission.

Legal Standard

Human Rights Law

Restrictions on visas for clergy and religious workers involve freedom of religion, as codified in article 18 UDHR and article 18 ICCPR, as well as the rights of religious minorities, as expressed in article 27 ICCPR.

The freedom of religion guaranteed by article 18 ICCPR includes the right "to manifest [one's] religion or belief in worship, observance, practice and teaching."[282] The Human Rights Committee has observed that "the practice and teaching of religion or belief includes acts integral to the conduct by religious groups of their basic affairs, such as the freedom to choose their religious leaders, priests and teachers [and] the freedom to establish seminaries or religious schools…."[283] Interpreting the equivalent provision of the ECHR, article 9, the European Court of Human Rights has repeatedly held that restrictions on clergy or religious worker visas or residency permits constitute an interference with a manifestation of religion.[284]

Under article 18.3 ICCPR, any limitations to these acts must be prescribed by law and necessary to protect public safety, order, health, morals, or the rights of others.[285] The HRC insists that article 18.3 be "strictly interpreted" such that "restrictions are not allowed on grounds not specified there, even if they would be allowed as restrictions to other rights protected in the Covenant, such as national security."[286] The equivalent provision of the ECHR, article 9.2, requires that any interference with manifestations of religion be "prescribed by law" and "necessary in a democratic society" for the preservation of public safety, order, health, morals, or the rights of others. Under ECtHR precedent, an interference is necessary in a democratic society if it corresponds to a pressing social need, is proportionate to the legitimate aim pursued, and is justified by relevant and sufficient reasons. The State bears the burden of proving these factors.[287]

Article 27 ICCPR guarantees persons belonging to religious minorities the right, in community with the other members of their group, to profess and practice their own religion.[288] The HRC has clarified that article 27 confers rights on all persons belonging to minorities which "exist" in a state party, including nationals, permanent residents, foreign workers (including religious workers), and visitors.[289] Article 27 requires states to take positive measures of protection against majority oppression by state and private actors. It further requires positive measures to ensure members of religious minorities are able to practice their religion in the community with the other members of the group, with the goal of ensuring the survival and continued development of the religious community.[290] These measures must be implemented in accordance with the Covenant's guarantees of non-discrimination and equal protection.[291]

The ECtHR ruled in 2006 that Russia's refusal to reregister the local branch of the Salvation Army, which resulted in its loss of legal status and made it impossible for its 25 foreign employees and seven non-Moscow Russian employees to obtain residence registration in Moscow, was an unjustified violation of the religious freedom of the organization's members in violation of article 9 ECHR. The Russian courts had upheld the refusal to re-register the organization, *inter alia*, on the basis that the organization's executive body included five non-Russian nationals with multiple-entry visas but no residence permits.[292]

In 2007, the ECtHR held Turkey responsible for acts carried out by the unrecognized Turkish Republic of Northern Cyprus (TRNC) that violated the religious freedom rights of Greek Cypriots, including restrictions on access to religious sites in TRNC-controlled territory and travel restrictions on Greek Cypriots living in TRNC-controlled territory for worship.[293] Additionally, the Court ruled that the refusal of the Turkish Cypriot authorities to allow additional Greek Orthodox priests to be appointed to the TRNC-controlled Karpas region, which consequently had only one priest, "prevented the organisation of Greek Orthodox religious ceremonies in a normal and regular manner" and thereby violated article 9 ECHR.[294]

In *Perry v. Latvia*, the ECtHR held that a prohibition on a foreign evangelical pastor from exercising his ministry as a condition of his residence permit renewal was not authorized by any provision of Latvian law and thus had not been "prescribed by law," in violation of article 9 ECHR.[295]

USCIRF Precedent

Russia

Following its visit to Russia in 2003, the Commission wrote to President George W. Bush to express concern over "disquieting events" that included "a recent conspicuous increase in the number of clergy and other religious workers denied visas or residency permits, even in cases of previous long-term residency in Russia."[296]

In keeping Russia on Tier 2 in 2015, the Commission condemned new restrictions on clergy and religious workers in occupied Crimea. It noted that, by late 2014, clergy without Russian citizenship, in particular clergymen not affiliated with the Russian Orthodox Church, were forced to leave Crimea; that Russia's Federal Migration Service had not extended residence permits to foreigners working with Crimean religious groups; and that Ukrainian Catholic priests who are not Crimean natives can work only for three months before they must leave and re-apply, reducing by half the number of priests in Crimea affiliated with the Kiev Patriarchate.[297]

Cyprus and Turkey

In listing Turkey as a Tier 2 country and in monitoring Cyprus, the Commission has repeatedly noted with concern the restrictions on clergy and laity crossing the UN Buffer Zone for purposes of worship. In 2015, the Commission commended the lifting of longstanding restrictions that had prohibited the Archbishop of the Greek Orthodox Church of Cyprus and the Grand Mufti of the Turkish Cypriot community from crossing the Buffer Zone.[298] Notably, the Grand Mufti, a Turkish national, had been excluded from areas under the control of the Republic of Cyprus government on the basis that he was a Turkish settler.

ANALYSIS

Israeli Visa Provisions

The 1952 Entry into Israel Law vests the Ministry of Interior (MOI) with discretion to grant and extend visas and residence permits, including clergy and religious worker visas, to non-Israeli nationals (other than new Jewish immigrants).[299] The Population and Immigration Authority (PIBA) is the MOI department responsible for approving and supervising entry and residency by foreign nationals.

Clergy visas, designated as A/3 visas in the Entry into Israel Law regulations, are granted for the purpose of fulfilling clerical duties in religious communities recognized in Israel, pursuant to the invitation of the religious institution.[300] The application must be submitted in Israel by the religious community or institution. The initial A/3 visa is issued by Israeli missions abroad upon MOI approval, while renewals are processed only in Israel.

Regarding recognized and unrecognized religious communities, the State Department's 2003 IRF report explained:

> Israeli law recognizes the "religious communities" as carried over from those recognized under the British Mandate. These are: Eastern Orthodox, Latin (Catholic), Gregorian-Armenian, Armenian-Catholic, Syrian (Catholic), Chaldean (Uniate), Greek Catholic Melkite, Maronite, Syrian Orthodox, and Jewish. Three additional religious communities have subsequently been recognized -- the Druze, the Evangelical Episcopal Church, and the Baha'i. The status of some Christian denominations with representation in the country has been defined by a collection of ad hoc arrangements with various government agencies. The fact that the Muslim population was not defined as a religious community is a vestige of the Ottoman period during which Islam was the dominant religion and does not affect the rights of the Muslim community to practice their faith. At the end of the period covered by this report, several of these denominations were pending official government recognition; however, the Government has allowed adherents of not officially recognized groups freedom to practice.[301]

Interference in Religious Activities

Recognized Religious Communities

The State Department, in its 2013 IRF report, observed the following Israeli restrictions on the issuance of clergy visas to recognized religious communities:[302]

- The MOI gave some Christian clergy members entry permits only for the West Bank, precluding their travel inside Israel, or entry permits only for Israel, precluding their travel in the oPt.

- Certain clergy were required to sign a declaration acknowledging that accessing areas under Palestinian control without appropriate authorization from the Coordinator of Government Activities in the Territories (COGAT) could result in deportation and a ten-year travel ban. Israeli government officials at the port of entry did not explain to such clergy members how to obtain such a permit. COGAT is the department of the Israeli Ministry of Defense that coordinates civilian issues between the Government of Israel, the Israel Defense Forces, international organizations, diplomats, and the Palestinian Authority.

- Arab Christian clergy serving in the West Bank, including East Jerusalem, are issued only single-entry clergy visas, complicating their travel, particularly to areas under their pastoral authority that are outside the West Bank. Thus, a clergy member who holds a single-entry A/3 visa forfeits the remainder of the residency period provided by the visa when leaving Israel and the oPt, even on pastoral business. To return, the clergy member's religious institution must repeat the A/3 visa application process or the clergy member must enter on a B/2 tourist visa, which is valid for up to three months. These restrictions severely interfere with the ministry of Church institutions which have pastoral jurisdiction beyond Israel and the oPt, such as the the Latin Patriarchate of Jerusalem, which has jurisdiction over Israel, the oPt, Jordan and Cyprus.

- Israel generally prohibited Arab Christian clergy from entering Gaza, including bishops and other senior clergy seeking to visit congregations or ministries under their pastoral authority.

- Clergy, nuns, and other religious workers from Arab countries faced long processing delays and/or denial of their visa applications.[303]

Religious officials and laity cite difficulties in obtaining Israeli visas and residency permits for Christian clergy as one factor driving increased Christian emigration from Israel and the oPt.[304] Other contributing factors include the limited ability of Christian communities in the Jerusalem area to expand due to building restrictions, Israeli government family reunification restrictions, and taxation problems.

Case Study: The Catholic Church and Cremisan

Despite the establishment of full diplomatic relations between Israel and the Vatican in 1993, Israeli restrictions on Catholic clergy and religious worker visas substantially interfere with the Church's institutions and ministries in the Holy Land. Further, Israel's ongoing construction of its Separation Wall through the Cremisan Valley threatens to interfere with the operations and ministry of the Roman Catholic institutions in Cremisan and the spiritual life of Palestinian Christian community in the Jerusalem and Bethlehem areas.

The Fundamental Agreement between the Holy See and the State of Israel, signed in December 1993, established recognition and full diplomatic relations between Israel and the Holy See.[305] The Agreement includes an Israeli commitment to respect the Status Quo in the Christian Holy Places and a mutual commitment to promote religious freedom and ensure access to the holy places.[306]

The Agreement has multiple provisions that obligate Israel to facilitate the entry and residency of Church clergy and laity. Israel recognized the Church's right to "train, appoint and deploy its own personnel in [its religious, moral, educational and charitable] institutions or for the said functions to these ends," while the Church recognized Israel's right to carry out its functions, which include "protecting the welfare and the safety of the people."[307] Israel further commits in the Agreement to the "continuing guarantee of the freedom of Catholic worship," while the parties jointly reaffirm the Church's right "to establish, maintain and direct schools of study at all levels" and "carry out its charitable functions through its health care and social welfare institutions."[308]

Despite these commitments, Israel imposed onerous restrictions on entry visas and residence permits for Catholic religious personnel during the second intifada. These restrictions and their effect on the Church's ministry prompted the then-Latin Patriarch of Jerusalem, Michel Sabbah, to establish an "Ad Hoc Committee charged with examining the problem of Catholic religious personnel whose visas had been requested from the Ministry of Interior of Israel but have not yet been granted" ("Committee"). The Committee's report to the Vatican's Apostolic Delegate to Jerusalem, submitted in March 2003, included the following findings:[309]

- 70 of the 86 clergy or religious workers whose visa applications were outstanding, or 81 percent, were nationals of neighboring Arab states. These religious personnel each held a *laissez-passer* issued by the Holy See with assurances that the Vatican's Diplomatic Representation had verified in each case that the motive for entry or residence was a bona fide religious, educational, or charitable purpose.

- Israeli visa policies "impede[d] the conduct of Christian worship in certain areas by denying pastors and assistant-pastors the right to minister to the flock." The report noted that five of the delegates with outstanding visas or residency permits were pastors serving the Latin Patriarchate's 21 parishes in Israel and the West Bank.

- These policies "jeopardize[d] the very existence" of the Latin Patriarchate's main seminary at Beit Jala in the West Bank, as Israel was withholding the visas of the seminary rector and virtually all its seminarians from Jordan. The Latin Patriarchate has 32 parishes in Jordan and two-thirds of its seminarians are Jordanian nationals.

- These policies were "contrary to the spirit of mutual respect and cooperation" envisaged in the Fundamental Agreement, and incompatible with Articles 10(a) and 10(d) of the Agreement, wherein the parties agreed to "negotiate in good faith a comprehensive agreement...on unclear, unsettled and disputed issues" and to avoid "actions incompatible with these commitments" during the pendency of negotiations, which to date have not been completed.

- As a result of Israel's refusal or failure to process these visas, the Committee found, "critical aspects of the life of the Church are being hampered, from the most upper-level of Church administration, to the daily operations of a wide variety of its institutions."

The Committee's report thus concluded that:

> the Israeli government, by its extensive restrictions on entry visas and temporary residence permits is currently in material breach of the principle of Freedom of Religion, as guaranteed by its own Declaration of Independence, the Universal Declaration of Human Rights, and the Fundamental Agreement Between the Holy See and the State of Israel.

By March 2004, the number of outstanding visas or residency permits for Catholic delegates had reached approximately 130, prompting Archbishop Pietro Sambi, then the Vatican's Apostolic Delegate in Jerusalem, to publicly rebuke an Israeli official for his government's failure to abide by its commitments with respect to clergy and religious worker visas.[310]

Further, Israel's construction of the Separation Wall through the Cremisan Valley jeopardizes the Church's ability to effectively maintain its institutions in Cremisan and serve the spiritual needs of its pastoral following, in violation of article 18 ICCPR.

The right to freedom of religion, as defined in international human rights law, encompasses the right to establish and freely access religious institutions that are integral to a faith's ministry, including schools, hospitals, and care facilities. The UN Human Rights Committee has commented that "the practice and teaching of religion or belief" as defined in art. 18(1) ICCPR "includes acts integral to the conduct by religious groups of their basic affairs, such as the freedom to choose their religious leaders, priests and teachers [and] the freedom to establish seminaries or religious schools...."[311] Similarly, the 1981 UN Declaration provides that freedom of thought, conscience, religion or belief embodies the rights to:

- "establish and maintain appropriate charitable or humanitarian institutions";

- "teach a religion or belief in places suitable for these purposes";

- "train...appropriate leaders called for by the requirements and standards of any religion or belief"; and

- "establish and maintain communications with individuals and communities in matters of religion and belief at the national and international levels."[312]

Under article 18(3) ICCPR, the right to freedom of religion can only be subject to limitations that "are necessary to protect public safety, order, health, or morals or the fundamental rights and freedoms of others."[313] Article 4 ICCPR, which governs derogations of Convention rights, expressly provides that "public emergency which threatens the life of the nation" (i.e. war) does not justify derogation from freedoms of religion.[314] The rights contained in the ICCPR remain applicable despite the existence of any state of armed conflict.[315] Derogation is only permissible in times of *bona fide* national emergencies, which are strictly construed.[316]

Consistent with human rights law, the Commission has identified interference with access to religious institutions as violations of religious freedom. It has held Turkey responsible for the inability of Orthodox Christians and other religious groups to access and hold services at their places of worship and cemeteries in Turkish-occupied Northern Cyprus, including those within designated military areas.[317] Further, the Commission has asserted that the scope of limitations established in the ICCPR should be interpreted narrowly.[318]

Beginning in 2002, Israel repeatedly confiscated privately-owned Palestinian land in Cremisan for the purpose of constructing the Wall, deemed illegal under international humanitarian law and human rights law in the 2004 ICJ Advisory Opinion.[319] Plans for the Wall's construction in Cremisan were announced in 2006. Since that time, the Salesians of Don Bosco, a Roman Catholic order which owns and operates a convent and monastery in Cremisan, along with the Beit Jala Municipality and 58 Palestinian Christian families who own land in the valley, have mounted a legal challenge and a diplomatic campaign against the Wall's construction. The Salesian monastery is famous for its vineyards and wine cellars, while the convent operates a primary school, kindergarten, and program for children with learning disabilities, which together provide education to about 450 Palestinian children, as well as extracurricular activities and summer camps for local children. The Salesians thus maintain that the Wall violates the Fundamental Agreement, wherein Israel "recognizes the right of the

Catholic Church to carry out its religious, moral, educational and charitable functions...."[320]

The Israeli Supreme Court issued its final ruling on the petitioners' legal challenge in April 2015.[321] The Court accepted their demand that the Salesian convent and monastery not be separated from each other and from their constituency in the Palestinian towns of Bethlehem, Beit Jala, Beit Sahour, and al-Walaja. Thus, the Court ordered that the convent and monastery both be placed on the "Palestinian" side of the wall. Subject to these requirements of continuity, however, the Court allowed the state to proceed with construction of the wall on privately-owned Palestinian land in Cremisan. The Israeli government began construction of this section of the wall in August 2015 without publicly disclosing its route, making it impossible to know whether the final route complies with the letter and spirit of the Court's April 2015 decision. Court petitions by the Salesians to halt construction until and unless the route is disclosed have been unsuccessful.

While the full consequences of the Wall's construction in Cremisan will thus only be known once its construction is complete, the Salesians fear that its route will run flush against the convent and its school, turning it into a flashpoint for confrontations and interfering with its educational and religious ministry. They also fear that the same considerations will interfere with their ability to work the agricultural lands and vineyards of the Convent and the Monastery, which help to fund their religious ministry. Accordingly, the Latin Patriarch of Jerusalem, Fouad Twal, has called the Wall's construction through Cremisan "a form of Christian persecution" that will lead to further Christian emigration from the Holy Land.[322]

Unrecognized Religious Communities

Clergy or lay workers affiliated with religious communities not recognized by Israel are not entitled to apply for A/3 visas and must obtain a B/2 visitor visa, which allows residency for up to three months but does not authorize work in Israel or the oPt.[323] While B/2 visas can in certain circumstances be extended or renewed within Israel through the MOI, in practice, B/2 visa holders "renew" their visas by exiting Israel and the oPt every three months and attempting to re-enter on a new visa. However, consecutive entries raise the suspicion of the Israeli authorities that the individual is living and/or working without authorization in Israel or the oPt, and thus increases the risk that the individual will be denied entry and may be subject to entry ban.[324]

CONCLUSION

Israel's laws, policies, and practices governing visas for clergy and lay religious workers fall short of the religious freedom standards set by the Commission and interfere with the spiritual life and ministry of religious institutions in Israel and the oPt.

PART TWO

PRESERVING THE SYSTEM OF
ETHNORELIGIOUS CONTROL

6

FACILITATING PUBLIC AND PRIVATE DISCRIMINATION THROUGH NATIONAL IDS THAT DISCLOSE RELIGIOUS AFFILIATION

In Israel and the oPt, every citizen or permanent resident aged 16 or older is required by law to carry an official identity card. All identity cards, whether Israeli or Palestinian, are issued in accordance with Israeli-controlled population registries.[325] As discussed in chapter 2, *supra*, the Israeli population registry classifies residents by recognized 'nationality' (Hebrew: *le'om*; Arabic: *qawmiya*), with the overwhelming majority of the population classified as Jewish or Arab.[326] Before 2005, the holder's *le'om* was also listed on the official ID card. Due to an intergovernmental dispute over registering Reform converts to Judaism as members of the Jewish *le'om*, the Israeli government has not listed *le'om* on identity cards since 2005.[327] However, the ID cards still clearly differentiate Jews from non-Jews, violating international religious freedom standards and facilitating a variety of forms of public and private discrimination.

LEGAL STANDARD

Human Rights Law

In *Sinan Işik v. Turkey*, a case referenced in the Commission's reporting on Turkey, the European Court of Human Rights explained why states must remove all indicia of ethnic or religious affiliation from identity documents. The applicant belonged to the Alevi community, of which some members regard themselves as Muslims and other members regard themselves observers of a different faith. Since 2006, Turkish law allowed citizens to request that the religion entry on their state-issued ID cards be changed or left blank. The state refused to change the applicant's listed religion from Muslim to Alevi, but argued that the option to list no religion was an adequate accommodation. The ECtHR disagreed, ruling that Turkey had violated article 9 ECHR and that complete removal of the religion entry on the ID card was the appropriate compliance measure. The Court emphasized that:

> the right to manifest one's religion or beliefs also has a negative aspect, namely an individual's right not to be obliged to disclose his or her religion or beliefs and not to be obliged to act in such a way that it is possible to conclude that he or she holds – or does not hold – such beliefs.[328]

The Court further reasoned that, where an ID card has a designated category to indicate religion, even indicating a blank space is itself a form of forcing an individual to disclose, against his or her will, information concerning an aspect of his or her religion or most personal convictions.[329] The Court noted two components of this violation: first, merely having to apply for religion to be deleted from civil registers requires revealing certain aspects of a person's attitude toward religion.[330] Second, the court observed that "when identity cards have a religion box, leaving that box blank inevitably has a specific connotation."[331] Thus, individuals choosing not to indicate their religion would "stand out, against their will and as a result of interference by the authorities, from those who have an identity card indicating their religious beliefs."[332]

The ECtHR also found it legally significant that the ID card was a "public document [which] had to be shown at the request of any public authority or private enterprise or in the context of any formality whatsoever requiring identification of the holder... [thereby exposing] the bearers to the risk of discriminatory situations in their relations with the administrative authorities."[333] Given the purpose and use of ID cards in such a manner, the court found that the ID card, even if the religion box was left blank, "constitutes de facto a document requiring the applicant to disclose his religious beliefs against his will every time he uses it."[334]

The U.N. Special Rapporteur on freedom of religion or belief asserts that, while the risk of abuse must "be weighed against the possible reasons for disclosing the holder's religion[,] ... any indication of one's religious affiliation on official documents should in general be on a voluntary basis."[335] The Rapporteur further notes that "it would be discriminatory to provide only the possibility to choose from a limited number of officially recognized religions."[336]

USCIRF Precedent

The USCIRF, in interpreting IRFA consistently with international human rights standards, has maintained that designating religious affiliation on official state identity cards is unacceptable because it carries a serious risk of abuse by facilitating religious discrimination. In its 2013 Report, the Commission condemned discrimination against the Baha'i minority in Egypt and urged the Egyptian government to "remove mention of religious affiliation from national identity documents."[337] In its 2014 Report, the Commission recommended that Turkey cease indicating religious affiliation on official identity documents by "remov[ing] the space listing religious affiliation on official identification cards to comply with the 2010 European Court of Human Rights ruling that it violates freedom of religion or belief under the European Convention."[338]

ANALYSIS

Although the IDs of Israeli citizens and permanent residents no longer list the holder's *le'om*, they still conspicuously differentiate Jews from Palestinians and other non-Jews. Only persons identified as Jewish in the population registry have their dates of birth listed according to the Hebrew calendar, while only Palestinians' IDs include the name of the holder's grandfather. These differentiations facilitate profiling based on ethnic/national origin and religion. They thereby violate the IRFA and international human rights standards, which consider such profiling to be unacceptable religious discrimination.

Until 2005, the Israeli ID card designated the holder's "*le'om*," which denotes "nationality" in the sense of ethnoreligious affiliation rather than citizenship (as discussed in chapter 2 *supra*). These "nationalities," which include Arab, Jewish, Druze, Bedouin, and Circassian, are still recorded in the population registry. The categorizations reflect the ambiguity between ethnic/national and religious identities within Israeli law and policy. For example, the Druze are traditionally regarded as a religious minority who are Arab by ethnicity or national origin.[339] All Jews are regarded as "Jewish" regardless of national origin, while Muslims may be categorized as Arab, Bedouin, or Circassian. Thus, listing *le'om* on ID cards reinforces the Israeli social policy of unifying the Jewish "nationality" while fragmenting the Arab Palestinian population by recognizing the Druze, Bedouin, and (more recently) Christian communities as distinct "nationalities" (discussed in chapters 9 and 10, *infra*).

Crucially, Israel's practice of listing the holder's *le'om* on the national ID was not abandoned to comply with human rights standards, but because of a dispute between the secular and religious camps within the Israeli government over whether individuals who completed Reform conversions to Judaism could be considered members of the Jewish *le'om*. As such, the practice is likely to be restored if and when this internal conflict in Israeli Jewish society is resolved. In 2002, then-interior minister Eli Yishai, a member of the ultra-Orthodox Shas party, eliminated the nationality entry on IDs altogether to avoid complying with a Supreme Court ruling that called for the nationality of Reform and Conservative converts to be identified as "Jewish."[340] In 2011, Yishai approved a regulation that would have reinstated the nationality entry for persons who were eligible for IDs prior to 2002, in contempt of the Court's ruling.[341] Yishai's order was blocked and the nationality entry on IDs remains filled with asterisks.

However, even these ID cards without a nationality entry conspicuously distinguish Jews from non-Jews because the birth dates of Jews are listed according to the Hebrew calendar, whereas the birth dates of non-Jews are listed according to the civil (Gregorian) calendar. Although Jewish Israelis may now request that their birth dates be listed according to the Gregorian calendar, the Hebrew calendar remains the default.[342] As members of the dominant majority in Israeli society, Jewish Israelis have no practical incentive to request such a change.[343] The UN Special Rapporteur on freedom of religion or belief has voiced concern over this practice.[344] Thus, the removal of *le'om* does not meet IRFA's standard of eliminating indicators of religious affiliation from official identification documents.

<u>Religious Identification Facilitates Segregation</u>

Indicating religious affiliation on identity cards invites religious-based discrimination in access to housing. In 2011, the Israeli Supreme Court decision affirming the Admissions Committees Law (discussed in chapter 2, *supra*) reinforced such discrimination. The Law permits the housing admissions committees of small communities, including those located on state-owned land, to reject applications from persons who are deemed "unsuitable to the social life of the community…or the social and cultural fabric of the town."[345] Although the statute forbids explicit discrimination on the basis of religion or race, the "social and cultural fabric" language covers a wide range of value judgments, including a potential resident's perceived support for Zionism – an easy proxy for discrimination against Palestinians.[346] The Law further invites such discrimination by stipulating that each admissions committee shall include a representative of the World Zionist Organization/Jewish Agency, a parastatal institution representing the Jewish diaspora and chartered to promote Jewish immigration and settlement (discussed in chapter 2, *supra*).[347]

Although religious discrimination in access to housing on public lands (whether administered by the State directly or a third party like the JNF) is ostensibly illegal following the Supreme Court's ruling in the *Kaadan* case (see chapter 2, *supra*), religious-based exclusion is common in practice. A number of court cases on discriminatory land allocation and home sales were, at the time of this submission, pending before the Israeli Supreme Court, including: HCJ 9205/04 *Adalah v. Israel Lands Administration* and HCJ 9010/04 *Arab Center for Alternative Planning v. Israel Lands Administration*, concerning the Jewish National Fund's refusal to transfer land rights to non-Jewish Israeli citizens. The Supreme Court also recently upheld the

Admissions Committee Law, which enables small Jewish communities to deny the residency applications of Palestinian citizens on the basis of unsuitability to the town's "social/cultural fabric," and the Israeli government's plan to demolish the unrecognized Palestinian Bedouin town of Umm al-Hiran to make way for a new Jewish community on the site.[348]

Religious Identification Facilitates Other Private Discrimination

Identifying cardholders' religious identity facilitates discrimination between private citizens, particularly with regards to housing and land ownership, even where such discrimination is expressly prohibited by law. ID cards that clearly distinguish between Jews and non-Jews particularly exacerbate discrimination in the context of certain types of transactions, such as police encounters and access to housing (as discussed above). Such transactions, which often involve the use of an ID card, tend to take place in the context of a power imbalance (e.g. police officer to civilian, housing admissions committee member to prospective homeowner) and are particularly susceptible to manifestations of religious or racial bias due to the subjective decisions which the powerful party must make (e.g., whether to use force, whether to allow someone to live in the community).

Religious Identification Facilitates Secondary Rights Violations

These forms of direct discrimination facilitated by ID cards also lead to or exacerbate deprivations of various rights that are fundamental to political participation in a democratic society. For example, discrimination in access to housing – the cumulative result of both individual and official acts of discrimination, including zoning and planning policies that privilege Jewish growth and development over non-Jewish growth and development – exacerbates the acute housing crisis facing Palestinian citizens. Whereas 900 new Jewish municipalities have been built since 1948, no new Arab towns have been approved in the last 67 years, with two exceptions in the case of forced relocations of Bedouins in the Naqab (Negev).[349] Meanwhile, the natural growth rate for the Palestinian population has long outpaced that of the Jewish population,[350] resulting in an acute, systemic housing crisis for Palestinian citizens.[351] These factors often drive Palestinian citizens of Israel to leave their hometowns to live in Jewish or mixed communities.

Housing circumstances largely determine one's access to other basic services and legal rights.[352] As a result of unequal access to land and housing, non-Jewish citizens suffer reduced access to the following services:

- Hospitals and healthcare: In 2011, the CESCR voiced its concern for infant and maternal mortality rates among Palestinians citizens of Israel, including Bedouins, while noting discrimination against Bedouin women and girls, particularly those living in unrecognized villages, with regard to education, employment, and health care. [353]

- Education: The Israeli government has historically spent considerably less *per capita* on education for Palestinian children than for Jewish children.[354] This discrimination contributes to significant disparities in high school graduation rates and university attendance (21.5 percent for Jews versus 11.5 percent for "members of other religions") between Jewish Israelis and Palestinians. Preschool attendance for Palestinian Bedouin children was the lowest in the country, while the dropout rate for Palestinian Bedouin high school students was the highest. [355]

- Employment: The UN Committee on Economic, Social and Cultural Rights (CESCR), in its 2011 concluding observations of its periodic review of Israel, noted persistent obstacles to employment for Palestinian citizens and the considerable unemployment gap between Jewish and non-Jewish Israeli citizens (noting that approximately 12 percent of Palestinian citizens are paid below the minimum wage). [356]

- Municipal services: The Israeli authorities have long refused to recognize the 60-year old Arab village of Dahmash and rezone its land for residential use. The result was the denial of basic services including drainage, functioning sewer systems, garbage collection, education, welfare, health, and postal services; home demolitions; and the deprivation of use of common spaces as parks or playgrounds. The Palestinian residents of Dahmash are denied recognition of their home addresses on their Israeli ID cards and are often refused services, including education, in neighboring Jewish localities.[357] In 2015, the village once again made the headlines as local inhabitants fought a plan by the state to demolish sixteen homes, as part of this ongoing refusal to recognize the village.[358]

CONCLUSION

Israel's practice of issuing ID cards with indicia that differentiate Jewish from non-Jewish citizens renders every transaction involving use of the ID card a nonconsensual disclosure of religious affiliation and facilitates various forms of public and private discrimination. The risk of discrimination based on religious affiliation is particularly acute in Israel and the oPt, where religious and ethnic tensions and discrimination are intertwined, with serious repercussions for a wide range of fundamental rights.

7

ORTHODOX CONTROL OVER PERSONAL STATUS MATTERS OF NON-ORTHODOX JEWS

The Orthodox establishment in Israel maintains a monopoly over marriage, divorce, conversions, and burials of all Jewish Israelis. (As used herein, 'Orthodox' includes Haredim (including Hasidim) and modern Orthodox.) Concessions to the Orthodox community that infused Orthodox principles into public life, which were made at the time of the state's establishment remain in effect today and perpetuate discrimination against non-Orthodox Jews. This special relationship between the State and the Orthodox establishment further translates into a lack of funding for rabbis, schools, and institutions affiliated with other Jewish traditions.

The State Department has expressed concern with Orthodox control over the personal status matters of non-Orthodox Jewish Israelis. [359] These concerns were echoed by the UN Special Rapporteur on freedom of religion or belief, who identified preferential treatment of Orthodox Judaism and Orthodox control over personal status matters as issues of concern for religious freedom in Israel.[360] The USCIRF has consistently expressed concern over single-denomination control over an entire faith and should apply the same principles with regard to Israel.

LEGAL STANDARD

Orthodox control over the personal status matters of non-Orthodox Jewish Israelis constitutes coercion that impairs one's freedom to adopt and manifest a religion or belief of choice, in violation of article 18 UDHR and article 18 ICCPR. Orthodox control over all Jewish marriages in Israel violates the freedom to marry and have a family, as guaranteed by article 16 UDHR and article 23 ICCPR. Israel's reservation to article 23 ICCPR with respect to personal status matters within the jurisdiction of its rabbinical courts does not excuse the discrimination against women in marriage and divorce proceedings within the rabbinical court system, which violates articles 2 and 26 ICCPR, as well as article 16 CEDAW.

Human Rights Law

Freedom of Religion

The guarantee in article 18(1) ICCPR of the right to adopt and manifest a religion encompasses the right to adopt and manifest "non-theistic and atheistic beliefs as well as the right not to profess any religion or belief."[361] As General Comment 22 of the Human Rights Committee highlights, the fact that a religion (or an interpretation thereof) is newly-established does not excuse discrimination against it, as "Article 18 is not limited in its application to traditional religions or to religions and beliefs with institutional characteristics or practices analogous to those of traditional religions."[362] Furthermore, the freedom to have or adopt a religion or belief also entails the freedom to retain one's religion or belief.[363]

Article 18(2) further guarantees that "no one shall be subject to coercion which would impair his freedom to have or to adopt a religion or belief of his choice."[364] The Human Rights Committee has noted that the freedom to manifest a religion or belief not only encompasses worship, observance, teaching and practice but also "such customs as the observance of dietary regulations" and the "participation in rituals associated with certain stages of life." As such, the manifestation of religion or belief through rituals such as marriage and burial is protected under Article 18.

Right to Marriage and Equality of the Spouses

Single-denomination control also implicates the freedom to marry and establish a family. Article 16 UDHR guarantees that every person, regardless of gender, race, nationality, or religion, has the right to marry and to have a family. This guarantee of equality applies at the time of entry into marriage, during the marriage, and at its dissolution. The equivalent ICCPR provision, article 23, provides that "the right of men and women of marriageable age to marry and to found a family shall be recognised" and that state parties "shall take appropriate steps to ensure equality of rights and responsibilities of spouses as to marriage, during marriage and at its dissolution."[365]

Israel has entered a reservation to article 23 ICCPR, disclaiming the application of the Covenant with regard to the personal-status law of its recognized religious communities:

> With reference to Article 23 of the Covenant, and any other provision thereof to which the present reservation may be relevant, matters of personal status are governed in Israel by the religious law of the parties concerned.
>
> To the extent that such law is inconsistent with its obligations under the Covenant, Israel reserves the right to apply that law.[366]

This reservation, entered on 30 October 1991 and still effective today, implicates the object and purpose test of treaty law, which dictates that a state may not make a reservation incompatible with the purpose of the treaty.[367] Additionally, treaty provisions which reflect peremptory norms, as well as norms that are accepted as customary international law, may not be the subject of reservations.[368] Applying these principles, the Human Rights Committee in its General Comment 24 on Reservations and Declarations has stated that "a state may not reserve the right ... to deny freedom of thought, conscience and religion," or "to deny to persons of marriageable age the right to marry."[369] Regarding the obligation under article 2(1) ICCPR to uphold nondiscrimination in the protection of Convention rights, the Committee has asserted that "a reservation to the obligation to respect and ensure the rights, and to do so on a non-discriminatory basis (article 2(1)) would not be acceptable."[370] Consequently, Israel's reservation is invalid to the extent that the application of confessional personal status law results in violations of these rights. As such, where the personal status law of a religious community would provide for discriminatory treatment on a protected basis enumerated in article 2(1), Israel has an obligation to bring such discrimination to an end.

The Committee has further declared in its General Comment 24 that a state cannot "reserve an entitlement not to take the necessary steps at the domestic level to give effect to the rights of the Covenant," thereby disclaiming its obligations under article 2(2).[371] In a similar vein, its General Comment No. 28, regarding the equality of rights between men and women under article 3 ICCPR, calls upon States to "ensure that traditional, historical, religious or cultural attitudes are not used to justify violations of women's right to equality before the law and to equal enjoyment of all Covenant rights."[372]

Moreover, the Committee has reiterated that any reservation is intended as a transitional measure, which the state should in time withdraw as it comes into compliance with the relevant provision.[373] Accordingly, the Committee has repeatedly urged Israel to "reconsider its position regarding its reservation to article 23 of the Covenant with a view to withdrawing it."[374]

Discrimination against Women

The compulsory jurisdiction of the Orthodox rabbinical courts over Jewish Israelis results in discrimination against women, which implicates Israel's obligations under CEDAW.

Article 2 CEDAW obligates state parties to take appropriate measures to "modify or abolish existing laws, regulations, customs and practices which constitute discrimination against women."[375] Similarly, in article 5, CEDAW signatories commit themselves to "modify the social and cultural patterns of conduct of men and women, with a view to achieving the elimination of prejudices and customary and all other practices which are based on the idea of the inferiority or the superiority of either of the sexes or on stereotyped roles for men and women."[376] Article 16 CEDAW applies these principles to personal status matters, such as the rights and responsibilities during marriage and its dissolution.[377] In particular, article 16 affirms that women and men have "[t]he same right to enter into marriage"[378] and "the same rights for both spouses in respect of the ownership, acquisition, management, administration, enjoyment and disposition of property, whether free of charge or for a valuable consideration."[379]

Israel has entered a reservation to article 16 CEDAW "to the extent that the laws on personal status which are binding on the various religious communities in Israel do not conform with the provisions of that article."[380] This reservation does not relieve Israel of its obligations under articles 1 and 2 CEDAW to ensure non-discrimination in all matters, including social and personal-status matters, on the grounds of sex.[381] The CEDAW Committee is "of the view that [Israel's] reservation to article 16 is impermissible as it is contrary to the object and purpose of the Convention. It also impinges on other fundamental articles of the Convention, including article 2, and implementation of the principle of substantive equality between women and men in all matters relating to marriage and family relations."[382] Accordingly, the Committee has called upon Israel to introduce an optional system of civil marriage and divorce, as well as harmonize religious laws currently governing personal status matters with the rights and obligations under the Convention.[383]

USCIRF Precedent

Russia and Sudan: Religious Monopoly / State Preference of Particular Sect

In previous cases, the USCIRF has indicated that state preference for certain religious communities and a monopoly by one denomination of a faith over the affairs of members of other denominations constitutes an interference with religious freedom.[384]

In listing Russia as a Tier 2 state, the USCIRF has expressed concern for the hegemony of the state-backed Moscow Patriarchate of the Russian Orthodox Church, which claims as members 60 percent of the state's population, and its consequences for the rights of religious minorities.[385] Russian laws and policies give preferential treatment to the Orthodox Church, including through onerous registration procedures for other religions and the empowerment of state officials to impede registration or obstruct the construction or rental of worship buildings, actively promoting its interests at the expense of other religious communities.[386] The

Commission labeled the prominence of the Orthodox Church, in conjunction with extremist acts of intolerance towards other religious communities, as a grave concern.[387]

While Orthodox hegemony in Israel does not necessarily engender religious discrimination of a severity equal to the situation in Russia, the Commission's precedent on Russia establishes that it is unacceptable for state support of one religious community to result in infringements on the religious freedoms of other religious communities. As stated by the Human Rights Committee in its General Comment No. 22 (and quoted in the USCIRF's International Human Rights Standards compilation), "if a set of beliefs is treated as official ideology in constitutions, statutes, proclamations of ruling parties, etc., or in actual practice," or if "a religion is recognized as a state religion or established as official or traditional, or that its followers comprise the majority of the population," such facts "shall not result in any impairment of the freedoms under article 18 or any other rights recognized under the ICCPR nor in any discrimination against adherents to other religions or non-believers."[388]

In Sudan, designated a CPC since 1999, the Commission has noted that the government routinely grants permission for the construction of mosques, often with state funds, while permission to build churches is impossible to obtain.[389]

Turkey: Religious Discrimination against Minority Sects

In keeping Turkey on the Tier 2 list, the USCIRF has condemned the treatment of the Alevis, whose houses of worship are not recognized by the State as religious sites. Alevis are not considered Muslims by the Turkish authorities and thus are denied state recognition and funding of their religious services.[390] The European Court of Human Rights found that Turkey had violated article 9 ECHR by excluding the Alevi community from its practice of covering the electricity costs of the houses of worship of its religious communities.[391] Noting this ruling, the USCIRF expressed its concern over Turkey's denial of state benefits to the Alevi faith and discrimination against its members.

In particular, when assessing whether the Alevi sect was discriminated against, the Commission seems to have followed HRC General Comments

18 and 22, which it considered applicable as indicated on its Human Rights Document communicated on its website.[392] The USCIRF here takes the position that "not every differentiation of treatment will constitute discrimination, *if the criteria for such differentiation are reasonable and objective and if the aim is to achieve a purpose which is legitimate under the ICCPR.*"[393] Furthermore, as already highlighted above, the communication also states that "[t]he fact that a religion is recognized as a state religion or established as official or traditional, or that its followers comprise the majority of the population, shall not result in any impairment of the enjoyment of any of the rights under the ICCPR, nor in any discrimination against adherents to other religions or non-believers."[394] In particular, "measures restricting eligibility for government service to members of the predominant religion, *or giving economic privileges to them, or imposing special restrictions on the practice of other faiths* are not in accordance with the prohibition of discrimination based on religion or belief and the guarantee of equal protection under ICCPR article 26."[395]

Burma/Sudan: Conversions

The USCIRF has previously expressed concern about practices that allow members of a majority faith to control and limit conversions of minority faiths.[396] More particularly, in Burma – a perennial CPC state – the USCIRF noted its concern about the authority of Buddhist state officials to approve or disapprove religious conversions of members of other faiths.[397] In 2014, four bills were considered that would impose restrictions on interfaith marriage and restrict religious conversion, which were also cause for concern.[398]

In Sudan, another perennial CPC state, the Commission has observed that "government policies and societal pressure promote conversion to Islam."[399] The Commission suggests that such promotion is coercive in the context of the Sudanese government's "policies of Islamization and Arabization" and its "systematic, ongoing, and egregious violations of freedom of religion or belief."[400]

Indonesia: Interfaith Marriages

The USCIRF has condemned obstacles to interfaith marriage and their coercive effect on conversion. In listing Indonesia on Tier 2 since 2003, the

Commission has condemned its 1974 marriage law, which legitimizes only those marriages conducted in accordance with the laws of the parties' religion. The ministry of religious affairs and other public entities have used this law to prohibit interfaith marriages entirely. The Commission expressed particular concern over the bureaucratic hurdles to interfaith marriage created by the law, which may compel one of the spouses to convert to facilitate the marriage.[401] The Commission concluded that the law thus "undermines the individual freedoms to practice a religion and marry a partner of one's choice."[402]

ANALYSIS

The exclusive jurisdiction of Orthodox-controlled rabbinical courts over the personal status matters of all Jewish Israelis, and the resulting lack of civil marriage and divorce, violates article 18 ICCPR insofar as it requires non-Orthodox Jews to conduct "such customs as … participation in rituals associated with certain stages of life" in accordance with the principles and traditions of Orthodox Judaism.[403]

Background

Orthodox control over the personal status matters of non-Orthodox Jews has its origin in the 1947 "status quo" compromise between the Zionist movement and the historically anti-Zionist Orthodox community. This compromise, which was reached during the mandate of the UN Special Committee on Palestine, ensured that the Orthodox community would not undermine the Zionist movement's call for a Jewish state. To secure Orthodox support, the Zionist movement pledged that the new Jewish state would abide by four fundamental commitments that remain in effect to this day:

- kosher food in all state-run kitchens;
- respect of and adherence to Shabbat in the public life;
- rabbinical control of marriage and divorce; and
- autonomy of religious schools, subject to the minimum requirements of compulsory education.[404]

In the early years of the state, an exemption of full-time yeshiva students from military service became part of the status quo.[405] These arrangements were codified in such laws as the 1948 Kosher Food for Soldiers Ordinance, mandating kosher food in army cafeterias; the 1951 Hours of Work and Rest Law, recognizing Shabbat as official day of rest; the 1953 Rabbinical Courts Jurisdiction (Marriage and Divorce) Law, establishing rabbinical jurisdiction over Jewish marriages and divorces; and the 1953 State Education Law, recognizing the autonomy of religious schools, legalizing yeshivas, and making religious schools and yeshivas eligible for government funding.

The leaders of the socialist-secular Labor Party that founded Israel and dominated its politics for its first three decades believed that Orthodox adherence would be unnecessary to preserve Jewish identity in a Jewish-majority state, and thus that the Orthodox population and its influence in society would progressively decline.[406] It has also been suggested that "in reaching consensus on issues of freedom of religion in both the Status Quo Agreement and in the Declaration of the Establishment of the State of Israel, 'state leaders did not consider religious pluralism within the Jewish people.'"[407] Whatever the original rationale for the status quo arrangements, the Orthodox community has grown significantly as a share of the population and in political power since 1948, and it has blocked attempts to reform these arrangements.[408]

Despite their growing numbers and influence, the Orthodox remain a distinct minority of the overall Jewish population of Israel. A 2009 Israel Democracy Institute (IDI) survey found that 15 percent of Israeli Jews identify as Orthodox (up from 11 percent in 1999) and 7 percent as Haredi (compared with 5 percent in 2009), compared with 32 percent who identified as traditional, 43 percent as secular but not anti-religious, and 3 percent as anti-religious (all down slightly from 2009).[409] Additionally, while the Reform and Conservative movements are traditionally associated with the Jewish diaspora, a 2012 IDI study found that 7.1 percent of Jewish Israelis identify with one of these traditions, while 9.7 percent neither identify with, nor feel represented by, any Jewish tradition.[410] A clear majority (61 percent) of respondents in the IDI study "agree" or "totally agree" that the Conservative and Reform movements should have equal status with the Orthodox in Israeli law and practice.[411] The non-Orthodox

Jewish population also includes communities outside the rabbinic Judaism tradition, including an estimated 35,000 Karaite Jews,[412] 10,000 to 20,000 Messianic Jews, and 750 Samaritans.

As the Orthodox population has grown, so has the Orthodox Rabbinate's control over the personal status matters of all Jewish Israelis.[413] Israel's rabbinical courts, which are comprised exclusively of Orthodox rabbis, adhere to an Orthodox interpretation of *halacha* (the body of Jewish religious laws) and require their full observance.[414] While Reform and Conservative Jews are allowed to practice their beliefs, they do not enjoy the right to marry or divorce in line with their non-Orthodox beliefs within Israel and are subject to Orthodox rabbinical court control of their personal status issues.[415] Marriages performed by persons other than authorized Orthodox rabbis (such as Reform or Conservative rabbis) are not legally recognized in Israel and consequently do not entitle a couple to a marriage certificate or other economic benefits in the fields of residence, health, education, insurance, and taxation.[416] The lack of civil procedures for marriage and divorce also affects Israeli citizens who self-identify as atheists or secular, and do not wish to observe religious personal status laws of any faith.[417] In order to marry, non-Orthodox Jews must undergo Orthodox-administered marriage counseling, which teach traditional Orthodox family roles.[418]

Religious court jurisdiction in Israel

Within Israel, the respective judicial authorities of the 14 recognized religious communities manage personal status law, such as marriage, divorce, maintenance,[419] and succession, in whole or in part.[420]

Upon its founding, Israel adopted a version of the Ottoman *millet* system, which was maintained by the British Mandatory government of Palestine. This *millet* system is a decentralized and pluralistic legal system that gives recognized religious communities compulsory judicial autonomy (i.e. exclusive jurisdiction) over personal status issues.[421] The 14 recognized religious communities are Armenian Catholic, Armenian Orthodox, Baha'i, Chaldaic (Catholic), Druze, Evangelical Episcopal (Anglican), Jewish, Maronite, Muslim, Greek Catholic, Greek Orthodox, Latin (Roman Catholic), Syrian Catholic, and Syrian Orthodox.[422] While religious authorities manage maintenance and succession in concurrence with civil courts, the respective judicial authorities of the 14 recognized religious communities have the judicial authority to manage marriage and divorce.[423]

Israel has maintained the basic tenets of the *millet* system while further entrenching rabbinical court authority over the personal status matters of its Jewish citizens.[424] While the Orthodox Chief Rabbinate and Rabbinical Courts were established in 1920 and asserted compulsory jurisdiction over the Orthodox community, non-Orthodox Jews could elect or decline membership in the recognized Jewish Community (*Knesset Israel*) over which the courts had jurisdiction.[425] After 1953, the *Knesset Israel* stopped registering Jewish citizens and residents of Israel, and the jurisdiction of rabbinical courts expanded to include the entire Jewish population. Accordingly, as Haim H. Cohn explains, "the question of who was a Jew for this purpose was to be determined by the rabbinical courts themselves, who did not – and by *halachic* norms could not – exempt secular Jews."[426] The 1953 Rabbinical Courts Jurisdiction (Marriage and Divorce) Law provides that all "matters of marriage and divorce of Jews in Israel, being citizens or residents of the State, shall be under the exclusive jurisdiction of the rabbinical courts."[427]

While the religious community recognized under Israeli law is that of Judaism rather than Orthodox Judaism, the Orthodox maintain a monopoly over the Chief Rabbinate and the rabbinical courts.[428] In effect, the non-Orthodox majority of the Jewish Israeli public is under the undemocratic control of the Orthodox rabbinical establishment.[429] Accordingly, the UN Special Rapporteur on freedom of religion or belief expressed concern in 2009 over the rabbinical courts' exclusive jurisdiction over all Jews, regardless of their religious, non-theistic, or atheistic beliefs.[430]

<u>Rabbinical control over personal status matters of Jewish Israelis</u>

Marriage and divorce

Israeli law does not provide for civil marriage; persons wishing to marry must undergo a religious ceremony within their religious community or marry outside the State.[431] Because the Orthodox rabbinical courts do not officiate the marriage of Jews to non-Jews, and civil marriage does not exist in Israel's confessional system, interfaith couples are prevented from marrying within Israel, unless one of the partners decides to convert.[432] Requiring conversion for one to marry his or her spouse of choice requires an individual to relinquish a core aspect of one's conscience, religion, or belief as a condition of exercising a fundamental right. As such, it constitutes an interference with religious freedom as defined under article 18 ICCPR. In addition, it also violates the right to marry freely and to found a family, without distinction as to gender, race, nationality, or religion, under article 16 UDHR.

For Jewish citizens in a relationship, if one partner is Jewish by patrilineal descent (and thus is considered Jewish only in the Reform tradition) or received a non-Orthodox conversion, the couple is denied permission to have an Orthodox marriage or must undertake the lengthy Orthodox conversion process.[433] This constitutes a type of coercion impeding the couple's "freedom to have or adopt a religion or belief of … choice."[434]

Between 250,000 and 300,000 Israeli citizens and permanent residents cannot marry in Israel because they do not belong to any recognized community and Israeli law does not establish a civil marriage option.[435] The UN Special Rapporteur on freedom of religion or belief observed in 2009 that Israeli law made "no domestic solution available for those who are ineligible to marry in Israel."[436] A Law on Spousal Agreements for Persons Without a Religion, adopted by the Knesset in 2010, did not create a viable civil option and has rarely been used.[437] In fact, the Law has been criticized for further entrenching the authority of the confessional personal status courts by giving recognized religious communities the power to veto a spousal agreement registration if it believes that one of the applicants is a member of its community and within the jurisdiction of its courts.[438] Thus, if only one of the applicants lacks a recognized religion, that applicant must convert or the couple must marry abroad. Consequently, between the Law's effective date of September 22, 2000 and January 5, 2015, only 112 couples were added to the Registry of Spousal Agreements.[439]

Rabbinical court discrimination against women

Due to Orthodox control over Jewish personal status matters, women who may not wish to conform to *halachic* gender norms are forced to do so.[440]

Of particular concern to the CEDAW Committee are the limited rights granted to women under mandatory Orthodox divorce proceedings.[441] According to *halacha*, a wife requires a written *get* by the husband to be allowed a divorce.[442] A *get* is a dated and witnessed divorced document in Jewish religious law, in which the husband expresses his intention to divorce his wife and sever all ties with her. Not only does this requirement cause serious problems if the husband disappears, voluntarily or not, without providing his wife with a *get,* but it also gives a husband undue power over the maintenance issue, as he can blackmail his wife into asking for lesser maintenance in exchange for a *get*.[443] Women not granted divorces are referred to as *aguna*, which means chained.[444] Concerns have also been raised by the CEDAW Committee on the retroactive invalidation of divorces by the Orthodox Rabbinate.[445] It should be noted that, under *halacha*, a husband who is not yet divorced may enter into a relationship and have children with another women without dire consequences.[446] However, if a woman who has not been divorced has children with another men, her children will be considered *mamzer* (impure) and will be prevented from Jewish marriage with a "non-*mamzer*" for ten generations.[447]

Civil marriage abroad, common law marriage, and cohabitation not reasonable alternatives

Israeli citizens may marry abroad in a civil marriage and having that civil marriage registered with the Ministry of Interior in Israel upon return.[448] However, financial obstacles can prevent recourse to this option for some citizens. In addition, while the civil marriage may be conducted abroad, Jewish citizens of Israel will still be subject to mandatory rabbinical jurisdiction if either spouse seeks a divorce.[449] This issue is of particular concern for women's rights groups, as divorce proceedings in the Rabbinical Court follow strict interpretations of *halacha* (such as the *get*, as explained above).[450] This system, which effectively forces some marriages to take place outside of Israel, is coercive and denies secular Jews of the ability to marry freely without being subject to religious prescripts which do not accord with their beliefs.

There have been attempts to narrow the legal gap between cohabitating couples and married couples, giving rise to a perception that cohabitation is a civil solution for those not wishing to engage in a religious marriage facilitated by one a recognized religious communities.[451] The Knesset has accepted the judicially-created "reputed spouse" doctrine by extending certain social rights and benefits to a reputed wife and, less commonly, to a reputed husband.[452] However, such extensive rights of cohabitating couples do not represent a solution to the Orthodox monopoly over personal status law and the lack of a civil marriage institution.[453] Israel law professor Zvi Triger notes that most of his students "believe that civil marriage or non-marital cohabitation are paths out of the grip of the rabbinical court." He characterizes those beliefs as "denial mechanisms" which "discourag[e] people from taking political responsibility over the religious monopoly in the area of marriage and divorce and from making a commitment to change the system."[454]

In particular, the rights conferred upon cohabitating couples are not equal to the rights of married couples. Furthermore, couples may have to endure lengthy procedures and may be required to reveal intimate details about their lives in order to prove the sincerity of their relationship.[455] Subsequently, in order to ensure that their rights are recognized by local authorities, couples may be subject to extensive proceedings and litigation.[456] Regardless, cohabitation is distinct from marriage: marriage remains an important social symbol and institution that should be accessible to everyone, irrespective of the individual's relationship with religion or lack thereof.[457]

Various civil society organizations concerned with the lack of civil marriage and the Orthodox monopoly over personal status matters have sought alternative ways to allow cohabitating couples to enter into relationships which provide legal benefits. An example is the Domestic Union Card (DU Card), an affidavit issued by an Israeli NGO, New Family, that purports to establish a couple's status as common-law spouses.[458] However, for the reasons discussed above, the DU Card does not replace a civil marriage. Further, DU Card holders may not receive the benefits and privileges associated with state-recognized marriages. For example, women in common-law relationships are not exempt from military service,[459] and the process of obtaining residency is lengthier and more complicated for a common-law spouse than for a spouse whose marriage is religiously endorsed. In addition, only couples married by a religious institution are eligible for tax benefits in case of pension, age, or disability.[460]

Conversions

The issue of conversions and the issue of personal status law are crucial to the debate on religious freedom in contemporary Israel; and both were identified by the American-based Jewish Religious Equality Commission (J-REC) as priority spheres of action.[461] The J-REC is a "broad-based initiative advocating for religious freedom and equality as a means of strengthening Israel's identity as a Jewish and democratic state that assures its ties with global Jewry. J-REC is a coalition of American organizations and individuals working with like-minded Israeli organizations that would mobilize support to create alternatives to the exclusive control of the Chief Rabbinate over personal status issues, notably, marriage and divorce and conversions to Judaism."[462] According to the 2013 IRF report and the 2009 report of the UN Special Rapporteur on freedom of religion or belief, the Chief Rabbinate and Rabbinic Court, even though legally obliged to recognize Reform or Conservative Jewish converts,[463] do not recognize Jews converted by a non-Orthodox body for the purpose of religious rulings on matters of personal status.[464]

Matters of personal status and burials are managed by the Orthodox rabbinical courts. In a functional sense,[465] converts under non-Orthodox streams of Judaism must be recognized as Jews by the Orthodox authorities.[466] Non-Orthodox conversions have been retroactively annulled on grounds of failure to maintain observance of *halacha* after conversion.[467] In 2008, the Supreme Rabbinical Court ruled that the retroactive annulment of the conversion of a married woman wishing to divorce her husband was valid, and that she could not be divorced under Jewish law as she in fact was not married under Jewish law since she was not really Jewish. The case also challenged the validity of about 40,000 conversions executed by Rabbi Haim Druckman during his tenure at the head of the Israeli state conversion program. In 2010, the Supreme Court overturned this particular denial of the effective conversion of Druckman's conversions, yet the court refrained from offering an opinion on the general legitimacy of the retroactive annulment of conversions.[468] Such a requirement stems from a strictly Orthodox interpretation of Judaism and forces converts in other streams to either convert according to Orthodox precepts or not receive the benefits and protections of Israeli citizenship as awarded to Orthodox Jews.[469]

This issue is of particular concern given that about 300,000 immigrants from the Soviet Union, who immigrated in the 1990s, and their descendants "qualified for Israeli citizenship because of their Jewish ancestry or family connections," but are not considered Jewish under the Orthodox interpretation of religious law, and therefore are unable to marry Jews in Orthodox Courts.[470] This issue was recognized by the previous Israeli cabinet, and a decision was made to "allow regional rabbis to establish local conversion courts, making them more approachable and closer to the communities they serve than the central rabbinical authority that has long monopolized the stringent conversion process."[471] Nonetheless, the current cabinet effectively overturned the decision in July 2015, thereby re-enforcing the central Orthodox authority over conversion.

Burial

The UN Special Rapporteur on freedom of religion or belief further expressed concern over Orthodox control of burial provisions. Most public cemeteries in Israel are Orthodox and nearly all the state cemeteries are controlled by the Rabbinate.[472] In addition, funeral services at public cemeteries must be led by Orthodox rabbis.[473] Not only does this limit the religious freedom of Reform and Conservative communities who might wish a Reform or Conservative rabbi to lead their funeral, but it is also of grave concern for non-Orthodox converts to Judaism or secular Jews who do not meet the *halachic* requirements of being Jewish yet wish a Jewish burial. These individuals are buried in a "separate plot" of the cemetery if such a plot is available.[474]

State Funding/Resources

There have been strong and credible allegations that "state resources reportedly favor Orthodox Jewish institutions," to the exclusion of non-Orthodox institutions.[475] In 2012 the State Prosecutor's office adopted a Supreme Court recommendation stating the State should pay the salaries of non-Orthodox rabbis in regional councils and farming communities,[476] but non-Orthodox rabbis are still excluded from state funding in many large cities.[477]

With regard to funding for structures of worship, educational establishments, and religious services such as conversions, the Reform and Conservative movements receive significantly less funding and state support than their Orthodox counterparts. [478]

Non-funding of Jewish minority "sects"

The Orthodox-run Ministry of Religious Affairs meets the religious needs of members of the Orthodox faith but will not meet those of minority Jewish sects, an allocation of resources which amounts to discrimination. As a result, the Karaite community in Israel meets its own religious needs, since it is not a recognized Jewish sect.[479] In May 2013, *The Economist* quoted the Chief Rabbinate as stating that "Israel is a Jewish state and Jews have superior rights, but the Karaites are not Jewish."[480]

CONCLUSION

The unique legal status accorded to Orthodox Judaism in Israeli law and state support for the Orthodox Rabbinate coerces non-Orthodox Jewish Israelis into abiding by Orthodox Judaism personal status principles, in violation of freedom of religion. In a 2009 note to the Human Rights Committee, the Government of Israel admitted that "it seems difficult to claim that 'freedom from religion' is fully protected, particularly for the Jewish population, due to the interpenetration of religion and Government in several forms." This "interpenetration" is characterized by a series of legal institutions and practices that apply, sometimes forcefully, Orthodox norms to the entirety of the Jewish population.[481]

8
DISCOURAGING PROSELYTISM AND FAILING TO PREVENT HARASSMENT BY ANTI-ASSIMILATION AND ANTI-MISCEGENATION GROUPS

Proselytism, understood here and throughout this section in its neutral sense,[482] has been defined as "expressive conduct undertaken with the purpose of trying to change the religious beliefs, affiliation, or identity of another."[483] As a manifestation of religion and as expressive conduct, the act of proselytizing implicates the protections of human rights law. Restrictions on certain, coercive forms of proselytism may be lawful if they are necessary to uphold a legitimate, *secular* state interest, such as maintaining public order or upholding the right of others to practice their religion or beliefs without coercion, and are proportionate to fulfilling those interests. However, such restrictions are often motivated by improper considerations, such as protecting the State's dominant religious tradition or political ideology, and must be carefully scrutinized. Restrictions on non-coercive forms of proselytism generally violate human rights law.

While Israeli law recognizes the right to proselytize, the Israeli government often discourages and obstructs proselytizers who seek (or are thought to seek) to convert Jewish Israelis to another religion. More significantly, Israel fails to protect members of evangelical faiths from harassment by private actors, including anti-missionary and anti-miscegenation groups. As a result, evangelical Christian movements and organizations feel compelled to abstain from proselytism within Israel.

Opposition to proselytism in Israel, at both public and private levels, is motivated by concerns over Jewish intermarriage and assimilation. Under international religious freedom standards, the notion of ethnic continuity is not a legitimate state interest that justifies limitations on manifestations of religion, including proselytism. Accordingly, Israel's practice of discouraging proselytism and the state's failure to prevent interference by private actors in non-coercive proselytizing constitutes a violation of religious freedom.

LEGAL STANDARD

The IRFA expressly protects some forms of proselytism, defining "arbitrary prohibitions on, restrictions of, or punishment for... changing one's religious beliefs and affiliation; [and] possession and distribution of religious literature, including Bibles"[484] as violations of religious freedom. The Act protects other forms of proselytism through incorporation by reference of the ICCPR and other human rights instruments, under which the right to proselytize is derived from the rights to manifest one's religion, change one's religion, express oneself and speak freely, and receive information. Accordingly, the Commission has consistently protested unjustified restrictions on proselytism as violations of religious freedom.

Human Rights Law

The right to proselytize, while not expressly guaranteed by most international human rights instruments, derives from, and is defined by, the freedom of religion and expression of both the proselytizer and the proselytized.

Freedom to manifest one's religion

Freedom of religion as articulated in article 18 ICCPR includes the right "to manifest [one's] religion or belief in worship, observance, practice and teaching." The UDHR and the 1981 UN Declaration have virtually identical formulations.[485] However, these instruments do not expressly establish a right to proselytize. A 1947 draft of what would become the UDHR and the ICCPR guaranteed the rights "to give and receive any form of religious teaching and to endeavor to persuade others of full age and sound mind of the truth of [one's] beliefs...."[486] The omission of this language from the final text of the ICCPR reflects "the sensitivities of states to the issues [proselytism] raises and the difficulty of delineating agreeable standards" to govern the practice.[487] None of the human rights instruments incorporated by reference under section 2(a) of the IRFA expressly guarantees the right to proselytize. Among other human rights treaties, only the American Convention expressly contains this right.[488]

Nevertheless, it is well-established that the right to proselytize is encompassed within the right to manifest one's religion.[489] As observed by Arcot Krishnaswami, former UN Special Rapporteur on prevention of discrimination and protection of minorities, "while some faiths do not attempt to win new converts, many of them make it mandatory for their followers to spread their message to all, and to attempt to convert others. For the latter, dissemination is an important aspect of the right to manifest their religion or belief."[490] Because "article 18 [ICCPR] is not limited in its application to ... practices analogous to those of traditional religions," all forms of proselytism, however unusual they may seem relative to "traditional" or "institutional" religious practices, are protected as manifestations of religion.[491]

Unlike the right to adopt and maintain a religion, however, the right to manifest one's religion is not absolute. Under article 18(3) ICCPR, manifestations of religion may be subject to limitations that are "prescribed by law" and are "necessary to protect public safety, order, health, or morals or the fundamental rights and freedoms of others."[492] The Human Rights Committee has cautioned that these permissible grounds for limitations must be "strictly construed" and cannot be based on principles deriving exclusively from a single religious, social, or philosophical tradition:

> The Committee observes that the concept of morals derives from many social, philosophical and religious traditions; consequently, limitations on the freedom to manifest a religion or belief for the purpose of protecting morals must be based on principles not deriving exclusively from a single tradition.[493]

In this regard, the UN Special Rapporteur on freedom of religion or belief has observed:

> Unlike the rights to convert and not to be forced to convert, which are protected unconditionally, the right to try to convert others by means of non-coercive persuasion can be limited in conformity with the criteria prescribed in article 18(3) [ICCPR]. However, the Special Rapporteur has the strong impression that many of the legislative or administrative restrictions imposed by States fall far short of satisfying those criteria. For example, vague and overly broad definitions of "proselytism", "unethical conversion" and related "offences" may create an atmosphere of insecurity in which law enforcement agencies can restrict acts of religious communication in an arbitrary manner.[494]

On the other hand, the Human Rights Committee has instructed that states cannot permit, under the guise of manifesting one's religion, "propaganda for war" or "advocacy of national, racial or religious hatred that constitutes incitement to discrimination, hostility or violence," which article 20 ICCPR prohibits.[495] In accordance with article 20, states must adopt laws to prohibit such incitement and make appropriate efforts to suppress it.[496]

Thus, international human rights law guarantees the right to engage in acts of proselytism as manifestations of religion, subject to such limitations that are consistent with article 18(3) ICCPR, including limitations necessary to protect the fundamental rights and freedoms of others and to prevent religious incitement.

Freedom to change and maintain one's religion

Human rights law also protects the right to change and maintain one's religion. The right to change religions may imply the right to freely receive information on other faiths and, by extension, the right to proselytize. Conversely, the right to maintain one's religion protects the "peaceful enjoyment" of that faith and may justify restrictions on coercive forms of proselytism.[497]

Article 18(1) ICCPR guarantees the right "to have or to adopt a religion or belief of [one's] choice."[498] The Human Rights Committee states that this provision "necessarily entails the freedom to choose a religion or belief, including the right to replace one's current religion or belief with another or to adopt atheistic views...."[499] Saudi Arabia led the opposition to the inclusion of an express right to choose one's religion in the ICCPR. Other Muslim and developing states, concerned that recognizing such a right would encourage missionary activity and foreign intervention, also opposed its inclusion.[500] The European Convention, the UDHR, and the 1981 UN Declaration expressly recognize the right to change one's religion.[501]

There is no clear international consensus on whether the freedom to change religion implies that others have the right to proselytize. For example, Malaysia has argued in international forums that its constitutional restrictions on non-Muslims' proselytism towards Muslims does not interfere with the ability of Muslims to change their faiths.[502] However, the European Court of Human Rights asserted in *Kokkinakis v. Greece* that the right to change one's religion under article 9 ECHR "would be likely to remain a dead letter" unless the right to encourage others to change faiths were also protected.[503] Similarly, the UN special rapporteur on freedom of religion or belief has urged that "States should repeal any criminal law provisions that penalize apostasy, blasphemy and proselytism as they may prevent persons belonging to religious or belief minorities from fully enjoying their freedom of religion or belief."[504]

On the other hand, the Human Rights Committee interprets the right to "have or to adopt" a religion to protect "the right to retain one's religion or belief."[505] Further, article 18(2) ICCPR guarantees that "no one shall be subject to coercion which would impair his freedom to have or to adopt a religion or belief of his choice."[506] While this right prohibits criminal law sanctions that penalize apostasy, blasphemy, and proselytism, it may also warrant restrictions on coercive or exploitative forms of proselytism that interfere with the peaceful enjoyment of one's religion. The ECtHR in *Kokkinakis* recognized that proselytism may implicate the right of others to maintain their religion without interference and that "improper" proselytism, as opposed to "true evangelism," may be limited on that basis.[507] The Court identified as possible forms of improper proselytism "offering material or social advantages," "exerting improper pressure on people in distress or need," "the use of violence or brainwashing," and other activities that are "not compatible with respect for the freedom of thought, conscience and religion of others."[508]

The common thread between these forms of improper proselytism is the use of tactics or the existence of circumstances that render the act coercive, such that it impairs the right of the proselytized to maintain their religion.[509] It follows that non-coercive forms of proselytism are protected and cannot be restricted on the grounds of protecting the religious freedom or other fundamental rights of others. Applying these principles, the Court in *Kokkinakis* ruled that Greece had not shown that the petitioner's door-to-door proselytism, which involved scripture reading and interpretation, was coercive and thus improper. His conviction under a Greek penal law prohibiting proselytism thus violated article 9 ECHR.

Freedom of expression

Proselytism is also protected by the right to freedom of expression and its corollary, the freedom to receive information, as guaranteed by article 19 ICCPR and similar provisions of other human rights instruments. The UN Special Rapporteur on the freedom of opinion and expression has observed that:

> as a general rule, States should not invoke any custom, tradition *or religious consideration* to avoid meeting their obligations with respect to the safeguarding of the right to freedom of opinion and expression.[510]

However, under human rights law, the lawful grounds for restricting freedom of expression are broader than the lawful grounds for restricting manifestations of religion. States are also afforded comparatively greater flexibility in regulating expression that may offend the religious convictions of others or pose a threat to public order than in regulating political speech or expression.

Restrictions on proselytism as a form of free expression must be evaluated in light of a state's overall regulation of expression. Thus, in a society in which "people are continually confronted with information designed to influence their political opinions, their moral values, and even their consumer choices, it might be inconsistent to otherwise overly restrict information designed to influence their religious choices."[511] For example, under U.S. constitutional law, the First Amendment's guarantee of free speech "embraces the right to distribute literature, and necessarily protects the right to receive it."[512] The U.S. Supreme Court has thus recognized that proselytism is protected both by the right to free expression and the right to receive information.[513] U.S. constitutional jurisprudence further holds that conduct undertaken as a manifestation of religious freedom and freedom of expression may be entitled to greater protection than either right, taken alone.[514] By contrast, "in societies where information is generally restricted and people must seek it out rather than be confronted by it, it may be more problematic to allow information on religion to flow freely."[515]

Thus, proselytism might be subject to greater restrictions where it is considered exclusively as a form of expression, rather than a manifestation of religion. For example, the ICCPR and other human rights instruments recognize national security as a permissible basis for restricting freedom of expression, but not the freedom to manifest one's religion.[516] Similarly, with regard to maintaining public order and protecting the rights of others, the ECtHR has held that states have a "wider margin of appreciation" in regulating speech or expression that may offend the "intimate personal convictions" of morals and religion than in regulating core political speech.[517] On that basis, the Court has upheld time, place, and manner restrictions on the distribution of works portraying religious figures and institutions in a manner likely to offend the religious feelings of others.[518]

USCIRF Precedent

In Laos, India, Malaysia, and Tajikistan, the Commission has found that arbitrary restrictions on peaceful, non-coercive proselytism, including the State's systemic failure to protect individuals engaged in proselytism from private acts of violence, constitute a violation of religious freedom.[519]

Laos

In listing Laos as a Tier 2 country since 2009, the Commission has found that the Laotian government actively discourages most forms of proselytism, notwithstanding a constitutional guarantee of freedom of religion. A 2002 Decree on Religious Practice allows the government to prohibit activities, including religious practices, that cause "social division" or "chaos." Pursuant to this decree, the Laotian government has imposed "registration requirements for all religious groups, limits on proselytizing, and controls on the printing of religious materials." As the 2015 USCIRF report describes:

> The Decree also contains vague prohibitions on activities that create "social division" or "chaos" and reiterates parts of the Lao criminal code arbitrarily used in the past to arrest and detain dissidents. Provincial officials routinely cite the social and familial divisions caused by the spread of Protestantism as justification for serious religious freedom abuses.

Local officials have used the "vague" quality of the decree to effectively restrict proselytism, subjecting proselytizers to arrest and detainment. Furthermore, converts to Christianity have been punished with loss of property and forced relocation. The decree is enforced in a "varying and unpredictable" manner, leading to further discrimination against proselytizers from minority religions, particularly Protestant Christians. Abuses are typically committed by provincial authorities, who are either ignorant of laws protecting religious freedom or fail to implement them. The Laotian government has proved "either unable or unwilling to fully curtail" violations of religious freedom. Accordingly, the Commission has advocated for creation of a "formal human rights mechanism" between the United States and Laos to address issues of ethnic and religious discrimination.

India

The Commission has listed India as a Tier 2 country since 2009 due largely to the State's failure to protect minority religious communities from violence by private actors, leading to a culture of impunity for sectarian violence. The Commission recognized that India, as a pluralistic, secular democracy, demonstrates religious diversity at all levels of government. Nonetheless, it has "long struggled to protect minority religious communities or provide justice when crimes occur, which perpetuates a climate of impunity." Christian missionaries and Hindus who convert to Christianity report frequent harassment and violence. According to the Commission, "local police seldom provide protection, refuse to accept complaints, rarely investigate, and in a few cases encourage Christians to move or hide their religion."

Violations are particularly common in Indian states that have adopted anti-conversion laws, misleadingly called "freedom of religion acts," which "require government officials to assess the legality of conversions out of Hinduism" and subject proselytizers to fines and imprisonment for using "force, fraud, or 'inducement' to convert another." Because convictions under these laws typically require little evidence, they "create a hostile, and on occasion violent, environment for religious minority communities." That environment deters individuals from manifesting their religion through proselytism. To address these violations, the Commission recommended that the U.S. government urge India to repeal its state anti-conversion laws and strengthen its police forces to prevent sectarian violence.

Malaysia

In Malaysia, deemed a Tier 2 country since 2014, it is illegal for non-Muslims to proselytize to Muslims, but the Ministry of Islamic Affairs has supported Muslim efforts to proselytize to non-Muslims. The USCIRF report draws attention to the arrest, detention, and forced "rehabilitation" of Shi'a, Ahmadis, Baha'i, and Darul Arqam (all offshoots of Islam banned as "deviant" Muslim sects), as well as Jehovah's Witnesses and Mormons, for their proselytizing activities. The USCIRF recommended that the U.S. government urge Malaysia to "cease the arrest of individuals involved in peaceful religious activity" and "end government efforts to police religious belief and expression."

Tajikistan

In Tajikistan, a recommended CPC since 2012, proselytism was criminalized by a 2009 religion law. Religious groups must obtain government approval for the production, import, export, sale, and distribution of religious materials. Consequently, unregistered religious groups may not possess, obtain, or distribute religious materials. The Ministry of Culture has confiscated religious texts it deems inappropriate. Government approval is also required for religious organizations to invite foreign co-religionists into the country, further complicating various forms of religious observance, including proselytism. Jehovah's Witnesses, who had long been denied registration, were banned in 2007 for "causing popular discontent."[520] Jehovah's Witnesses have been detained, fined, and even deported for their unregistered religious activity, and their texts have been confiscated.[521]

ANALYSIS

The Commission, as well as the treaty bodies of the human rights instruments incorporated by reference in the IRFA, has found that arbitrary prohibitions or restrictions on religious conversions constitute violations of religious freedom. While Israeli law allows individuals of all faiths to convert, this right is not protected since the State fails to prevent private actors from discouraging (sometimes by coercive means) Jewish Israelis from converting to another faith or marrying a non-Jew.

Israeli Law on Proselytism, Religious Conversions, and Racial Incitement

Israeli law allows members of all religions to proselytize provided they do not offer a material benefit as an inducement to conversion or target minors whose parents are not adherents of the proselytizer's religion.[522] The 1977 Penal Law Amendment (Enticement to Change Religion) prohibits the exchange of money or other material benefit as a means to induce conversion.[523] Offenders may be sentenced to up to five years in prison. According to an instruction from the Attorney General, however, prior authorization by the state attorney is required to prosecute under this law. As of 1998, the law had never been applied.[524] In response to a mailing campaign by an American evangelical organization, a Knesset bill was introduced in 1997 that would have substantially restricted missionary activity. The bill was opposed by the government and was not adopted.[525]

Religious conversions are governed by a British Mandatory law, the 1927 Religious Community (Change) Ordinance.[526] Given that membership in a religious community determines the applicable personal status law in Israel's confessional system, the Ordinance requires that all changes in religion be registered. Further, for purposes of religious court jurisdiction, the conversion must be approved by the head of the individual's new religious community.[527]

Israeli criminal law prohibits racist incitement, defined as expression advocating the "persecution, humiliation, degradation, the display of enmity, hostility or violence, or the causing of riots against a public or parts of a population, all because of their color, racial affiliation, or ethnic [or] national origin."[528] Under Israeli jurisprudence, racist expression, even if framed in academic or theoretical terms, constitutes incitement if the accused intended, knew, or could reasonably foresee that the expression posed a risk to public safety and security, given all relevant circumstances.[529]

State Interference with Proselytism

Hostility to missionary activity

The State Department's 2013 IRF report makes the following observations regarding proselytism in Israel:

> Despite the legality of proselytism, the government generally discourages proselytizing and encourages the popular perception that it is illegal. The [Ministry of Interior] occasionally cites proselytizing as a reason to deny student, work, and religious visa extensions, as well as to deny permanent residency petitions.

Prior State Department reports have documented cases in which individuals suspected of missionary activity are detained at the airport, required to post bail, and forced to renounce proselytism.[530] In other instances, Christian clergy members are issued visas limiting them to the West Bank (excluding East Jerusalem) or prohibiting them from entering the West Bank, restrictions which may interfere with their ministry and potential evangelism (see chapter 5, *supra*).[531] Members of religious groups that are not recognized within Israel's confessional system – including several Protestant churches, such as the Lutherans, Baptists, and Quakers – face additional bureaucratic hurdles.[532]

State support of anti-assimilation initiatives

Israeli governmental authorities also provide funding and support for anti-assimilation initiatives, which reflects strong anti-assimilationist sentiment of the Israeli public. Public attitudes in Israel towards interfaith marriages between Jews and non-Jews are very negative, especially towards marriages between Israeli Jews and Israeli Palestinians; and women or men in interfaith unions are often harassed.[533] This anti-assimilationist sentiment was captured in a 2011 Ministry of Immigrant Absorption media campaign, which included videos and print advertisements in several U.S. cities warning Israeli expatriates that they and their children will lose their national and religious identities unless they return to Israel.[534] The campaign was cancelled under pressure from American Jewish organizations.[535]

In February 2010, the Ministry of Immigrant Absorption, the Tel Aviv-Yafo Municipality, and the World Congress of Bukharan Jews jointly launched an "aid program" for Jewish "distressed immigrant girls" who are romantically involved with Palestinian or non-Jewish foreign men.[536] The program was piloted in Tel Aviv neighborhoods with substantial Palestinian and immigrant populations. A Municipality employee explained that the program targeted "the trend of scores of Jewish girls getting together with minority men and with migrant workers, and then getting into trouble with their families and the families of the minority men, that often ostracize them for being Jewish."[537] According to the Israeli daily *Maariv*, the Absorption Ministry provided 75 percent of the program's funding, while the Tel Aviv-Yafo Municipality contributed NIS 250,000.

The Israeli Ministry of Social Affairs also funds a hostel for "at-risk" Jewish women, primarily women formerly involved in relationships with Palestinian men. The hostel is operated by Hemla ("Mercy"), a registered NGO with ties to the anti-assimilation group Lehava and, by extension, the racist political party Kach, which is banned in Israel and designated as a terrorist organization in the United States. Between 2005 and 2011, Hemla received between NIS 600,000-700,000 in annual funding – about half its annual budget – from the Ministry of Social Affairs, earmarked for the "treatment, support and personal and social rehabilitation" of the women residing in its hostel.[538] The organization's director, Rachel Baranes, has explained that "Hemla was established for the purpose of building a warm home in order to help girls – saving Jewish girls from assimilation, whether it's foreign workers, Arabs, [or] people with no connection to our religion."[539]

Failure to Prevent Harassment and Incitement against Evangelical Faiths

Under international human rights law, advocacy of religious hatred that constitutes incitement to discrimination, hostility, or violence cannot be protected as a manifestation of one's religion. On the contrary, states have an obligation to prohibit such incitement and take appropriate measures to suppress it.[540]

The State Department's 2013 IRF report observes Israel's failure to suppress incitement and threats of violence by anti-assimilation and anti-miscegenation groups:

> Societal attitudes toward missionary activities and conversion were generally negative. Most Jews opposed missionary activity directed at Jews, considering it tantamount to religious harassment, and some were hostile to Jewish converts to Christianity. Messianic Jews and Jehovah's Witnesses were reportedly harassed regularly by Yad L'Achim and Lev L'Achim, Jewish religious organizations opposed to missionary activity and intermarriage. There were no violent attacks against Messianic Jews or Jehovah's Witnesses.
>
> Yad L'Achim offered assistance to Jewish women in "escaping" situations of cohabitation with Arab men, in some cases reportedly facilitating the kidnapping of children away from the women's spouses. The anti-intermarriage organization Lehava established a hotline for citizens to inform on Jewish women who were suspected of having romantic relationships with Arab men and made the names and phone numbers of the men available to facilitate members of the general public contacting them and discouraging intermarriage. Lehava also allegedly collected the identification numbers of the Jewish women.[541]

The private anti-missionary and anti-miscegenation organizations identified in the State Department report – *Yad L'Achim* and *Lehava* – interfere with the right of evangelical non-Jewish communities and individuals in Israel to manifest their religion through legitimate, non-coercive forms of proselytism. Further, these organizations routinely engage in advocacy of religious hatred that constitutes incitement as defined in article 20(2) ICCPR and other human rights instruments. Israel bears responsibility for its failures to defend the right to lawfully proselytize against interference by private actors and to effectively suppress religious incitement.

These organizations feel particularly threatened by, and therefore target, Messianic Jews. Messianic Judaism is, in the movement's own words, a "Biblically based movement of people who, as committed Jews, believe in Yeshua (Jesus) as the Jewish Messiah of Israel of whom the Jewish Law and Prophets spoke."[542] Estimates of the number of Messianic Jews in Israel vary widely – from 6,000 to 20,000 members – because community leaders and members do not self-identify or disclose their prayer locations out of fear of harassment or persecution.[543] In 2010, a Jewish extremist confessed to placing a bomb, packaged as a gift for the Jewish holiday Purim, at the home of a Messianic Jewish family in the West Bank settlement of Ariel.[544]

Yad L'Achim

Yad L'Achim ("Hand to Brothers") is an anti-missionary and anti-assimilationist organization. According to its English website, its anti-assimilationist department undertakes "military-like rescues" of Jewish women who are romantically involved with Arab men or foreign workers, moving them to "safe houses" throughout Israel, "where they can build new lives for themselves."[545] Yad L'Achim activists regularly harass Messianic Jews and Jehovah's Witnesses, and pressure landlords, employers, and state officials to assist its campaign against what it considers to be "dangerous cults."[546] Contributions by American donors to Yad L'Achim are tax-deductible through its U.S. affiliate, Yad L'Achim Peyle Israel.[547]

As documented annually in the State Department's IRF reports, Yad L'Achim and other elements in the Orthodox Jewish community have succeeded in denying Jehovah's Witnesses and Messianic Jews of the use of public facilities and in disrupting events, all ostensibly in violation of Israeli law. For example, Jehovah's Witnesses were unable to continue to hold meetings in the Ra'anana municipality after a city council member publicly requested that such venues refrain from renting their spaces for missionary purposes.[548] In April 2015, a Jehovah's Witnesses seminar was again cancelled in Ra'anana under pressure from Yad L'Achim, which claimed that the event was a "mass baptism."[549] In canceling the event, the municipality cited the possibility of public disorder and "real fear" that Jehovah's Witnesses would attempt to convert minors from Judaism.[550] The Lod District Court ruled that the cancelation violated the right to freedom of religion and ritual. In response, the municipality appealed to the Supreme

Court to issue an injunction against the event.

Evangelicals face harassment – which often goes unpunished – from members of the Orthodox Jewish community.[551] In 2009, for example, a group of Orthodox Jews beat a group of Messianic Jews handing out religious pamphlets on the street.[552] In 2010, a group of approximately 200 Orthodox Jews disrupted a Jehovah's Witnesses religious assembly by shouting, throwing stones, and smashing windows.[553] Similarly, in 2011, a group of approximately 15 Orthodox Jews disrupted a Jehovah's Witnesses meeting and assaulted one of the meeting's attendees.[554] No arrests were made in any of these cases. Jehovah's Witnesses claim that government officials, including soldiers and police, have told them that proselytizing is illegal.[555] Jehovah's Witnesses further claim that verbal and physical assaults are so common that they ceased reporting them because authorities failed to follow up on past complaints. Indeed, public officials have occasionally supported Orthodox anti-missionary activity. For example, in 2008, the deputy mayor of Or Yehuda, near Tel Aviv, organized a book-burning of New Testaments distributed by Messianic Jews.[556]

Lehava

Lehava (literally "Flame," and the Hebrew acronym for "Prevention of Assimilation in the Holy Land") is an anti-assimilation organization with an anti-miscegenation focus. Founded in 2009, Lehava gained notoriety in August 2014 for staging a protest outside a mixed Jewish-Palestinian wedding.[557] Later that year, two Lehava activists were arrested and convicted for an act of arson at an Arabic-Hebrew bilingual school, the Max Rayne Hand-in-Hand School, in West Jerusalem. While the Israeli government has considered declaring Lehava an illegal organization, to date, no action has been taken against the group.[558]

Lehava is closely associated with the state-funded NGO Hemla. A 2011 investigation by the Israeli newspaper *Haaretz* found that several of Lehava's "leading and prominent activists" also worked for Hemla. Most notably, Lehava director Ben-Zion Gopstein concurrently served as Hemla's public relations director.[559] Gopstein is a follower of the late Rabbi Meir Kahane and was a member of Kahane's *Kach* party, which is outlawed in Israel and designated as a terrorist organization in the United States.

Gopstein was placed in administrative detention in 1994 for his involvement in Kahanist organizations. The November 2014 arson attack at a bilingual school, mentioned above, was carried out by two Lehava activists, brothers Shlomo Twito and Nahman Twito. They were convicted of arson and sentenced to 24 and 30 months in prison, respectively. In the wake of the arson attack, Gopstein was arrested on suspicion of incitement to racism, but was released three days later.[560] In June 2015, members of a Jewish extremist group calling itself "The Revolt," which is led by Kahane's grandson, Meir Ettinger, carried out an arson attack at the Church of the Multiplication on the Sea of Galilee.[561] Gopstein publicly sanctioned the church burning as a legitimate means of eliminating idol worship during a panel discussion with yeshiva students.[562]

Despite their records of inciting and perpetrating violence, Israel has failed to take meaningful legal action against Lehava or Gopstein for incitement to racial hatred and violence. In October 2014, the Israel Religious Action Center (IRAC), the legal advocacy arm of the Reform Movement, petitioned the Supreme Court for an order compelling the attorney-general to indict Gopstein for incitement to racism. According to the Center director, IRAC submitted "40 to 50 complaints [...] against Lehava and its leaders" to the attorney-general's office over a four-year period and received only one substantive response.[563] Additionally, following Gopstein's remarks endorsing church-burning, the Custody of the Holy Land, which administers the Catholic Church's property in Israel and the oPt, wrote to the attorney-general to urge that Gopstein be indicted. The Assembly of Catholic Ordinaries of the Holy Land, representing the heads of the Catholic rites in Israel and the oPt, filed a police complaint against him.[564] To date, however, Gopstein has not been charged. In August 2015, the Shin Bet, which bears statutory responsibility for recommending that groups be designated as illegal or terrorist organizations, concluded that it lacked sufficient grounds for declaring Lehava an illegal organization.[565]

Self-Censorship by Evangelical Faiths

Public concern over Christian proselytism of Jewish Israelis is rooted in the same anti-assimilationist sentiment that drives these extremist groups. The

Israeli government acquiesces to this pressure, and forces evangelical faiths to abandon this part of their ministry as a condition of operating in Israel. Thus, for example, Christians United for Israel, a Christian Zionist organization led by U.S. pastor John Hagee with a membership comprised almost entirely of evangelical Christians, has repeatedly declared that proselytism is "unacceptable" for its members.[566] This public pressure and state acquiescence, which all but vitiates the legal right to proselytize, are epitomized by the controversy surrounding the construction of Brigham Young University's Jerusalem Center on Mount Scopus.

Case Study: Brigham Young University's Jerusalem Center

BYU, which is owned and operated by the Church of Jesus Christ of Latter-day Saints (informally, the Mormon Church), inaugurated a study-abroad program in Jerusalem in 1966 and announced plans to build a dedicated study-abroad center in 1979. BYU was registered with Israeli authorities as a university association and made oral commitments to refrain from proselytism in an effort to facilitate the center's establishment. In March 1984, BYU and the Israel Land Administration entered into a renewable 49-year lease for a plot of Palestinian refugee land on Mount Scopus that had been transferred to the Custodian of Absentee Property.[567] However, in early 1985, opposition led by Yad L'Achim and other Orthodox groups nearly forced BYU to abandon the project. As BYU professor Blair Van Dyke recounted:

> Yad L'Achim was the most outspoken Orthodox Jewish group to oppose the Jerusalem Center. Other like-minded groups, like Am Israel Hai and Agudat Yisrael, lent considerable support to the opposition as well. ... Yad L'Achim was certain that Mormon claims that the Center would be used for university purposes were a ruse. They identified Mormonism as one the most aggressive and successful Christian proselytizing organizations in the world, and thus established a very aggressive defense. They prolifically churned out hundreds of articles, editorials, interviews, political cartoons, press releases, and reports of lectures opposing the Center that they felt "unveiled" Mormon intentions. Their efforts were calculated to protect Jews in Israel and the greater Diaspora from what they saw as an insidious Mormon threat. Additionally, they engaged radio and television, public rallies,

documentaries, debates, and public protests that effectively conveyed their opposition to the Mormon building project to Israelis and to media markets abroad. Their sole intention was to block the construction of the "Mormon University" (as the Jerusalem Center came to be known by locals). ...

The documented history of their attacks against the Mormons reveals an uncommonly fierce campaign. Their arguments were usually laced, if not saturated in, ad hominem including dehumanizing caricature, abusive verbal exchange, and threats of physical harm—even murder.[568]

This campaign included incitement and threats of violence that spanned from Israel to the United States:

In July 1985, the Mormon Center in the consular section of East Jerusalem was vandalized. Veiled death threats were made against [Jerusalem Mayor Teddy] Kollek, and pamphlets were distributed in ultra-Orthodox areas of Jerusalem likening him to Hitler and Haman. A program on army radio labeled the Mormons "enemies of Israel, a fifth column, a cancer in the body of the nation." In the United States, multiple LDS churches and meeting centers received anonymous bomb threats warning them to "get out of Israel." One congregation in Washington, D.C., received such a call while its 200 members were in the middle of worship.[569]

In May 1985, Orthodox anti-missionary groups demanded that the Mormons provide formal written guarantees that they would not proselytize in Israel.[570] The Israeli government, through Knesset Interior Committee chairman Dov Shilansky, capitulated to this demand. The director of BYU's Jerusalem study abroad program, David Galbraith, called this demand "demeaning," but the University acceded when it became clear that the Israeli government would halt construction without a written commitment.

Thus, in August 1985 BYU, "at the request of the Interior Committee of the Knesset," pledged that, "[i]n harmony with the law and consistent with our own past policy and practice, students, faculty, and staff connected with the Institution will not be permitted to engage in proselytizing activities in Israel."[571] In accordance with this undertaking, all students at BYU's Jerusalem Center must abide by a Non-Proselytizing Agreement, which sweepingly prohibits virtually all discussion of the Mormon faith with non-Mormons while in Israel or the oPt:

Any activities that could be construed as aimed at inducing, encouraging or leading people in Israel, the West Bank or Gaza to investigate any religion for possible conversion are strictly contrary to the desires of the government and people of Israel and to the commitments made by Brigham Young University, the Jerusalem Center for Near Eastern Studies, and The Church of Jesus Christ of Latter-day Saints. I will not distribute, either directly, by mail or by internet, any materials pertaining to the Church or its doctrines within Israel or Palestine. I will not discuss the Church or its doctrines or answer any questions regarding the Church or its doctrines with individuals who reside in the Holy Land or who may be visiting there. I will not invite guests who are not LDS to attend Church services held in the Holy Land. I understand the assurances and commitment of the Church, University, and the Jerusalem Center not to proselyte within Israel or Palestine and agree to abide by them. These restrictions on proselytizing also apply to all Arab countries and Turkey.[572]

This commitment to refrain from proselytizing did not end the controversy. In December 1985, the ultra-Orthodox Agudat Yisrael introduced a no-confidence motion in the government, despite being part of the governing coalition. In response, Prime Minister Shimon Peres appointed a ministerial cabinet committee to make recommendations on the fate of the BYU Center. The committee found no improprieties on the part of the Mormon Church in its registration and land acquisition, nor any evidence that it had violated its pledge to abstain from missionary activity. Over 150 U.S. congressmen, including the Democratic and Republican caucus chairmen, signed a letter urging the Israeli government to permit the Center's completion.[573] In August 1986, Israel's deputy attorney-general ruled that there was no legal basis for halting construction of the Center.[574] Accordingly, the committee recommended that the government allow construction to be completed, but urged that the university's lease be amended to incorporate the non-proselytism commitment.

The Center was completed in 1988 and opened in 1989. However, "those early days of suspicion and censure," which yielded the comprehensive non-proselytism agreement, "made it hard to envision a positive role for the BYU Jerusalem Center in interfaith relations, even after it opened its doors."[575]

The public backlash against the Mormon Church and the resulting complications with state authorities regarding the establishment of BYU's Jerusalem Center set a precedent that evangelical faiths have since followed: self-censorship is the cost of operating in Israel, despite the legal right to proselytize. Religious communities that have refused to forgo missionary activity integral to their faiths, such as Jehovah's Witnesses and Messianic Jews, have paid a heavy price in harassment by anti-missionary groups.

CONCLUSION

Israel's discriminatory policies discourage proselytizers from engaging with Jews. These policies, combined with police inaction and widespread social hostility towards missionary activities, create an environment in which non-Jewish proselytizers are routinely harassed, assaulted, and prevented from exercising their right to freedom of religion.

PART THREE

PROMOTING THE FRAGMENTATION OF ARAB PALESTINIAN IDENTITY

9
VIOLATING ARAB PALESTINIAN MINORITY RIGHTS BY RECOGNIZING AN ARAMEAN NATIONALITY

Israel regards its Jewish "nation" (*le'om*) as an indivisible unit. The state makes no distinction between Jews who identify with Orthodoxy in its various forms (Modern, Haredi, Hasidic Haredi), Reform Jews, Conservative Jews, non-*halachic* Jews from the former Soviet Union, non-rabbinic Jews such as Karaites and Samaritans, and secular Jews. Nor does the state recognize ethnic minorities, such as Sephardic,[576] Mizrahi[577] and Yemenite Jews, or linguistic minorities, such as Russian- and Amharic-speaking communities,[578] as national minorities.

In contrast, Israel recognizes and has historically encouraged divisions within its Palestinian population, particularly with respect to the Druze and Bedouin communities. Most recently, Israel granted recognition to an Aramean nationality – a national minority that does not objectively exist – as a means of encouraging the fragmentation of Palestinian society by promoting an exceedingly small segment of the Christian Arab community that identifies with the Israeli state and its institutions, most notably its military, rather than the Palestinian minority. Thus, recognition of an Aramean nationality, far from being a *bona fide* positive measure of protection of an objectively-established national minority, deliberately interferes with the internal affairs of the Palestinian national minority and

126

its exercise of internal self-determination, to which it is entitled as an indigenous population. As explained herein, this recognition must be understood in the context of Israel's broader campaign to create cleavages within its Palestinian national minority.

Recognition of an Aramean nationality violates the principles set by the Israeli Supreme Court in *Tamarin* and *Ornan* cases: that the existence of a nationality must be based on objective criteria as well as subjective self-identification. As a political initiative associated with right-wing parties that reject recognition of the Palestinian population as a native community with collective rights, recognition of an Aramean nationality violates both the letter and the spirit of human rights law, which seeks to protect *bona fide* national minorities and demands equal treatment of minority groups.

LEGAL STANDARD

Article 27 ICCPR requires states not to interfere with the right of ethnic, religious, or linguistic minorities "to enjoy their own culture, to profess and practise their own religion, or to use their own language." Although article 27 is framed in negative terms, the Human Rights Committee has clarified that states may be required to undertake "positive measures of protection" to ensure "the existence and the exercise of this right."[579] Recognition as a national minority (or "nationality" in Israel, where citizenship and nationality remain distinct concepts; *see* chapter 2, *supra*) is a fundamental positive measure, one that is often linked to some measure of self-government.

Thus, in Israel, the Palestinian minority seeks to be recognized as an native national community and to exercise the internationally-recognized collective rights of native populations, including the right to internal self-determination. In this regard, the UN Declaration on the Rights of Indigenous Peoples states that "indigenous peoples, in exercising their right to self-determination, have the right to autonomy or self-government in matters relating to their internal and local affairs...," as well as the right "to maintain and strengthen their distinct political, legal, economic, social and cultural institutions, while retaining their right to participate fully, if they so choose, in the political, economic, social and cultural life of the State."[580] However, a state's obligations towards a national minority do not depend on recognition, as "the existence of an ethnic, religious or linguistic minority in a given State party does not depend upon a decision by that State party but requires to be established by objective criteria."[581]

The purpose of such positive measures, including recognition, must be "to protect the identity of a minority and the rights of its members to enjoy and develop their culture and language and to practise their religion, in community with the other members of the group."[582] To avoid abuses of this principle, positive measures of protection towards national minorities under article 27 ICCPR must (1) be based on reasonable and objective criteria and (2) comply with requirements of equality and nondiscrimination:

> it has to be observed that such positive measures must respect the provisions of articles 2.1 and 26 of the Covenant both as regards the treatment between different minorities and the treatment between the persons belonging to them and the remaining part of the population. However, as long as those measures are aimed at correcting conditions which prevent or impair the enjoyment of the rights guaranteed under article 27, they may constitute a legitimate differentiation under the Covenant, provided that they are based on reasonable and objective criteria.[583]

Linguistic minorities require such protections because, as observed by the UN's independent expert on minority issues, states often view the desire to maintain minority languages as "divisive and counter to State ideologies and policies to promote national identity, national unity, integration and territorial integrity."[584] Recognition of a linguistic minority is generally linked with other positive measures to preserve their language, which include bestowing official status on the language and offering education to linguistic minorities in their mother tongue.[585]

Analysis

Refusal to Recognize a Secular, Binational Israeli Nationality

The distinction between Israeli citizenship rights and Jewish national rights is central to the State's systematic discrimination against its Palestinian citizens, as discussed in chapter 2, *supra*. The category of nationality was used in the first Israeli census of 1949, and has since become a device to facilitate the superior legal status of Jewish Israelis relative to Palestinian citizens of Israel.[586] As discussed *supra*, Israel defies contemporary state practice in which citizenship and nationality are understood synonymously as effective links to a territorially-defined "nation" – the state. Rather, in Israel, nationality and the privileges associated exclusively with Jewish nationality create different classes of citizenship. Recognizing an Israeli nationality open to both Jews and Palestinians would complicate, if not imperil, this system of Jewish national privileges that is central to the Israeli ethnocracy. Consequently, the Israeli government and Supreme Court have consistently refused to recognize an Israeli nationality.

The Supreme Court first disavowed the existence of an Israeli nationality in its 1972 *Tamarin* decision.[587] The petitioner, George Tamarin, a Jewish immigrant from Yugoslavia, relied on the Court's decision in *Shalit*, which held that membership in an Israeli nationality, like the Jewish nationality, could only be determined by a *bona fide* statement of self-identification (*see* chapter 2, *supra*). Tamarin averred that upon his immigration to Israel in 1949, "there was still only a nucleus of the process of creation of the Israeli identity, and [he] was not sufficiently rooted in it," but by 1970, "a crystallized Israeli identity" had come into existence to which he belonged "by all the subjective criteria," including "identification, sense of belongingness, loyalty and [a] declaration to that effect."[588] The Court reasoned that "there is no significance in the criterion of subjective feeling…regarding his belonging to a certain nation, unless it is possible to determine, according to any criteria, that that nation exists."

The Court maintained that the existence of a nationality is determined objectively, based on "the ethnic attributes and cultural assets that single out a national group and make it different than other national groups," and also subjectively, by "the sympathetic attitudes with which members of the national group regard those attributes and assets," as ascertained by a sense of interdependence and common responsibility. It found that Tamarin had failed to prove that "there is a sizeable group of people in Israel who lack, or have lost, that same deep feeling of Jewish interdependence or common responsibility." Even if such a group existed "barely twenty-three years after the establishment of the State," the Court added, their request to recognize an Israeli nationality was, like the American Confederacy, an attempt to "secede from the Jewish people" on a basis inconsistent with national self-determination. The Court thus concluded that "[t]here is no Israeli nation separate from the Jewish people."

In 2013, the Court again refused to recognize an Israeli nationality, this time on a petition brought by Israeli professor Uzzi Ornan and his fellow members of the *Ani Israeli* (I am an Israeli) movement. Unlike Tamarin, Ornan was born in Mandatory Palestine and became an Israeli citizen upon the state's establishment. Ornan argued that Israel's Declaration of Establishment created an Israeli nationality, comprised of "members of 'the independent Hebrew nation in their land" and "members of the Arab nation who reside in the State of Israel," but not including the Jewish diaspora.[589] Thus, he argued, "the entire citizenry of Israel amounts to its constituent nationality, and therefore, negating the existence of an Israeli nationality is tantamount to negating the existence of the State of Israel as a sovereign democratic state." Further, Ornan urged that "nationality" in the modern sense, recognized in international human rights law, including the right to a nationality under article 15 UDHR, is not "a religious or ethnic nationality" but "the state's nationality in the legal sense."[590]

The Court, per Judge Uzi Vogelman, restated the reasons identified in *Tamarin* for why the existence of an Israeli nationality had to be proven by objective factors: the "immensely wide" implications such recognition would have on "Israel's relations with diaspora Jews" and "perceptions among the various groups within the State of Israel and the relations between them."[591] Ornan failed to prove that "the general public's perception of "nationality" has changed since the *Tamarin* ruling."[592] Regarding Ornan's assertion that an Israeli citizen's nationality in its modern sense is Israeli, the Court stated simply that "distinction between citizenship and nationality is not new" and rejected the "unification of these two terms" for the "ideological purpose" urged by Ornan.[593]

Judge Meltzer, who agreed that Ornan's insistence on a distinct Israeli nationality was inaccurate, explained that Ornan's argument was foreclosed by "constitutional datum" establishing Israel as a "Jewish and democratic state," and by international recognition of Israel's Jewish character, as established by (1) the 1947 UN Partition Plan, which provided for a Jewish state in Mandatory Palestine; (2) the "moral recognition of the Jewish people's right to self determination within a national framework"; and (3) state practice, which "rejects the argument that the democratic system necessitates a nationally 'neutral state.'"[594] One characteristic of the state's Jewish character is its "responsibility for the fate of the entire Jewish people, since it was founded as a manifestation of all-Jewish solidarity."[595] Accordingly, he found "no justification for the 'unification' of the separate nationalities and their legal merger into a new general 'Israeli nationality', since this would run contrary to Israel's Jewish nature as well as its democratic nature."[596]

The State's insistence upon a singular Jewish identity and consequently its refusal to recognize a secular, binational Israeli nationality contrasts with its recognition and promotion of multiple "nationalities" within its Palestinian citizenry, as discussed in chapters 9 and 10, *infra*.

Recognition of an Aramean Religious and Linguistic Minority

Israel's recognition of an Aramean nationality based on the self-identification of certain Christian Arab Palestinians is not based on reasonable, objective criteria. It also violates the requirements of equality and nondiscrimination in minority protection because Israel denies such recognition based on the self-identification to larger, defined, and established groups within its Jewish "nationality."

International human rights law as expressed in article 27 ICCPR, and Israeli law as established in *Tamarin* and *Ornan*, both require that the existence of a national minority (or "nationality" in Israeli law) be established by objective criteria as well as subjective self-identification. According to the leaders of the Aramean recognition initiative, Aramean identity is based on ethnicity, religion, and language. None of these bases can be objectively substantiated. Self-identified Arameans cannot be distinguished on ethnic or religious grounds from other Christian Palestinians in Israel, an overwhelming majority of whom reject the existence of an Aramean national minority. The principal objective criteria for the existence of (and membership in) a linguistic minority is actual use of the language, at least in private.[597] Despite an Israeli government-promoted "revival" of Aramean language education, there is no Aramean-speaking community in Israel. Thus, whether premised on ethnicity, religion, or language, an Aramean national minority cannot be established by objective criteria. Nor is there a "sizeable group of people in Israel" with a "deep feeling" of Aramean "inter-dependence and common responsibility," as the Israeli Supreme Court has found necessary for recognition of a national minority or "nationality."[598]

Instead, recognizing a distinct Aramean nationality reinforces Israel's selective "protection" of Arab minorities, which advances its social policy objective of marginalizing Palestinian nationalism among its Arab citizens. Israel's efforts to fragment and weaken a national minority clearly established by objective criteria – the Palestinian population, defined principally by national origin (see chapter 2, *supra*) – by declaring that each of its religious and linguistic traditions constitutes a separate "nationality" (*le'om*) violates the letter and spirit of article 27 ICCPR. Notably, the principals of the Aramean initiative are associated with right-wing parties which oppose the creation of a Palestinian state in the oPt and recognition of the collective, national rights of the native Palestinian minority within Israel.[599]

Registration Requirements for Aramean Nationality

In Israel, citizens and permanent residents are classified on the population registry according to a limited set of recognized religions,[600] without the option to be unaffiliated or atheist. As discussed in chapter 2, *supra*, a foundational and essential feature of the Israeli ethnocracy is the construction of an ethnoreligious Jewish nationality rather than of an Israeli nationality.[601] Since Israel's first census in 1949, the State's second most substantial population, Palestinians, have been classified by their Arab nationality in the population registry. These classifications are also included on the national ID cards that adults must carry at all times (a source of religion-based discrimination, as discussed in chapter 6, *supra*.

On September 17, 2014, then-Israeli interior minister Gideon Saar signed an order directing the Administration of Border Crossings, Population and Immigration (PIBA) to recognize an Aramean nationality in the population registry.[602] Under the order, applicants are eligible to be registered as Aramean if they establish (1) national origin in the Middle East, (2) they are conversant in the Aramean language, and (3) are a member of one of the following Christian denominations: Maronite, Orthodox Aramaic, Syriac Catholic, Greek Orthodox, or Greek Catholic (Melkite).[603] The first person registered under the order, on October 21, 2014, was 2-year old Yacoub Halul. Yacoub's father, Shadi Halul, is the principal of the Maronite Christian group, Amram, which applied to the State for recognition of the Aramean nationality.[604] The conjunctive requirements of national origin, linguistic knowledge, and religious affiliation reflect the historical narrative of the initiative's founders, as expressed by Halul:

> We have existed in this region for thousands of years. We accepted Christianity, but then had Arabic forced upon us during the Arab conquest, just as local Jews did. But we preserved our language in churches and other cultural settings.[605]

As discussed *infra*, the governing bodies of the Eastern churches in the Holy Land, as well as Palestinian Christian political leaders, reject this narrative and deny the existence of an Aramean national minority in Israel based on ethnic, religious, or linguistic identity.

Recognition of Aramean Nationality not Based on Reasonable, Objective Criteria

In human rights law it is accepted that the existence of a minority is a question of fact that must be established by objective factors and subjective self-identification.[606] While there is no single accepted definition of a minority, the working definition of former UN Special Rapporteur on prevention of discrimination and protection of minorities, Francesco Capotorti, is often invoked:

> A group numerically inferior to the rest of the population of a State, in a non-dominant position, whose members - being nationals of the State - possess ethnic, religious or linguistic characteristics differing from those of the rest of the population and show, if only implicitly, a sense of solidarity, directed towards preserving their culture, traditions, religion or language.[607]

Israeli law, as defined in the *Tamarin* and *Ornan* cases, similarly holds that "the ethnic attributes and cultural assets that single out a national group are objective factors" that must be proved by the party seeking recognition.[608]

In *Tamarin*, the Supreme Court described recognition of a new "nationality" as an expression of the principle of self-determination, which "is intended for nations and not fragments of nations. Otherwise, total national and social disintegration could ensue."[609]

The persons eligible for registration as Aramean under the September 17, 2014 government order do not meet these objective criteria. As the registration criteria make clear, eligible "Arameans" do not possess ethnic or religious characteristics differing from the existing "Arab nationality" – the Palestinian national minority in Israel, which includes an estimated 161,000 Christians, roughly 10 percent of the Israel's total Palestinian population of 1.674 million.[610]

The principal objective criteria for the existence of a linguistic minority is actual use of the language by its putative members, at least in private. There is no such Aramean-speaking population in Israel, as Halul admits when he speaks of wanting to "resurrect" or "revive" the language.[611] While certain Palestinian Christian communities, including the Maronites and the Syrian Orthodox, have recently initiated neo-Aramaic elementary and adult education classes in both Israel and the oPt, these efforts have not produced an actual Aramean-speaking community, as exist elsewhere in the Levant.

Rather, Aramean exists in Israel and the oPt as the liturgical language of certain Eastern Christian churches. Clergy affiliated with these Eastern churches, who are the principal (and virtually the exclusive) community in Israel and the oPt with knowledge of the language, overwhelmingly reject the existence of an Aramean linguistic minority. The Justice and Peace Commission of the Assembly of the Catholic Ordinaries of the Holy Land, which includes the Maronite, Melkite, and Syriac Catholic Churches, issued the following statement explaining the origins of the Arameans and denying the existence of an Aramean ethnic or linguistic national minority:

> Arameans were an ancient people that dwelt in the Middle East. Their language, Aramaic, was the lingua franca of the Assyrian, Babylonian and Persian Empires. It was adopted by the Jews in the Babylonian Exile and has remained important for them until today because a large part of the rabbinic tradition was written in Aramaic. Some streams of Christianity adopted a form of Aramaic, known as Syriac, and it remains a liturgical language for some Eastern Churches until today.

> Arabs who live today in Greater Syria have spoken different languages over the centuries: Aramaic, Greek and Arabic. Today, the unique language in daily use throughout the area is Arabic (except for tiny pockets where some form of colloquial Aramaic is preserved). Today, we, in Israel, we are Christian Palestinian Arabs.[612]

Dr. Amnon Ramon, a Jewish Israeli expert on the state's policy toward the Christian churches, has similarly dismissed the Aramean initiative as "an attempt to invent a new nationality."[613]

Accordingly, the existence of an Aramean national minority in Israel cannot be established by the objective criteria required under human rights law, including article 27 ICCPR, and recognized in Israeli jurisprudence. Accordingly, the state's decision to extend recognition to an Aramean nationality cannot be based on reasonable, objective criteria. Carving an Aramean nationality out of the Arab Palestinian nationality while denying recognition to objectively-established minority groups among citizens of Jewish nationality thus violates Israel's obligation under human rights law to uphold equality and nondiscrimination in the protection of national minorities.

<u>Recognition of an Aramean Nationality Violates the Native National Community Rights of Palestinians</u>

Because Palestinians are the native national community in Israel, their guaranteed right under article 27 ICCPR "to enjoy their own culture" must be read in conjunction with the internationally-recognized additional protections owed to indigenous populations. The UN Declaration on the Rights of Indigenous Peoples provides that "indigenous peoples and individuals have the right not to be subjected to forced assimilation or destruction of their culture."[614] To safeguard this right, the UN Declaration calls for effective mechanisms for the prevention of "any action which has the aim or effect of depriving them of their integrity as distinct peoples, or of their cultural values or ethnic identities."[615]

Contrary to these principles, recognition of an Aramean nationality is a manifestation of Israel's divide-and-rule strategy towards its Palestinian citizens.[616] The recognition of Arameans as a separate nationality further divides the Palestinian people along sectarian lines.[617]

The leaders of the Aramean recognition initiative also lead the state-supported campaign to promote Arab Christian enlistment in the Israeli armed forces. Both initiatives are linked to right-wing Israeli political parties, whose members speak openly about using Christian citizens as a "counterbalance" to the Muslim population, which they view as more fervent in its Palestinian nationalism.[618]

The Aramean initiative's founder and leader is Shadi Halul, the director of the Aramaic Maronite Heritage Center and the Israeli Aramaic Christian Association. Halul is a retired captain in the Israeli armed forces who ran in the 2015 Knesset elections on the candidate list of the far-right *HaBayit Hayahudi* (Jewish Home) party. *HaBayit Hayahudi* is unequivocally hostile to Palestinian interests. It calls for Israel to annex Area C of the West Bank (which represents over 60 percent of its territory), opposes a Palestinian state or any further Israeli withdrawal from the West Bank, and conditioned its participation in the 2013-2015 coalition government on passage of the Basic Law: Israel of the Nation-State of the Jewish People (discussed in chapter 2, *supra*), which would constitutionalize the denial of internal self-determination to Israel's Palestinian native minority.[619]

Halul is also a leading figure in the Israeli Christians Recruitment Forum, a government-sponsored initiative announced by Prime Minister Netanyahu in August 2013 to promote voluntary service in the Israeli armed forces by self-described "Christian Israelis" – Palestinian Christian citizens of Israel.[620] The Forum is closely associated with Fr. Gabriel Naddaf, a Greek Orthodox priest.[621] In April 2014, the Israeli military began distributing voluntary enlistment forms to Palestinian Christian youths of recruitment age (in Israel only, not within the oPt).[622] These forms are similar to the mandatory conscription notices distributed to Jewish Israelis and male members of the Druze community.[623] The Palestinian Christian leadership in Israel and the oPt, including the Orthodox Patriarch of Jerusalem, Atallah Hanna, and the Latin Patriarch Emeritus of Jerusalem, Michel Sabbah, denounced the initiative and encouraged young Palestinian Christians to "throw [the enlistment forms] away and not to engage with them in any way."[624]

The fringe views driving the Aramean recognition and related Christian military recruitment efforts are antithetical to the views of an overwhelming majority of Palestinian citizens of Israel. In the 2015 elections, 82 percent of Palestinian citizens voted for the Joint List political alliance.[625] The alliance's platform calls for "an end [to] the occupation of all territories conquered in 1967," "the establishment of a sovereign, independent Palestinian state" on that territory, and "full national and civic equality for the Arab-Palestinian public in Israel as a native minority with collective and individual rights."[626] Further, the Joint List vows to "fight to annul compulsory military service for the Arab-Druze community, and against all programs of military recruitment and national service for young Arab people."

Israeli state support for these fringe initiatives can also be seen in its heavy-handed suppression of opposition to these initiatives among the Palestinian community. A young Palestinian Christian citizen of Israel, Ghassan Munair, was arrested and placed under house arrest for alleged incitement after posting to Facebook a photo of Fr. Naddaf and then-Israeli finance minister Yair Lapid with the caption:

> For the sake of freedom of speech and transparency, the faces and names of the 'honorable' that appear in the following photos are the ones who want to enlist your sons against your people – keep this in mind.

Similarly, Abir Kopty, a former Nazareth city council member, was summoned for interrogation over a blog post critical of the initiative.[627] (These investigations contrast with the State's failure to investigate and prosecute incitement by Jewish anti-assimilationist and anti-miscegenation groups against non-Jews, discussed in chapter 8, *supra*.)

The UN Declaration on the Rights of Indigenous Peoples further provides that "States shall consult and cooperate in good faith with the indigenous peoples concerned through their own representative institutions in order to obtain their free, prior and informed consent before adopting and implementing legislative or administrative measures that may affect them."[628] Instead, Israel has enlisted fringe figures from the Palestinian community to support these initiatives, while bypassing Palestinian representative institutions. Indeed, the Aramean recognition and Christian recruitment initiatives have been condemned in near-universal terms by Palestinian religious and political leaders in Israel and the oPt:

- National Coalition of Christian Organizations in Palestine
"The use of army service to divide the Arab population against itself is detrimental to the interests of the Arabs as a community."[629]

- Christian Orthodox Institutions in Jerusalem and the Palestinian Territories
"Those who call for recruitment and encourage Christian youth to join the occupation army do not represent the church and do not represent Christians of whom the majority reject the army recruitment in its entirety."[630]

- Latin Patriarch of Jerusalem, Fouad Twal
"At the individual level, everyone is free to act as they wish. But I think that this proposal is pursuing the goal of dividing the Arab community in its interior, tearing the community of Muslims and Christians who always live together, and the goal of affirming that Christians are not Arabs. Christians here, as I, too, are one hundred per cent Christian and one hundred per cent Arab. No one can change that and make false papers. Nobody can believe another line. If someone has accepted this proposal, shall bear the responsibility of it. Unfortunately, one always finds some weak individuals who, under pressure or promise of money, can do this."[631]

- Latin Patriarch Emeritus of Jerusalem, Michel Sabbah
"A new Christian issue has been raised inside Israel: there are voices among Christians, encouraged by the authorities, who have begun to say "we are not Arabs, we are Arameans". Where does this imaginative discourse come from? Perhaps it has its roots in an imagined past: it is true that some of us, Christians, spoke Aramaic, centuries ago, like the Jews. However, history has been ongoing and has transformed situations and peoples. Today, we are what we are: Palestinians, Arabs and Christians. Resurrecting some distant past does not automatically separate one from his or her people. When one is faced by a difficult present, it is not always healthy to escape into a "mythical" past and bury oneself in it. It is usually best to face the present challenges and to help others to face these challenges. On the other hand, I would say to a Christian Palestinian who now claims to be Aramean and not Arab: If you want to express a special loyalty to Israel, start being loyal to yourself. If you are not loyal to yourself you will be loyal to no one. I do not think this "flight of imagination" will be of any help to Israel. Loyalty does not mean providing Israel with more soldiers in the army or more collaborators in society. It is no help to the Christians, even if some of them will profit as individuals, getting jobs, admissions to universities and so on. This "flight of imagination" is rather an added element of confusion and internal dissention, inside Israel and among the Christian Palestinian Israeli citizens.[632]

- Catholic Ordinaries of the Holy Land
  Come back to your senses. Do not harm your people, because of idle promises and personal egoistic gain. By adopting such a position, you do not benefit yourselves nor do you benefit Israel. Israel is in need of Christians who have heard Jesus' teaching: "Blessed the peace makers". Israel does not need Christians who have deformed their identity, who position themselves as enemy of their own people and who become soldiers for war. This does not produce peace, neither for you nor for any other Israeli. Serve yourselves, serve your people and serve Israel in remaining faithful to the truth, i.e. faithful to your identity as Christians, as Palestinians and as peacemakers. Promote peace among yourselves, among Palestinians and Israelis.

The Aramean recognition initiative, along with the Christian recruitment initiative with which it is affiliated, must be understood as an element of the State's broader campaign to divide Christians and Muslims within the Palestinian population.

CONCLUSION

The recognition of the Aramean nationality, carved out of the native Arab Palestinian population, is implemented in a societal context where the state identifies separate nationalities only among non-Jewish citizens. The Jewish population, which includes members who speak many different languages, have different geographical origins, and are affiliated with different traditions of Judaism, is instead treated as an indivisible whole. In this context, the new measure of registering Arameans as a separate nationality clearly reveals Israel's intent to divide the Palestinian population and constitutes a discriminatory policy itself. The recognition of an Aramean nationality therefore violates (1) the requirement in human rights law that measures of protection for national minorities be based on objective, reasonable criteria; (2) the principles of equality and nondiscrimination in minority protection; and (3) the internal self-determination of the Arab Palestinians, an indigenous population in Israel, by interfering in its integrity, promoting counter-majoritarian initiatives, and bypassing its recognized representatives.

10

DENYING PALESTINIAN DRUZE CITIZENS OF ISRAEL THE RIGHT TO CONSCIENTIOUSLY OBJECT TO SERVING AGAINST FELLOW ARAB PALESTINIANS

The Druze are a religious minority that comprise eight percent of the Arab population of Israel and 1.6 percent of the state's overall population. The Druze faith was borne out of the Shi'a Islamic tradition and the Druze are part of the Arab population by language, culture, and history. However, since the 1930s, the Zionist (and later Israeli) establishment have sought to redefine the Druze as a "nation" distinct from the rest of the Palestinian population, whose interests align with the state rather than Palestinian nationalism. As a result, the degree of affiliation by Druze with Palestinian or Israeli identities varies widely. Some Druze self-identify as Palestinians and others as Israelis.

All Druze men of military age, whatever their self-identification, are subject to mandatory military service, with effectively no possibility of exemption under claims of conscientious objection. Even so, some Druze men object to completing military service in the oPt, as doing so, they feel, would mean taking up arms against their fellow Palestinians. The Israeli military's "conscience committee" rejects claims of conscientious objection based on a refusal to serve in the occupied territory, irrespective of the objector's national origin. The Israeli government and judiciary have upheld the military's position. In many cases, Druze conscientious objectors have been subjected to repeated imprisonment for their objection.

Other segments of the Palestinian population are exempted *en masse* from military service and thereby relieved of the duty of serving against their fellow Palestinians in the oPt. Even so, Israel denies that its Druze citizens may validly identify as Palestinians, despite their linguistic, cultural, and historical ties. This unequal treatment of self-identified Palestinians of Druze faith violates religious freedom, which includes the right to conscientiously object to military service and the right to be treated equally to conscientious objectors of other faiths.

LEGAL STANDARD

Human Rights Law

Conscientious objection to compulsory military service is derived from the guarantee of freedom of thought, conscience and religion in article 18 ICCPR and article 18 UDHR, as explained by the Human Rights Committee in General Comment No. 22:

> The Covenant does not explicitly refer to a right to conscientious objection, but the Committee believes that such a right can be derived from article 18, inasmuch as the obligation to use lethal force may seriously conflict with the freedom of conscience and the right to manifest one's religion or belief. When this right is recognized by law or practice, there shall be no differentiation among conscientious objectors on the basis of the nature of their particular beliefs; likewise, there shall be no discrimination against conscientious objectors because they have failed to perform military service.[633]

The UN Human Rights Council reaffirmed, in a 2012 resolution, "the right of everyone to have conscientious objection to military service as a legitimate exercise of the right to freedom of thought, conscience and religion" and called "upon all States to continue to review, as appropriate, their laws, policies and practices relating to conscientious objection to military service."[634] The Council's predecessor, the UN Commission on Human Rights, adopted Resolution 1998/77 on conscientious objection, which called upon states:

> to establish independent and impartial decision-making bodies with the

task of determining whether a conscientious objection is genuinely held in a specific case, taking account of the requirement not to discriminate between conscientious objectors on the basis of the nature of their particular beliefs;

The resolution further emphasized that:

States should take the necessary measures to refrain from subjecting conscientious objectors to imprisonment and to repeated punishment for failure to perform military service, and recalls that no one shall be liable or punished again for an offence for which he has already been finally convicted or acquitted in accordance with the law and penal procedure of each country[.][635]

The European Court of Human Rights recognized in *Bayatyan v Armenia* that the right to conscientious objection is protected by article 9 ECHR:

opposition to military service, where it is motivated by a serious and insurmountable conflict between the obligation to serve in the army and a person's conscience or his deeply and genuinely held religious or other beliefs, constitutes a conviction or belief of sufficient cogency, seriousness, cohesion and importance to attract the guarantees of Article 9.[636]

The Court, noting that all member states of the Council of Europe, except Turkey, had recognized *de jure* the right to conscientious objection, held that article 9 prohibits prosecuting a genuine conscientious objector for refusal to perform military service if he or she is willing to perform alternate civilian service:

The imposition of a penalty on the applicant, in circumstances where no allowances were made for the exigencies of his conscience and beliefs, could not be considered a measure necessary in a democratic society. Still less can it be seen as necessary taking into account that there existed viable and effective alternatives capable of accommodating the competing interests, as demonstrated by the experience of the overwhelming majority of the European States.[637]

In *Savda v Turkey*, the ECtHR further ruled that the guarantees of article 9 require states to establish a procedure for examining conscientious objection claims that meets the due process requirements of article 6 ECHR.[638] The Court thus held that requiring an objector to defend his claim of conscientious objection before a military tribunal violates the right to a fair trial under article 6. While the inclusion of a single military officer on a three-judge panel was not *per se* a due process violation, the Court found that a tribunal composed entirely of military personnel lacked the impartiality and independence required by the Convention.

Additionally, the UN General Assembly, invoking the freedom of thought, conscience and religion under article 18 UDHR, has "recognize[d] the right of all persons to refuse service in military or police forces which are used to enforce apartheid."[639] As noted in chapter 2, *supra*, the separate legal regimes for Israeli Jews and Palestinians within the occupied West Bank is increasingly identified as a form of apartheid, as defined in international criminal law. [640]

USCIRF Precedent

The Commission has condemned, and continues to monitor closely, violations of the right to conscientious objection in several countries, including Kyrgyzstan, Belarus, Turkmenistan, and South Korea.

In the case of Kyrgyzstan, the Commission has expressed concern that the Kyrgyz religion law, which imposes onerous registration requirements for religious communities and acknowledges claims of conscientious objection to military service by members of recognized religious groups only, thus excluding non-traditional Muslim, Protestant, and other minority religions.[641] In Belarus and Turkmenistan, the Commission has expressed concern over the absence of legal provisions governing conscientious objection.[642]

The Commission's scrutiny in this regard is not limited to illiberal regimes: it has denounced South Korea's practice of imprisoning Jehovah's Witnesses and other conscientious objectors for violating its Military Service Act. Offenders incur an 18-month imprisonment and a criminal conviction that disqualifies the individual from taking national certification exams for civil service positions.[643]

Furthermore, in conjunction with the Tom Lantos Human Rights Commission and Amnesty International USA, the USCIRF has developed the "Defending Freedom Project," which aims to protect "prisoners of conscience" around the world. Regarding the classification of detained conscientious objectors as prisoners of conscience, Amnesty International stated:

> A person who for reasons of conscience or profound conviction arising from religious, ethical, moral, humanitarian, philosophical, political or similar motives refuses to perform armed service or any other direct or indirect participation in wars or armed conflicts and is imprisoned as a direct result of his or her refusal to serve is considered by Amnesty International to be a prisoner of conscience unless such a person has also refused to perform alternative civilian service which is no longer than the length of military service or is otherwise not punitive in nature. There is no such alternative civilian service in Israel.[644]

While Israel has an alternative national service (*Sherut Leumi*), conscientious objectors who are denied exemptions are not given the option of participating in this service.[645]

ANALYSIS

Conscientious Objection in Israel

Israel's Defense Service Law subjects all citizens, male and female, to recruitment for mandatory military service at age 18.[646] The Law allows for exemptions to be granted for medical reasons and to women who are married, have children, or are pregnant.[647] The Law vests the Ministry of Defense with discretion to exempt or defer individuals from service.[648]

Men may only be exempted from military service on grounds of conscientious objection through an exercise of the Ministry's discretionary authority.[649] The Israeli Supreme Court has repeatedly upheld the military's policy of granting exemptions to male conscripts with a *bona fide* "general objection to bearing arms and fighting in wars" but refusing objections to "specific" conscientious objectors – those with "an objection to a specific war or military operation," including the occupation of the West Bank and Gaza.[650] For women, the Law provides for exemptions for "reasons of conscience or reasons connected with her family's religious way of life."[651] However, in 2004, the Israeli Supreme Court ruled that "reasons of conscience" as used in the Law do not include moral objections to military practices and policies, but rather require evidence of religious or traditional constraints that prevent a woman from performing military service.[652]

Declared conscientious objections are a relatively new and growing phenomenon in Israel. Historically, the Israeli military "made substantial efforts to downplay the significance of refusals," preferring to resolve undeclared refusals through an accommodation within the objector's military unit.[653] Declared refusals to serve, backed by organized movements such as *Yesh Gvul* ("There is a Limit") and *Ometz LeSarev* ("Courage to Refuse"), began with the Lebanon War (1982-1985) and grew markedly during Israel's repression of the first Palestinian *intifada* (1987-1991).[654]

In the early 1980s, the Israeli military first responded to requests to conscientiously object by "adopt[ing] a hard-line policy of trial and prison term."[655] The military acknowledged this policy in a 1980 Supreme Court case, *Algazi v. Minister of Defense*, wherein counsel for the military stated:

> Army authorities had assured objectors that they would be stationed according to their wishes... as long as acts of refusal was an isolated phenomenon. Now the policy has changed. What had once been sporadic instances of refusal that IDF was willing to tolerate, has changed in its nature and become an organized protest whose aim is to turn the IDF... into the battleground for a kind of confrontation which the army should not be associated with.[656]

Subsequently, the army formed an internal committee to review conscientious objection claims. As described by Israeli law professor Leora Bilsky:

> The "conscience committee" was formed in 1995 by the IDF chief of personnel. Its formal purpose was to better organize the policy for exempting individuals based on conscientious objections, which was unclear up to that point. The committee is chaired by an officer from the personnel unit and consists of a legal representative from the military attorney general unit and members of regulation and behavioral science units, as well as one civilian member, usually a philosophy professor. The committee employs the distinction, which preceded its establishment, between "pacifism" and "selective" or "political" objection. According to this distinction, "pacifists," defined as people who object to any type of

military service, are exempted from army service, while "selective objectors," who refuse to take part in specific military actions, are not. [657]

Out of roughly 180 cases that the conscience committee heard between 1995 and 2004, it recognized only six applicants as genuine pacifists and thus eligible for an exemption.[658] In practice, conscientious objector status is granted solely on religious grounds, whereas reasons of conscience, based on moral, ethical, or political considerations, are not considered sufficient to exempt an individual from military service.[659]

The UN Human Rights Committee has determined that the "conscience committee" lacks independence, given that all but one of its members are military officials, and that Israel's practice of imprisoning individuals who refuse to serve in the armed forces may violate the *ne bis in idem* ("double jeopardy") principle, in breach of articles 14 and 18 ICCPR.[660]

The Druze, Israel, and Palestinian Identity

The relationship between the Druze community, the State of Israel, and the Palestinian national movement is a complicated subject that cannot be fully explicated here. For our purposes, it suffices to observe that the "natural" pre-Zionism relationship between the Druze and other Arab Palestinians and the degree to which Israel has sought to manipulate that relationship are subject to debate.[661] Among the issues disputed in these narratives is whether the 1956 conscription agreement actually reflected the will of the Druze community of that era, and if so, whether today's Druze citizens of military age should be bound by that decision.

According to the Israeli narrative, the Palestinian Druze never identified with other Palestinians or the Arab nationalist movement that developed in response to Zionism. Rather, Palestinian Druze naturally cooperated with the Zionist movement in the late Mandate period, during the 1948 War, and after Israel's establishment. This cooperation culminated in the 1956 conscription agreement, which was reached at the request of the Druze leadership. Given the unique role of military service in Israeli society, the conscription agreement helped to forge a Druze-Israeli consciousness that explains the historic divergence of Druze from other elements of Palestinian society in Israel. As observed by sociologist Lisa Hajjar, the

Israeli narrative presents "the state-sponsored transformation of their status from quasi Muslim sect to Druze 'nation'" as a "historic realization of nationhood comparable to that which Zionism provided for Jews," with the consequent understanding that "only those individual Druze who are confused about their true identity as Druze would identify with or support Arab or Palestinian nationalism in the conflict against Israel."[662]

The contemporary Druze narrative, in the tradition of Israel's "New Historians," relies on declassified state records to challenge this account. According to this narrative, the Zionists began to cultivate ties with the Druze during the 1936 Arab Rebellion, as part of a greater strategy of building alliances with non-Sunni Muslim communities to challenge Arab nationalism. Most Druze thus maintained a neutral or pro-Zionist posture during the 1948 War.[663] Nevertheless, the Druze were subject to land confiscations in the War's aftermath, as were the Muslim and Christian elements of Palestinian society; and these confiscations threatened their agriculture-based lifestyle and means of subsistence. Israel conditioned their access to land and other state benefits on military service. Conscription was agreed to by an unrepresentative elite Druze leadership and met with considerable resistance. The Israeli government manipulated factions within the Druze community, while competing Druze leaders sought to consolidate power through relations with the Israeli establishment. This manipulation was expressed in Israel's 1957 recognition of a Druze "nationality," the 1963 decision to grant the Druze autonomy in personal status matters, and the 1976 creation of a separate Druze educational system and curriculum.[664]Additionally, the Druze community is the only non-Jewish religious community in Israel to have a religious council, which is funded by the state and serves as the court of appeal for the Druze personal-status courts. [665]

Today, the degree of affiliation by Druze with Palestinian or Israeli identities varies widely, as demonstrated by the political views of Druze members of the Knesset. MKs Ayoob Kara and Hamad Amar are members of the right-wing Likud and Yisrael Beitenu parties, respectively, and identify as Druze Israelis. They support full Druze engagement with state institutions, including the security forces. In contrast, MK Abdullah Maaruf, a member of the Jewish-Arab non-Zionist party Hadash, was one of the first Druze conscientious objectors in Israel and is a leader of the Arab

Druze Initiative Committee, which supports Druze conscientious objectors and "challenges the militarization of Druze education."[666] Similarly, former MK Said Nafaa is a Druze Arab nationalist who represented the Arab democratic party *Balad* in the Knesset between 2007 and 2013.[667]

This analysis is limited to Druze in Israel. Syrian Druze living in the Golan Heights, which Israel has occupied since 1967 and brought under Israeli civil law, administration, and jurisdiction in 1981, have overwhelmingly refused Israeli citizenship and thus are not subject to mandatory military service.[668] As detailed by Hajjar, the Israeli government allowed the Druze population to stay in the occupied Golan (roughly 6,500 persons, while an estimated 130,000 non-Druze Syrian Arabs were expelled) in the expectation that the Syrian Druze would integrate with their coreligionists in Israel, and it established policies to that end. However, the Syrian Druze "did not willingly accept efforts to nationalize their sectarian identity, or see themselves politically as part of some 'Druze collectivity' which would negate or override their status as Syrian citizens living under Israeli occupation."[669] Relations between the Syrian Druze and the Druze in Israel remain "cool," and the two communities have very low rates of intermarriage.[670]

Conscientious Objection in the Druze Community

Druze conscientious objection remains an exception to the rule: Druze enlistment rates remain above national average in Israel.[671] However, the growing number and prominence of declared objectors reflects a strengthening Palestinian identity among Arab citizens of Israel, including the Palestinian Druze, and explains the state's intransigent denial of Druze conscientious objection claims.

اطفال رفح

RAFAH'S CHILDREN (1971)

SAMIH AL-QASIM

To the one who digs his path through the wounds of millions
To him whose tanks crush all the roses in the garden
Who breaks windows in the night
Who sets fire to a garden and museum and sings of freedom.
Who stomps on songbirds in the public square.
Whose planes drop bombs on childhood's dream.
Who smashes rainbows in the sky.

Tonight, the children of the impossible roots have an announcement
for you,
Tonight, the children of Rafah say:
"We have never woven hair braids into coverlets.
We have never spat on corpses, nor yanked their gold teeth.
So why do you take our jewelry and give us bombs?
Why do you prepare orphanhood for Arab children?
Thank you, a thousand times over!
Our sadness has now grown up and become a man.
And now, we must fight."

*Al-Qasim (1939 – 2014), a renowned Palestinian poet and author,
is regarded as the first Druze declared conscientious objector.
He refused induction and was imprisoned in 1959.*

From the outset, Druze conscientious objection has been linked to Palestinian identity. The renowned Palestinian poet and author Samih al-Qasim, who refused induction and was imprisoned in 1959, is regarded as the first Druze declared conscientious objector. Druze conscientious objectors have been supported since 1972 by the Druze Initiative Committee, which has also sought to reinstate the draft exemption for Druze men. More recently, a new generation of self-identified Palestinian Druze has launched a movement, *Urfod – Sha'abik Biyhimik* (Refuse – Your

People Will Protect You), to support conscientious objectors through moral support, legal assistance, and scholarship programs. One of *Urfod's* founders is the Palestinian Druze poet and author Alaa Muhanna, who avoided military service in the late 1990s by deliberately failing a mental aptitude exam and thereby receiving a "Profile 21" exemption (permanently unfit for military service). Muhanna said of his decision: "I grew up as a Palestinian, I came from a political family that taught me about my identity. I knew as a child that I wasn't going to the army."[672]

As noted by Amnesty International, the Druze leadership still regards "military service as an entry card to Israeli society" and places "strong social pressures on young Druze not to object or at least not to attribute their objection to reasons of conscience."[673] Regarding the Druze conscientious objection movements, Sheikh Muwaffak Tarif, the spiritual leader of the Druze community in Israel, has stated: "like every society, Druze society too has extremist, subversive elements who try to stir up the youth, with one goal: to break the alliance between the Druze community and the State of Israel."[674]

Because of these pressures, many Druze conscientious objectors site economic or family reasons for refusing to serve. Thus, reliable figures on the number of *bona fide* conscientious objectors in the Druze community are unavailable. An Amnesty International investigation conducted in 1991, during the first Palestinian *intifada*, identified 22 Druze men who had been convicted or detained pending trial that year alone for refusing to serve. Some of these objectors declared their reasons of conscience at trial; others invoked economic and family reasons; but information available to Amnesty suggested that several of the latter group were motivated by reasons of conscience.[675]

According to Amnesty, at least six conscientious objectors were imprisoned in Israel during 2014.[676] Among them there was Omar Sa'ad, an 18-year-old Druze musician from al-Maghar village in northern Israel, who was convicted and sentenced seven times and spent 150 days in prison before being declared unsuitable and exempted from further service. Upon release from his seventh and final imprisonment, Sa'ad issued the following statement:

I was sentenced 7 times for a period of 150 days, and 46 days ago between home and hospital, and every time before sending me out to prison, they ask me the same question: Why [do] you refuse to serve in the IDF? My answer was always the same: I refuse because I am an integral part of the Palestinian Arab people. Refuse because your army is an army of occupation. Refuse because I am the owner of principle and conscience. I make peace with my musical instrument and I refuse to replace it with a weapon that generates death, and does not differentiate between a child, a woman, a man and an old man. So how can you ask me to kill, occupy and arrest my people? My weapon is my musical instrument and will not be replaced by any another weapon.[677]

Saad's case was highlighted in the 2014 final report of the UN Special Rapporteur on human rights in the occupied territory, Richard Falk.[678]

Blanket Exemption for Haredi Jews

While there are almost no exemptions for Druze men, Haredi Jews (ultra-Orthodox) have been exempted from military service since Israel's establishment. This *en masse* exemption was part of a greater accommodation agreed between the secular Zionist movement and the *Agudat Yisrael* movement, representing the Haredi population in Mandatory Palestine.[679] Haredi objections to service are "based on various religious and cultural arguments, such as the compelling interest of studying in Yeshiva, an objection to the existence of a Jewish state, and the concern of secularization during the army service."[680] Haredi women are exempted under section 39(c) of the Defense Service Law, which exempts women prevented from serving by "reasons connected with her family's religious way of life." Haredi men, by administrative practice of the Ministry of Defense, receive deferrals as long as they are engaged in full-time Torah study and do not hold paid employment.

Despite successful legal challenges to the Haredi exemption[681] and overwhelming public support for Haredi conscription,[682] attempts at reform have repeatedly been defeated. Most recently, in March 2014, the Knesset adopted a law that would have established mandatory conscription for most Haredi males by 2017 and subjected them to the standard criminal sanctions for refusal to serve.[683] However, following the 2015 elections, the

Prime Minister agreed, in the current government's coalition agreement, to nullify the law's provisions regarding criminal sanctions.[684] Further, on November 23, 2015, the Knesset amended the conscription law to postpone obligatory enlistment on full-time yeshiva students from 2017 to 2020.[685] Ironically, Haredi enlistment seems to have decreased substantially in response to the enactment of the Law, which is now effectively unenforceable.[686] Thus, the discrimination between Druze and Haredi communities with regard to exemptions from military service remains as stark as ever.

Druze Mandatory Military Service without Conscientious Objection Constitutes Multiple Forms of Discrimination

Israel's procedures and practices in claims of conscientious objection fall short of international human rights standards, particularly the lack of independence of the conscience committee and the repeated imprisonment of conscientious objectors. The state's conscription of male Druze citizens also constitutes impermissible discrimination in two ways. Firstly, as the only segment of the Arab Palestinian minority that is subject to compulsory military service, the Druze are denied equal treatment and nondiscrimination within a national minority, as required by articles 2.1, 26 and 27 ICCPR.[687] Even accepting *arguendo* Israel's characterization of the Druze as a "nation" separate from the Arab Palestinian nationality, the same ICCPR provisions obligate Israel to uphold equal treatment and nondiscrimination as between national minorities. Secondly, Druze and non-Orthodox Jewish conscientious objectors who refuse to serve based on their secular humanist views are discriminated against relative to Haredi (ultra-Orthodox) Jewish citizens, who, in practice, are exempted *en masse* from military service based on their religious views.

CONCLUSION

Israel's conscription practices violate the guarantee of freedom of thought, conscience, and religion enshrined in article 18 ICCPR and recognized by USCIRF precedent. The Israeli military's conscience committee does not meet accepted standards of impartiality and independence, and requiring a conscript to defend a conscientious objection claim before a military tribunal violates the right to a fair trial. Further, Israel's practice of repeatedly imprisoning conscientious objectors is incompatible with the due process principle of *ne bis in idem*.

By denying Druze claims of conscientious objection based on a refusal to serve against fellow Arab Palestinians, Israel effectively denies their membership in the Palestinian minority despite clear linguistic, cultural, and historical ties. In contrast, Haredi Jews are exempted *en masse*, without individualized assessment, based on various religious and cultural reasons – including the perceived secularizing effect of military service – that are not grounded in general pacifism. This unequal treatment of self-identified Druze Palestinians further violates Israel's obligation to uphold equality and nondiscrimination in protecting freedom of conscience.

11
CONCLUSION

The common thread running through the religious freedom violations documented in this report is the goal of expanding and consolidating ethnoreligious territorial control over Israel/Palestine while maintaining the dominant, privileged status of the Jewish population relative to the Palestinian population, both within Israel and in the oPt. In other words, these religious freedom violations are, in fact, structural elements of the Israeli ethnocracy. In that regard, Israel bears substantial similarities with Russia and Turkey, states upon which the Commission has reported extensively (all of the following quotes are taken from the Commission's annual reports on these states) and currently lists as Tier 2 countries.

Russia: While Russia is ostensibly a constitutional democracy, the state represses opposition parties and organizations, including minority religious institutions. Nearly three-quarters (74 percent) of Russians view themselves as Orthodox while 7 percent identify as Muslim.[688] Although "the Russian constitution guarantees a secular state and equal legal status for all religions ... the Moscow Patriarchate of Russian Orthodox Church (ROC)– which claims 60 percent of Russians as adherents – is especially favored; it has agreements with various state agencies and receives the most state subsidies of any religious group. 'Non-traditional' religious groups do not receive state subsidies. Officials often refer negatively to religious and other minorities, abetting an intolerant climate." That climate is characterized by "rising xenophobia and intolerance, including anti-Semitism, [which] are linked to violent and lethal hate crimes that often occur with impunity."

Additionally, Russia's "illegal annexation" of Crimea, which "President Putin sought to justify [through] the shared Orthodox 'culture, civilization, and human values' of Russia and Ukraine," has precipitated greater violations of religious freedom on the peninsula, including persecution of Muslim Tartars, visa restrictions on non-ROC Christian clergy and non-Russian Muslim imams, and vandalism of Ukrainian Orthodox churches and Jewish synagogues.

Turkey: While Turkey is ostensibly a parliamentary democracy, Turkish secularism interferes substantially with freedom of religion. The Turkish constitution gives the state "pervasive control over religion and denies full legal status to all religious communities."[689] The state, in turn, limits the rights of all faiths" to own and maintain places of worship, train clergy, and offer religious education." Over 90 percent of Turkey's population is Muslim, including 15 to 25 percent who are Alevis. Alevis are denied representation in the state's Directorate for Religious Affairs (*Diyanet*) and are thus denied accommodation of their religious and cultural practices. Alevi gathering spaces (*cemevi*) are not considered legal houses of worship by the Turkish government and thus cannot receive the legal and financial benefits associated with such status. Further, Alevis are subject to compulsory Sunni Islamic religious education, violating the right of Alevi parents to have their children education consistent with their own religious convictions.

While Turkey's non-Muslim religious minority communities total less than 1 percent of the population, they are "diverse" and "historically and culturally significant." However, Turkish secularism has historically proven "particularly detrimental to the smallest religious minority communities and their ability to perpetuate their faiths." The Turkish government provides financial subsidies to nearly 400 non-Muslim places of worship and has restored Christian and Jewish houses of worship and heritage sites. However, "Turkey denies religious minority communities the ability to train clergy in the country." Further, it interferes in the internal affairs of the Greek Orthodox Church by stipulating that only Turkish citizens can serve in the Church's Holy Synod, selectively denying applications for dual citizenship for prospective Synod members, and maintaining the closure of the Church's Halki seminary.

Further, through its occupation of Northern Cyprus, Turkey bears responsibility for "the inability of Orthodox Christians, other religious communities, and clergy to access and hold services at their places of worship and cemeteries in the north, particularly those in Turkish military bases and zones; [and] the disrepair of churches and cemeteries and issues relating to the preservation of religious heritage, such as iconography, mosaics, and other religious symbols."[690]

Israel: While Israel is ostensibly a parliamentary democracy, the state's laws, policies and practices seek to maximize and consolidate Jewish territorial control over Israel/Palestine and a system of rights and privileges exclusive to its Jewish population. While the Israeli Jewish and Arab Palestinian populations of Israel/Palestine are virtually equal, at 6.3 million each, Israeli laws, policies and practices deny equal rights to the Palestinian population under its control – both Muslims and Christians, both citizens of Israel and noncitizen residents of the oPt. Parastatal organizations exercise sovereign functions of land ownership, development, and settlement exclusively for the Jewish people, thereby limiting Palestinian access to land and housing. Only Jewish holy places are registered and afforded legal protection under Israeli law, leaving Christian and especially Muslim holy places vulnerable to neglect and commercial exploitation. Israel has encroached on Muslim self-governance of the Al-Aqsa Mosque Compound by ending coordination with Jordan and denying the Waqf its historic right to regulate the entry of non-Muslim visitors to the Compound. This interference has emboldened "Temple movements," that seek to assert Israeli sovereignty and Jewish national rights over the Compound in ways that would further marginalize or eliminate Muslim self-governance at the Compound and provoke sectarian and nationalist violence. Further, Israeli restrictions on clergy visas have interfered with the ministry of Christian institutions in Israel and the oPt.

Israel maintains this system of ethnoreligious dominance by preserving the unity of the Jewish population while promoting the fragmentation of the Palestinian population. To that end, the state refuses to recognize a non-sectarian Israeli nationality or confessional, ethnic and linguistic minorities within the Jewish population. Further, the state upholds the agreement made between the Zionist movement and the Orthodox community prior to the state's establishment, which provides for Orthodox control of the personal status matters of the entire Jewish population, including non-Orthodox Jews, and exempts Haredi Orthodox en masse from military conscription on grounds unrelated to pacifism, such as the perceived secularizing effect of military service.

Conversely, Israel pursues a divide-and-conquer strategy relative to the Palestinian population under its control. Thus, the state has recognized an Aramean nationality that is not a *bona fide* religious or linguistic minority as defined by international human rights law and is overwhelmingly rejected by Palestinian Christian institutions and clergy. Similarly, Druze citizens of Israel who identify as Palestinians and refuse to contribute to the occupation of their fellow Palestinians in the oPt are denied conscientious objector status and are subject to repeated imprisonment. Since 2003, Palestinian citizens of Israel and Palestinian residents of East Jerusalem have been generally banned from living in Israel or East Jerusalem with a Palestinian spouse from parts of the oPt other than East Jerusalem. The proposed Basic Law: Israel as the Nation-State of the Jewish People, which the current Israeli government is committed to adopting, would define Israel as the state of the Jewish people alone, affirmatively denying the right of the Palestinians in Israel to internal self-determination consistent with its status as a native national community.

Given Israel's similarities with Russia, Turkey and other states documented annually in the Commission's reports, as analyzed herein, Israel's total absence in the Commission's reporting is conspicuous. The unmistakable impression of a double standard undermines the Commission's ability to engage effectively with states regarding their religious freedom practices, particularly in the Arab and Muslim worlds. The authors of this report hereby express their hope that this report will lead the Commission to undertake its own, comprehensive report of religious freedom in Israel and the occupied Palestinian territory, a report that is consistent with religious freedom standards enshrined in international human rights law and the Commission's precedent.

NOTES

[1] USCIRF, Ambassador-at-Large for International Religious Freedom, Testimony before the Subcommittee on International Operations and Human Rights House Committee on International Relations (Oct. 6, 1999), http://www.uscirf.gov/advising-government/congressional-testimony/testimony-robert-seiple.

[2] USCIRF, "Statement on Pope's Visit to Holy Land" (May 23, 2014), http://www.uscirf.gov/news-room/press-releases/statement-pope-s-visit-holy-land.

[3] Confirmed or suspected attacks by Israeli civilians against non-Jewish holy places in the West Bank include the Benedictine Abbey of the Dormition in East Jerusalem (2012, 2013, 2016, vandalism) and mosques in the Palestinian communities of Yasuf (arson, 2009), al-Lubban al-Sharqiyya (arson, 2010), Beit Fajar (arson and vandalism, 2010), al-Mughayyir (vandalism, 2011; arson, 2014), Qusra (arson, 2011), Birzeit (vandalism, 2011), Yatma (vandalism, 2011), Burqa (arson, 2011), Bnei Naim (arson, 2011), Deir Istiyya (arson, 2012 and 2014), Jaba'a (arson, 2012), Tuqu'a (vandalism, 2013) and Aqraba (vandalism, 2014).

Confirmed or suspected attacks by Israeli civilians against non-Jewish holy places within Israel include the Greek Orthodox Monastery of the Cross in West Jerusalem (vandalism, 2012), the Jerusalem Baptist Narkis Street Congregation in West Jerusalem (vandalism, 2012), the St. George Romanian Orthodox Church in West Jerusalem (vandalism, 2014), and the Church of the Multiplication in Tabgha (arson, 2015), and mosque in the Palestinian communities of Tuba-Zangariyye (arson, 2011), Umm al-Qutuf (vandalism, 2013), Baqa al-Gharbiyye (vandalism, 2013), Umm al-Fahm (arson, 2014), and Fureidis (vandalism, 2014). See Lara Friedman, "'Price Tag' Escalation Timeline," Americans for Peace Now (Feb. 10, 2016), https://peacenow.org/entry.php?id=1077.

[4] Yesh Din, "Law Enforcement on Israeli Civilians in the West Bank: Yesh Din Monitoring Update, 2005-2015" (Oct. 2015), http://www.yesh-din.org/userfiles/Datasheet_English_Oct%202015.pdf. As a matter of policy, the Israel Police does not publish figures on incidents in which Israeli civilians harmed Palestinians or Palestinian property. (Id.)

[5] Yesh Din, Law Enforcement on Israeli Civilians in the West Bank, supra n. 4.

[6] See, e.g., "USCIRF Denounces Attack on Ismaili Muslims in Pakistan" (May 14, 2015), http://www.uscirf.gov/news-room/press-releases/uscirf-denounces-attack-ismaili-muslims-in-pakistan ("The Pakistani government must redouble its efforts to confront militant groups that target minority religious communities.... The perpetrators and planners must be brought to justice.").

[7] In contrast to the USCIRF, American Jewish organizations have noted the Israeli

government's failure to take responsibility for Jewish extremist violence against Palestinians. For example, the Anti-Defamation League has observed,

> [m]ost of these attacks include the phrase "price tag" and are accompanied by hateful and racist slogans, the name of an illegal settlement, or a reference to an Israeli casualty of Palestinian terrorism, the implication being that the violent incident is the "cost" of Israeli government action on settlements or for anti-Israeli violence.

(Anti-Defamation League, "Price Tag and Extremist Attacks in Israel" (Aug. 5, 2015), http://www.adl.org/israel-international/israel-middle-east/content/backgroundersarticles/price-tag-attacks.html.) The ADL communiqué identifies the perpetrators of these attacks as "extremist Israeli Jews," including "so-called 'hilltop youth' – teenage Israeli settlers who are involved in establishing 'outposts' outside of existing settlements the victims as "Israeli Arabs and Palestinians," and their motive as "reprisal for Israeli government action against illegal settlement activity." It further identifies the party responsible for investigating, prosecuting and ultimately stopping such attacks as the Israeli government, noting that a new Israeli police unit dedicated to price-tag attacks "has thus far had minimal success."

[8] United Nations Office for the Coordinator of Humanitarian Affairs, "Key figures on the 2014 hostilities" (June 2015), http://gaza.ochaopt.org/2015/06/key-figures-on-the-2014-hostilities/.

[9] Holy Land Christian Ecumenical Foundation, "His Beatitude Patriarch Fouad Twal of Jerusalem Weighs in with the White House on International Religious Freedom" (July 23, 2014), http://hcef.org/790793937-his-beatitude-patriarch-fouad-twal-of-jerusalem-weighs-in-with-the-white-house-on-international-religious-freedom/.

[10] Rachel Partain, "Latin Patriarch Bridges Talks Between White House and Roman Catholic Church to Extend Hand to the Situation in Gaza," Arab America (July 23, 2014), http://www.arabamerica.com/latin-patriarch-bridges-talks-between-white-house-and-roman-catholic-church-to-extend-hand-to-the-situation-in-gaza/.

[11] Oren Yiftachel, Ethnocracy: Land and Identity Politics in Israel/Palestine (2006) 3.

[12] International Religious Freedom Act of 1998, Public Law 105–292, as amended, 22 U.S.C. §§ 6401 et seq. [hereinafter "IRFA"], sec. 102(2).

[13] Geneva Convention (IV) relative to the protection of civilian persons in time of war, Aug. 12, 1949, 75 UNTS 973 [hereinafter "Geneva Convention IV)"] provides that the rights of protected persons (i.e. the Palestinian population of the oPt) under the Convention cannot be renounced by the individual himself (art. 8), derogated from by special agreement between state parties to the Convention (art. 7), or otherwise denied by the occupying power, including through annexation of

the occupied territory, changes to its institutions and government, or agreement between the occupying power and the authorities of the occupied territory (art. 47).

[14] See Israel-PLO Interim Agreement on the West Bank and the Gaza Strip, Sept. 28, 1995, 36 ILM 650 (1997) [hereinafter "Interim Agreement"] art. I, sec. 1 ("Israel shall transfer powers and responsibilities as specified in this Agreement from the Israeli military government and its Civil Administration to the [Palestinian] Council in accordance with this Agreement. Israel shall continue to exercise powers and responsibilities not so transferred.") See also Omar Dajani, Stalled Between Seasons: The International Legal Status of Palestine During the Interim Period, 26 Denv. J. Int'l L. & Pol'y 27 (1997).

[15] Geneva Convention (IV), supra n. 13, art. 47 ("Protected persons who are in occupied territory shall not be deprived, in any case or in any manner whatsoever, of the benefits of the present Convention by any change introduced, as the result of the occupation of a territory, into the institutions or government of the said territory, nor by any agreement concluded between the authorities of the occupied territories and the Occupying Power, nor by any annexation by the latter of the whole or part of the occupied territory.")

[16] Legal Consequences of the Construction of a Wall in the Occupied Palestinian Territory, Advisory Opinion, 2004 ICJ 131 (July 9, 2004) [hereinafter "Construction of a Wall"], para. 102-113 (affirming applicability of international human rights instruments to which Israel is a party within the oPt). The UN General Assembly reaffirms this principle in its annual resolution regarding Israeli practices affecting the human rights of the Palestinian people in the Occupied Palestinian Territory, including East Jerusalem. See, e.g., GA Res. 70/90, UN Doc. A/RES/70/90 (Dec. 15, 2015) ("Recalling also the International Covenant on Civil and Political Rights, the International Covenant on Economic, Social and Cultural Rights and the Convention on the Rights of the Child, and affirming that these human rights instruments must be respected in the Occupied Palestinian Territory, including East Jerusalem").

[17] USCIRF Annual Report [hereinafter "USCIRF Report"], 2013. All USCIRF Reports referenced herein can be found at http://www.uscirf.gov/reports-briefs/annual-report. See also id., dissent by Commissioners William J. Shaw and Azizah Al-Hibri ("We strongly object to the inclusion of Northern Cyprus in the chapter report on Turkey. Northern Cyprus is not an official territorial or governmental part of Turkey.") For the European Court of Human Rights precedent on which the Commission relies, see Loizidou v. Turkey (Preliminary Objections), App. No. 15318/89, [1995] ECHR 10 (Mar. 23, 1995), para. 62-63 ("Bearing in mind the object and purpose of the Convention, the responsibility of a Contracting Party may also arise when as a consequence of military action - whether lawful or unlawful - it exercises effective control of an area outside its national territory. The obligation to secure, in such an area, the rights and freedoms set out in the Convention derives from the fact of such control whether it be

exercised directly, through its armed forces, or through a subordinate local administration. ... In this connection the respondent Government have acknowledged that the applicant's loss of control of her property stems from the occupation of the northern part of Cyprus by Turkish troops and the establishment there of the 'TRNC'.")

[18] 2015 USCIRF Report. Shortly after Russian forces occupied Crimea, Russian-backed authorities of the newly-proclaimed 'Republic of Crimea' held a referendum on whether to join the Russian Federation or remain part of Ukraine under the 1992 Crimean constitution. Nearly 97 percent of voters in the referendum, which was widely condemned and declared void by the international community, supported integration into Russia.

[19] Thomas J. Reese and Daniel I. Mark, "Losing Their Religion in Crimea," Foreign Affairs (Apr. 15, 2015) ("There is no question that Russia bears the responsibility. It instituted discriminatory laws at home, and those spread to Crimea. ... Certainly the international community should continue to demand that Russia withdraw from Ukraine.").

[20] 2015 USCIRF Report.

[21] See GA Res. 67/19, ¶ 2, UN Doc. A/RES/67/19 (Dec. 4, 2012), recognizing, as a nonmember state, the State of Palestine on the 1967 occupied territory. The United States voted against the resolution.

[22]See State Department, Office of the Spokesperson, "Regarding Palestinian Efforts to Accede to the Rome Statute of the International Criminal Court" (Jan. 8, 2015), available at http://www.state.gov/r/pa/prs/ps/2015/01/235695.htm ("The view of the United States is that the Palestinians have not yet established a state.")

[23] IRFA sec. 202(b) (emphasis added).

[24] U.S. federal courts have repeatedly held that the PLO and PA do not enjoy sovereign immunity under the FSIA. See, e.g., Ungar v. Palestine Liberation Organization, 402 F.3d 274 (1st Cir. 2005).

[25] The Consulate represents the United States in Jerusalem, the West Bank, and the Gaza Strip. Its jurisdiction does not include the occupied Golan Heights, which is covered by the Embassy in Tel Aviv.

[26] See, e.g., Letter to Assistant Secretary Posner regarding U.S State Department's Human Rights Country Report for Israel (Dec. 1, 2009), http://www.alhaq.org/attachments/article/270/Lt-to-Secy-Posne.pdf ("Israel's human rights abuses are presented in an incidental format woven in between Palestinian-on-Palestinian human rights abuses so that it is difficult to ascertain whether the [Israeli] abuses taking place are part of a consistent pattern of human rights violations...") The signatories to the letter are prominent human rights organizations in the oPt and Israel as well as three U.S. organizations: Center for

Constitutional Rights, National Lawyers Guild, and American-Arab Anti-Discrimination Committee (ADC).

[27] U.S. Department of State, Country Reports on Human Rights Practices [hereinafter "State Department Human Rights Report"], Israel and The Occupied Territories, 2013 (emphasis added). Unless otherwise specified, references herein to the annual Human Rights Report are to the Israel and The Occupied Territories report. The 2014 Country Reports were released on June 25, 2015 and are the most recent release at the time of writing. (See http://www.state.gov/secretary/remarks/2015/06/244358.htm.) All Human Rights Reports referenced herein can be found at http://www.state.gov/j/drl/rls/hrrpt/humanrightsreport.

[28] U.S. Department of State, Annual Report to Congress on International Religious Freedom [hereinafter "State Department Religious Freedom Report"], Israel and The Occupied Territories, 2013. Unless otherwise specified, references herein to the annual Religious Freedom Report are to the Israel and The Occupied Territories report. The 2014 Religious Freedom Report was released on October 14, 2015 and is the most current release at the time of writing. (See http://www.state.gov/secretary/remarks/2015/10/248198.htm.) All Religious Freedom Reports referenced herein can be found at http://www.state.gov/j/drl/irf/rpt/index.htm.

[29] As stated by the Secretary of State in 2013, "the United States of America views all of the settlements as illegitimate." See "Kerry: US views all settlements as illegitimate," YNet News (Dec. 8, 2013), http://www.ynetnews.com/articles/0,7340,L-4416902,00.html.

[30] As of May 2015, the Israeli settler population in the West Bank (including East Jerusalem) was estimated at 547,000, corresponding to 8.7 percent of Israel's Jewish population of 6.3 million. See B'Tselem, "Statistics on Settlements and Settler Population," http://www.btselem.org/settlements/statistics. The annual growth rates of the settler population and overall population in Israel are 4.4% and 1.9% percent, respectively. Id.

[31] Law and Administration Ordinance, 1948, as amended, sec. 11(B). Before its 1967 amendment, the Ordinance declared that Israeli law would apply to "any part of Palestine which the minister of defense has defined by proclamation as being held by the Israel Defense Forces."

[32] Cabinet Resolution Regarding the Disengagement Plan (Jun. 6, 2004), Addendum A, para. 1(3) ("In any future permanent status arrangement, there will be no Israeli towns and villages in the Gaza Strip. On the other hand, it is clear that in the West Bank, there are areas which will be part of the State of Israel, including major Israeli population centers, cities, towns and villages, security areas and other places of special interest to Israel."), available at

http://www.mfa.gov.il/mfa/foreignpolicy/peace/mfadocuments/pages/revised%20disengagement%20plan%206-june-2004.aspx.

[33] See generally Michael Karayanni, Conflicts in a Conflict: A Conflict of Laws Case Study on Israel and the Palestinian Territories (2014) (analyzing "how personal jurisdiction doctrine accommodated Israel's policy of control over the [oPt].")

[34] John Dugard and John Reynolds, Apartheid, International Law, and the Occupied Palestinian Territory, 24 Eur. J. Int'l L. 867 (2013) [hereinafter "Apartheid, International Law and the oPt"].

[35] See, e.g., UN Human Rights Council, Report of the Special Rapporteur on the situation of human rights in the Palestinian territories occupied since 1967, Richard Falk, UN Doc. A/HRC/25/67 (Jan. 13, 2014), ¶¶ 51-77; UN Human Rights Council, Report of the Special Rapporteur on the situation of human rights in the Palestinian territories occupied since 1967, John Dugard, UN Doc. A/HRC/4/17 (Jan. 29, 2007), ¶¶ 49-50, 58-63; Dugard and Reynolds, Apartheid, International Law, and the oPt, supra n. 34; Russell Tribunal on Palestine, Findings of the Final Session (Mar. 16-17, 2013), § 2; Beyond Occupation: Apartheid, Colonialism and International Law in the Occupied Palestinian Territories (2012).

[36] IRFA, sec. 3(13).

[37] UN General Assembly, Declaration on the Elimination of All Forms of Intolerance and of Discrimination Based on Religion or Belief, UN Doc. A/RES/36/55 (Nov. 25, 1981) [hereinafter "1981 UN Declaration"]; Peter Danchin, U.S. Unilateralism and the International Protection of Religious Freedom, 41 Colum. J. Transnat'l L. 33, 56 (2002). Lex ferenda refers to an interpretation of the law that is normative or aspirational – what the law ought to be – rather than declarative of existing law (lex lata).

[38] The Oslo Accords, although not treaties in the traditional sense, are nevertheless considered legally-binding international agreements between subjects of international law. As such, they are understood to be governed by treaty law principles. See Geoffrey R. Watson, The Oslo Accords: International Law and the Israeli-Palestinian Peace Agreements (2000). For specific commitments, see Israel-PLO Declaration of Principles on Interim Self-Government Arrangements, 32 I.L.M. 1525 (1993) [hereinafter "Declaration of Principles"], art. IV ("The two sides view the West Bank and the Gaza Strip as a single territorial unit, whose integrity will be preserved during the interim period"); Israel-PLO Interim Agreement on the West Bank and the Gaza Strip (1995), art. XXXI(7) ("Neither side shall initiate or take any step that will change the status of the West Bank and the Gaza Strip pending the outcome of the permanent status negotiations.")

[39] See ILC Guiding Principles Applicable to Unilateral Declarations of States Capable of Creating Legal Obligations, ILC Report, UN Doc. A/61/10 (2006), art. 1 ("Declarations publicly made and manifesting the will to be bound may have the

effect of creating legal obligations. When the conditions for this are met, the binding character of such declarations is based on good faith; States concerned may then take them into consideration and rely on them; such States are entitled to require that such obligations be respected.").

[40] IRFA sec. 3(13)(A)(i)-(v) (including, among violations of religious freedom, infringements on freedom of expression, assembly, and association, due process violations (including the right to be free of inhuman or degrading treatment), and breaches of privacy and family life in the teaching of religious practices); see Danchin, supra n. 37, at 74-75.

[41] IRFA sec. 3(13)(B) (including in the definition of violation of religious freedom "any of the following acts if committed on account of an individual's religious belief or practice: detention, interrogation, imposition of an onerous financial penalty, forced labor, forced mass resettlement, imprisonment, forced religious conversion, beating, torture, mutilation, rape, enslavement, murder, and execution.")

[42] Hague Convention (IV) Respecting the Laws and Customs of War on Land and Its Annex: Regulations Concerning the Laws and Customs of War on Land, 18 October 1907, 187 CTS 227 [hereinafter "Hague Regulations"]; Construction of a Wall, supra n. 16, at ¶ 89 (observing that Hague Regulations are binding on Israel as customary international law).

[43] Geneva Convention (IV), supra n. 13, art 4.

[44] For Security Council resolutions establishing the applicability of Geneva Convention (IV) to the oPt, see, e.g., SC Res. 446, UN Doc. S/RES/446 (Mar. 22, 1979); SC Res. 471, ¶¶ 2,4, UN Doc. S/RES/471 (June 5, 1980); SC Res. 607, ¶ 1, UN Doc. S/RES/607 (Jan. 5, 1988).

[45] Construction of a Wall, supra n. 16, at ¶ 106 (international human rights instruments are applicable "in respect of acts done by a State in the exercise of its jurisdiction outside its own territory", particularly in occupied territories). Israel argues that the human rights treaties to which it is a party only apply to the territory over which it claims sovereignty. It further argues that most West Bank Palestinians live in "Area A", under the jurisdiction of the Palestinian Authority, and thus that Israel is not responsible for implementing the treaty in those areas. The UN Human Rights Committee and other UN human rights treaty bodies have consistently rejected these arguments and held that Israel's human rights treaty obligations extend to the oPt in its entirety. See, e.g., UN Human Rights Committee, Concluding Observations on the fourth periodic report on Israel, UN Doc. CCPR/C/ISR/CO/4 (Nov. 21, 2014), ¶ 5.

[46] Construction of a Wall, supra n. 16, at ¶ 106 ("the protection offered by human rights conventions does not cease in case of armed conflict"); id. at ¶ 102-13; see also Armed Activities on the Territory of the Congo (Dem. Rep. Congo v.

Uganda), 2005 I.C.J. 168, ¶¶ 216-20 ("The Court thus concludes that Uganda is internationally responsible for violations of international human rights law and international humanitarian law committed by the UPDF and by its members in the territory of the DRC and for failing to comply with its obligations as an occupying Power in Ituri in respect of violations of international human rights law and international humanitarian law in the occupied territory."); Vienna Convention on the Law of Treaties, May 23, 1969, 1155 UNTS 331, art. 31(3)(c) (requiring treaty parties interpreting their obligations to take into account "any relevant rules of international law applicable in the relations between the parties.")

[47] Cyprus v. Turkey, App. No. 25781/94, Judgment (May 10, 2001) para. 245-246.

[48] See Restatement (Third) of the Foreign Relations Law of the United States (1987), § 102, Comment K and Reporter's Note 6 (recognizing "international crimes" resulting from the violation of certain preemptory norms, including "rules prohibiting genocide, slave trade and slavery, apartheid and other gross violations of human rights, and perhaps attacks on diplomats.").

[49] International Law Commission, Draft Articles on Responsibility of States for Internationally Wrongful Acts, with commentaries, in Report of the International Law Commission, 53rd Session, UN Doc. A/56/10 (2001) [hereinafter "ILC Draft Articles on State Responsibility"] ¶¶ 76 et seq. and Commentary, Art. 40, ¶ 5, http://legal.un.org/ilc/texts/instruments/english/commentaries/9_6_2001.pdf.

[50] ILC Draft Articles on State Responsibility, supra n. 49, Commentary Art. 40, ¶ 8, n. 651.

[51] ILC Draft Articles on State Responsibility, supra n. 49, Commentary Art. 40, ¶ 4.

[52] Report of the Special Rapporteur on the situation of human rights in the Palestinian territories occupied since 1967, Richard Falk, supra n. 35, ¶ 51, http://unispal.un.org/UNISPAL.NSF/0/06AE69A80B959A3D85257C86006D89 A7; Report of the Special Rapporteur on the situation of human rights in the Palestinian territories occupied since 1967, John Dugard, supra n. 35, p. 3.

[53] Report of the Special Rapporteur on the situation of human rights in the Palestinian territories occupied since 1967, Richard Falk, supra n. 35, ¶¶ 77-78.

[54] Palestine Order-in-Council, 1922, art. 83.

[55] See Ariel L. Bendor and Michael Sachs, The Constitutional Status of Human Dignity in Germany and Israel, 44 Israel L. Rev. 24, 29 (2011); see also HCJ 262/62 Peretz v Kfar Shmaryahu 16 P.D. 2101 (1962) (municipality obligated to rent community halls to non-Orthodox Jews for religious services).

[56] HCJ 292/83 Temple Mount Faithful v. Jerusalem Police, 38(2) P.D. 449, 454 (internal citations omitted).

[57] See also Bendor and Sachs, supra n. 55, at 44 ("the Basic Laws do not mention the right to equality, freedom of speech, freedom of religion and conscience, the right to apply to law courts, the freedom to strike, and the rights to education and health, among others. … The Knesset was presented – both before and after adopting the two Basic Laws – with proposals to create a comprehensive constitutional charter of all human rights, but it rejected this option. It was impossible to reach an agreement on the inclusion of additional rights within the Basic Laws.")

[58] Basic Law: Human Dignity and Liberty, 1391 LSI 150 (1991-1992), art. 2

[59] Basic Law: Human Dignity and Liberty, supra n. 58, art. 4

[60] Basic Law: Human Dignity and Liberty, supra n. 58, art. 1 (as amended by Basic Law: Human Dignity and Liberty - Amendment, 1994, SH No. 90).

[61] Penal Law, 1977, articles 170-174 (Offenses Against Sentiment of Religion and Tradition); see generally Shmuel Berkowitz, The Legal Status of the Holy Places in Jerusalem (1997) 28-37 (analyzing provisions).

[62] Yiftachel, "Ethnocracy: The Politics of Judaizing Israel/Palestine", Constellations, Vol. 6, 364-391 (1999).

[63] Adalah, The Inequality Report: The Palestinian Arab Minority in Israel (2011) 31, http://www.adalah.org/uploads/oldfiles/upfiles/2011/Adalah_The_Inequality_Report_March_2011.pdf.

[64] Rassem Khamaisi, "Territorial Dispossession and Population Control of the Palestinians," in Surveillance and Control in Israel/Palestine: Population, Territory and Power (2010) 335, 344.

[65] Israel's status as a democracy, ethnic democracy, or ethnocracy has been the subject of extensive scholarly and popular debate. See, e.g., Yiftachel, Ethnocracy, supra n. 11; Oren Yifchael and As'ad Ghanem, "Understanding Ethnocratic Regimes: the Politics of Seizing Contested Territories" Political Geography 23: 647-676 (2004); Nur Maslha, The Bible and Zionism: Invented Traditions, Archaeology and Post-Colonialism in Palestine-Israel (2007); Sammy Smooha, "The Model of Ethnic Democracy: Israel as an Jewish and Democratic State," Nations and Nationalism 8(4): 475-503 (2002); As'ad Ghanem, Nadim Rouhana and Oren Yiftachel, "Questioning 'Ethnic Democracy': A Response to Sammy Smooha," Israel Studies 3(2) 253-267 (1998); Aeyal Gross, "All Signs Point Toward Ethnocracy, Not Democracy, in Israel," Haaretz (Nov. 17, 2014) http://www.haaretz.com/israel-news/.premium-1.626809; Ben White, "Is Israel a democracy or an ethnocracy?," New Statesman (Feb. 5, 2012), http://www.newstatesman.com/blogs/the-staggers/2012/02/jewish-state-citizens-israel; Gershom Goreneberg, "Is Israel a Democracy?," American Prospect (Dec. 4, 2009), http://prospect.org/article/israel-democracy-0.

[66] Kuric and others v. Slovenia, App. No. 26828/06, [2012] ECHR 1083 (June 26, 2012).

[67] Kuric, supra n. 66, at para. 384-396.

[68] 2014 USCIRF Report

[69] 2015 USCIRF Report

[70] United Nations High Commissioner for Refugees, "2015 UNHCR Country Operations Profile – Myanmar", http://www.unhcr.org/pages/49e4877d6.html.

[71] 2015 USCIRF Report.

[72] 2015 USCIRF Report (emphasis added).

[73] 2014 USCIRF Report.

[74] 2014 USCIRF Report.

[75] See generally Rashid Khalidi, Palestinian Identity: The Construction of Modern National Consciousness (1997).

[76] Ayelet Shachar, Whose Republic? Citizenship and Membership in the Israeli Polity, 13 Georgetown J. Int'l L. 233, 245 (1999).

[77] HCJ 58/68 Shalit v. Minister of Interior, 23(2) PD 477.

[78] Law of Return (Amendment No. 2), 1970, 24 LSI 28, sec. 4(B).

[79] Central Conference of American Rabbis, Resolution on Patrilineal Descent, https://www.jewishvirtuallibrary.org/jsource/Judaism/patrilineal1.html; see also Union for Reform Judaism, "How does Reform Judaism define who is a Jew?," http://www.reformjudaism.org/practice/ask-rabbi/how-does-reform-judaism-define-who-jew.

[80] In this regard, Yiftachel argues that "the breaching of Israeli borders with settlement activity and the involvement of world Jewry in internal politics have eroded the territorial and civil meaning of the term 'Israeli,' and simultaneously strengthened the (non-territorial and ethno-religious) Jewish collective identity. This process has grave implications for democracy, principally because it bypasses the institution of territorial citizenship, on which a democratic state must be founded." Yiftachel, Ethnocracy: The Politics of Judaizing Israel/Palestine, supra n. 11.

[81] Dugard and Reynolds, Apartheid, International Law, and the oPt, supra n. 34, at 890; see also Shachar, Whose Republic?, supra n. 76, at 235 n. 15 ("the Zionist view of the Jewish people ... conceptualized the 'Jewish problem' not as a religious or social problem, but rather as a national problem. ... This nationalist perception of the Jewish people is modernist and secularized. It has never been the only way to

think about membership in the Jewish people, nor has it been accepted by all branches of Judaism.")

[82] Dugard and Reynolds, Apartheid, International Law, and the oPt, supra n. 34, at 890; Khalidi, Palestinian Identity, supra n. 75, at 144 (discussing the formation of Palestinian national consciousness during World War I and the years following, and its "interrelation with broad, transnational foci of identity, in particularly Arabism and Islam, with other potent regional and local loyalties.")

[83] Palestinian National Charter, Resolutions of the Palestine National Council, July 1-17, 1968, article 1.

[84] Palestinian National Charter, supra n. 83, articles 5-6.

[85] Mitri Raheb et al., Palestinian Christians in the West Bank: Facts, Figures and Trends (2012).

[86] Dugard and Reynolds, Apartheid, International Law, and the oPt, supra n. 39, at 890.

[87] Dugard and Reynolds, Apartheid, International Law, and the oPt, supra n. 39, at 889 (emphasis added).

[88] Declaration of Establishment of the State of Israel, 1 LSI 7 (1948).

[89] For a historical overview of the relationship between nationality and citizenship, see Alison Kesby, The Right to Have Rights: Citizenship, Humanity, and International Law (2012) 43-46.

[90] Nottebohm Case (Liechtenstein v. Guatemala); Second Phase, 1955 ICJ 4.

[91] European Convention on Nationality, ETS 166 (Nov. 6, 1997). art. 3(2).

[92] Bronwen Manby, Citizenship Laws in Africa: A Comparative Study (2d. ed. 2010) at ix; see generally Kesby, The Right to Have Rights, supra n. 89, at 47-90.

[93] For expression by Israel's Palestinian minority of the rights of recognition as a native national community and internal self-determination, see Adalah, "Democratic Constitution," (2007) http://www.adalah.org/uploads/oldfiles/Public/files/democratic_constitution-english.pdf; Mada al-Carmel, "Haifa Declaration" (2007), http://mada-research.org/en/files/2007/09/haifaenglish.pdf. See also Hassan Jabareen, "Hobbesian Citizenship: How the Palestinians Became a Minority in Israel," in Multiculturalism and Minority Rights in the Arab World (2014) 189-219.

[94] See Israeli Ministry of Justice, Draft Basic Law: Israel as the Nation-State of the Jewish People, art. I(2), http://www.justice.gov.il/StateIdentity/InformationInEnglish/Documents/BasicLawBill.pdf.

[95] Barak Ravid and Jonathan Lis, "U.S. Responds to 'Jewish Nation-state' Bill: Israel Must Stick to Its Democratic Principles," Haaretz (Nov. 24, 2014), http://www.haaretz.com/israel-news/1.628327.

[96] Tamar Pileggi, "Ministers debate softened version of 'Jewish state bill,'" Times of Israel (July 12, 2015), http://www.timesofisrael.com/knesset-committee-to-debate-new-version-of-jewish-state-law/.

[97] Israel Ministry of Foreign Affairs, "Acquisition of Israeli Nationality," http://www.mfa.gov.il/mfa/aboutisrael/state/pages/acquisition%20of%20israeli%20nationality.aspx.

[98] 2007 State Department Human Rights Report.

[99] Ayelet Shachar, "Whose Republic? Citizenship and Membership in the Israeli Polity," 13 Georgetown Journal of International Law 233, 234 (1999).

[100] World Zionist Organization - Jewish Agency (Status) Law, 1952, 7 LSI 3, sec. 5.

[101] Shachar, Whose Republic?, supra n. 76, at 235 (emphasis in original).

[102] Shachar, Whose Republic?, supra n. 76, at 238.

[103] Israel Citizenship Law, 1952, sec. 2(b)(2).

[104] Committee on Economic, Social and Cultural Rights, Concluding Observations: Israel, UN Doc. E/C.12/1/Add.90 (May 23, 2003), para. 18.

[105] Citizenship Law (Amendment No. 4), 1980. The amendment also granted birthright citizenship to their children.

[106] Shachar, Whose Republic?, supra n. 76, at 254.

[107] See Human Rights Watch, "Forget About Him, He's Not Here": Israel's Control of Palestinian Residency in the West Bank and Gaza (2012) at 18 (270,000-390,000 estimate); see also BADIL Resource Center for Palestinian Residency & Refugee Rights, Survey of Palestinian Refugees and Internally Displaced Persons, Vol. VIII, 2013-2015 (2015) [hereinafter "BADIL Survey of Palestinian Refugees"] 53 (240,000 Palestinians made refugees for the first time in 1967).

[108] BADIL Survey of Palestinian Refugees, supra n. 107, at 53.

[109] HRW, Forget About Him, He's Not Here, supra n. 107, at 17.

[110] BADIL Survey of Palestinian Refugees, supra n. 107, at 33 (estimating number in 2014 at over 1.1 million).

[111] BADIL Survey of Palestinian Refugees, supra n. 107, at 53.

[112] Israel-PLO Interim Agreement, supra n. 14, annex III, appendix I, article 11.

[113] HRW, Forget About Him, He's Not Here, supra n. 107, at 23.

[114] HRW, Forget About Him, He's Not Here, supra n. 107, at 22-25.

[115] HRW, Forget About Him, He's Not Here, supra n. 107, at 26-46.

[116] Report of the Special Rapporteur on the situation of human rights in the Palestinian territories occupied since 1967, Richard Falk, supra n. 35, para. 78.

[117] Asem Khalil, Palestinian Refugees in Arab States: A Rights-Based Approach (2009) 8; Abbas Shiblak, "Stateless Palestinians," 26 Forced Migration Review 8-9 (2006).

[118] See generally Mutaz Qafisheh, "Citizens of the State of Palestine and the Future of Palestinian Refugees: Legal and Political Scenarios," in Palestine Membership in the United Nations: Legal and Practical Implications (2014) 45-133.

[119] Convention Relating to the Status of Stateless Persons, Sept. 28, 1954, 360 UNTS 117, art. 1(1).

[120] Anis Kassim, "The Palestinians: From Hyphenated to Integrated Citizenship," in Citizenship and the State in the Middle East (2000) 201, 204-205 (discussing Israeli court decisions deciding that Palestinian citizenship was rendered "devoid of substance," "not satisfactory" and "inappropriate to the situation following the establishment of Israel.")

[121] Asem Khalil, Palestinian Refugees in Arab States, supra n. 117, at 1; Kassim, "The Palestinians: From Hyphenated to Integrated Citizenship," supra n. 120, at 207.

[122] Kassim, "The Palestinians: From Hyphenated to Integrated Citizenship," supra n. 120, at 211-214 (discussing Jordan's denaturalization of Palestinians since 1988); Khalil, Palestinian Refugees in Arab States, supra n. 117, at 22-23; see also Human Rights Watch, Stateless Again: Palestinian-Origin Jordanians Deprived of Their Nationality (2010) 17.

[123] Khalil, supra n. 117, at 39; see also United States Citizenship and Immigration Services, "Palestine/Occupied Territories: Information On Passports Issued By The Palestine National Authority" (Dec. 17, 1998), http://www.uscis.gov/tools/asylum-resources/resource-information-center-52 ("the U.S. Department of State, the United States does not recognize Palestine as a country, and therefore the Palestinian Authority Passport/Travel Document does not confer citizenship.")

[124] Manby, supra n. 92, at x.

[125] Nationality and Entry into Israel Law (Temporary Order), 2003, as amended, English translation at http://www.hamoked.org.il/items/1140_eng.pdf.

[126] Jonathan Lis, "Knesset Extends Law Banning Palestinian Family Reunification," Haaretz (June 17, 2015), http://www.haaretz.com/news/diplomacy-defense/.premium-1.661438.

[127] Nationality and Entry into Israel Law (Temporary Order), 2003, supra n. 125, art. 3(2) ("if [the Minister of Interior] is convinced that the said resident identifies with the State of Israel and its goals, and that the resident or his family members performed a meaningful act to advance the security, economy, or another matter important to the state....").

[128] HCJ 7052/03 Adalah et al. v. Minister of Interior, [2006] 2 TakEl 1754 (Decision of May 14, 2006), English translation at http://www.hamoked.org/files/2011/4489_eng.pdf.

[129] Society of St. Yves, "Palestinian Families Under Threat: 10 Years of Family Unification Freeze in Jerusalem" (Dec. 2013) at 15, http://www.saintyves.org/uploads/files/10_years_freeze_of_family_unification_in _jerusalem.pdf.

[130] HaMoked, "The humanitarian committee advising the Minister of Interior in a rare and exceptional decision: a Palestinian woman married to an East Jerusalem resident who suffers from multiple sclerosis will receive temporary status in Israel" (Aug. 25, 2015), http://www.hamoked.org/Document.aspx?dID=Updates1538. As of late 2010, the committee had elected to discuss only 290 of 770 applications received. See HCJ 1193/15 Ziyadah v. Minister of Interior and the Committee for Special Humanitarian Affairs, Petitioners' Petition for Order Nisi (Feb. 17, 2015), para. 24, http://www.hamoked.org/files/2015/1159741_eng.pdf.

[131] Yoav Peled, The Challenge of Ethnic Democracy: The State and Minority Groups in Israel, Poland and Northern Ireland (2003) 138.

[132] 2013 State Department Human Rights Report.

[133] International Covenant on Civil and Political Rights, Dec. 16, 1966, 999 UNTS 171, art. 17 and 23 [hereinafter "ICCPR"]; see Human Rights Committee, Concluding observations on the fourth periodic report of Israel, supra n. 45, para. 21 ("The Committee reiterates that the Citizenship and Entry into Israel Law (Temporary Provision) should be revoked and that the State party should review its laws, practices and policies with a view to bringing them in line with its obligations under articles 23 and 26 of the Covenant.")

[134] International Convention on the Elimination of All Forms of Racial Discrimination, Dec. 21, 1965, 660 UNTS 195, art. 5(d)(v) [hereinafter "CERD"]; see Committee on the Elimination of Racial Discrimination, Concluding observations: Israel, UN Doc. CERD/C/ISR/CO/14-16 (Mar. 9, 2012), para. 18 ("The Committee reiterates its concern at the maintenance of discriminatory laws especially targeting Palestinian citizens of Israel such as the Citizenship and Entry into Israel Law (Temporary Provision). ... The Committee is particularly concerned at the recent decision of the High Court of Justice, which confirmed its constitutionality (Articles 2 and 5 of the Convention).")

[135] International Covenant on Economic, Social and Cultural Rights, Dec. 16, 1966, 993 UNTS 3, art. 10 [hereinafter "CESCR"]; see Committee on Economic, Social and Cultural Rights, Concluding observations: Israel, UN Doc. E/C.12/ISR/CO/3 (Dec. 16, 2011), para. 20 ("The Committee urges the State party to guarantee and facilitate family reunification for all citizens and permanent residents irrespective of their status or background, and ensure the widest possible protection of, and assistance to, the family.").

[136] Nationality and Entry into Israel Law (Temporary Order), 2003, supra n. 125, Explanatory Note to Section 2.

[137] See International Committee of the Red Cross, "Expert Meeting: The Use of Force in Armed Conflicts: Interplay Between the Conduct of Hostilities and Law Enforcement Paradigms" (2013) at 11, https://www.icrc.org/eng/assets/files/publications/icrc-002-4171.pdf ("IHL also contains other specific rules for the use of force outside conduct of hostilities operations, such as the obligation of the Occupying Power to maintain public order and safety.") (Emphasis added.)

[138] Yoav Peled, "Citizenship Betrayed: Israel's Emerging Immigration and Citizenship Regime," 8 Theoretical Inquiries in Law 603, 610-611 (2007). Peled, an Israeli political scientist who has traditionally defined Israel within its pre-1967 borders as an ethnic democracy rather than an ethnocracy, contends that the state is "moving steadily from ethnic democracy towards a form of state that strongly resembles an ethnocracy." Id. at 607.

[139] HCJ 7052/03 Adalah et al. v. Minister of Interior, supra n. 128, Opinion of J. Cheshin, para. 3.

[140] See, e.g., HCJ 9132/07 Al-Bassiouni v. Prime Minister, para. 12

[141] Peled, Citizenship Betrayed, supra n. 138, at 616.

[142] Cabinet Decision No. 3805 (June 26, 2005), quoted in Peled, Citizenship Betrayed, supra n. 138, at 604.

[143] Advisory Committee for the Examination of an Immigration Policy for the State of Israel, Interim Report (Feb. 2, 2006) (unpublished) (Hebrew), quoted in Peled, Citizenship Betrayed, supra n. 138, at 615.

[144] Peled, Citizenship Betrayed, supra n. 138, at 613.

[145] Peled, Citizenship Betrayed, supra n. 138, at 613.

[146] HCJ 7052/03 Adalah et al. v. Minister of Interior, supra n. 128, Opinion of J. Hayut, para. 2.

[147] HCJ 7052/03 Adalah et al. v. Minister of Interior, supra n. 128, Opinion of J. Procaccia, para. 28.

148 HCJ 7052/03 Adalah et al. v. Minister of Interior, supra n. 128, Opinion of J. Cheshin, para. 62 (emphasis added).

149 Committee of Economic, Social and Cultural Rights, Concluding Observations: Israel, UN Doc. E/C.12/1/Add.27 (Dec. 4, 1998), para. 11.

150 Mandate for Palestine (1922), art. 4 ("An appropriate Jewish agency shall be recognised as a public body for the purpose of advising and co-operating with the Administration of Palestine in such economic, social and other matters as may affect the establishment of the Jewish national home and the interests of the Jewish population in Palestine, and, subject always to the control of the Administration to assist and take part in the development of the country.")

151 World Zionist Organization – Jewish Agency for Israel (Status) Law (1952), art. 4.

152 Chaim Levinson, "West Bank Settlers Suing WZO Settlement Division for Overcharging on Property Fees," Haaretz, June 30, 2015, http://www.haaretz.com/news/israel/.premium-1.663707. In June 2015, a class-action lawsuit on behalf of settlers was filed against the WZO, alleging that the Settlement Division is "exploiting its monopoly position in running the property registry" in West Bank settlements by charging illegally high registration fees. Id.

153 For a complete critical history of Jewish National Fund, see Walter Lehn, "The Jewish National Fund," Journal of Palestine Studies, Vol. 3, No. 4 (1974).

154 Jewish National Fund, "Our History," http://www.jnf.org/about-jnf/history/.

155 Jewish National Fund, "Our History: The Second Decade, 1911-1920," http://www.kkl.org.il/eng/about-kkl-jnf/our-history/second-decade-1911-1920/.

156 A Survey of Palestine: Prepared in December, 1945 and January, 1946 for the Information of the Anglo-American Committee of Inquiry (1991) at 566. See also Amiram Barka, "Buying the State of Israel," Haaretz, Feb. 10, 2005, http://www.haaretz.com/print-edition/features/buying-the-state-of-israel-1.149767 (setting the JNF's land ownership before the 1948 War at 640,000 dunums).

157 GA Res. 194, art. 11, UN Doc. A/RES/194 (III) (Dec. 11, 1948).

158 Michael R Fischbach, Records of Dispossession: Palestinian Refugee Property and the Arab-Israeli Conflict (2003) 58-68.

159 Fischbach, Records of Dispossession, supra n. 158, at 67.

160 Absentees' Property Law (No. 20) 1950, sec. 19; Development Authority (Transfer of Property) Law, 1950.

161 Keren Kayemet Le-Israel Law (No. 3) 1953, sections 3, 8-10; unofficial English translation at

http://www.adalah.org/uploads/oldfiles/Public/files/Discriminatory-Laws-Database/English/05-Jewish-National-Fund-Law-1953.pdf.

[162] Keren Kayemet Le-Israel Law, sec. 6 (granting JNF Israel the status of a local authority under the Land (Acquisition for Public Purposes) Ordinance, 1943).

[163] Section 22 of the 1943 Ordinance (http://mykammar-law.com/pdf_laws/landEn.pdf) allows for the High Commissioner, as executive of the Palestine (Mandate) Administration (the powers of which are vested in the government in Israeli law) to expropriate private property on behalf of a municipal corporation, local council or other local authority if such expropriation is, in the government's sole discretion, "likely to prove useful to the public."

[164] Hussein Abu Hussein and Fiona McKay, Access Denied: Palestinian Land Rights in Israel (2003) 152.

[165] Basic Law: Israel Lands, 14 LSI 48 (1960), art. 1.

[166] Jewish National Fund, "Our History: The Second Decade, 1951-1960," http://www.kkl.org.il/eng/about-kkl-jnf/our-history/sixth-decade-1951-1960/.

[167] See J. David Bleich, Contemporary Halakhaic Problems (1977) 27-32.

[168] Thabat Abu Rass, "Arab Towns in the 'Little Triangle,'" in Urban Ethnic Encounters: The Spatial Consequences (2003) 69-70.

[169] Adalah, The Inequality Report, supra n. 63, at 23.

[170] HCJ 6698/95 Kaadan v. Israel Lands Administration (Judgment, Mar. 10, 2000), para. 10.

[171] Kaadan, supra n. 170, para. 35, 39.

[172] Kaadan, supra n. 170, para. 39.

[173] Kaadan, supra n. 170, para. 40(B).

[174] Lucy Ash, "Battling against Israeli 'apartheid', BBC News (Dec. 23, 2004), http://news.bbc.co.uk/1/hi/world/middle_east/4111915.stm.

[175] See Adalah, Critique of the Draft Bill - Israel Land Administration Law (Amendment No. 7) 2009" (July 21, 2009), http://www.adalah.org/uploads/oldfiles/newsletter/eng/jul09/Position_Paper_on_Land_Reform_Bill_july_2009.pdf.

[176] Cooperative Societies Ordinance (Amendment) (No. 8), 2011, English translation at http://www.adalah.org/uploads/oldfiles/Public/files/Discriminatory-Laws-Database/English/12-Admissions-Committees-Law-2011.pdf.

[177] Adalah, Press Release: "In the wake of the Knesset Constitution, Law and Justice Committee's approval of the Admissions Committees Law: Adalah: There are now 695 communities in Israel where Arab citizens of the state are forbidden to live" (http://www.adalah.org/en/content/view/7086).

[178] Cooperative Societies Ordinance (Amendment) (No. 8), supra n. 176, para. 2 (adding sec. 6(C) to the Cooperative Societies Ordinance, which provides in relevant part, "[a]n admissions committee is entitled to refuse to accept a candidate for a community town based on one or more of these considerations only: ... (4) The candidate is not suitable for the social life in the community....; (5) The candidate's lack of compatibility with the social-cultural fabric of the community town, when there is reason to assume that this would harm this fabric[.]")

[179] HCJ 2504/11 Adalah: Legal Center for Arab Minority Rights in Israel v. The Knesset. (Decision, September 17, 2014).

[180] See Absorption of Discharged Soldiers Law, 1994 and its Amendment No. 7 (Benefits for Discharged Soldiers), 2008 (granting any registered university or college student who has completed his/her military service and resides in a designated "National Priority Area" such as the Naqab (Negev), the Galilee, or West Bank settlements a "compensation package" including full tuition for the first year of academic education, a year of free preparatory academic education, and student housing benefits); Shachar, Whose Republic?, supra n. 76, at 260; Adalah, The Inequality Report, supra n. 63, at 14.

[181] See Adalah, Discriminatory Laws Database, http://www.adalah.org/en/law/index, listing several proposed discriminatory laws relating to military service, including the Contributors to the State Bill, approved by the Knesset's Ministerial Committee for Legislation on June 16, 2013, which would institute preferential treatment to citizens completing military or civil service, including preference in hiring, salaries, student housing, higher education and allocation of land for housing. The bill states that such preferential treatment shall not be considered discrimination as prohibited by Israeli law. See also Israel Democracy Institute, "The Contributors to the State Bill: Contributing to the Jewish-Arab Divide," Oct. 29, 2013, http://en.idi.org.il/analysis/articles/the-contributors-to-the-state-bill-contributing-to-the-jewish-arab-divide.

[182] Adalah, The Inequality Report, supra n. 63, at 14.

[183] Shachar, Whose Republic?, supra n. 76, at 260.

[184] See Isabel Kershner, Some Israelis Question Benefits for Ultra-Religious," N.Y. Times (Dec. 28, 2010), http://www.nytimes.com/2010/12/29/world/middleeast/29israel.html (stating the Israel spends $30 million annually on stipends to kollel (seminary) students).

[185] Shachar, Whose Republic?, supra n. 76, at 271.

[186] Shachar, Whose Republic?, supra n. 76, at 262.

[187] See Walter Zander, "Truce on the Temple Mount," New Outlook, July/August 1976, pp. 14-19, http://www.walterzander.info/acrobat/Truce%20On.pdf ("The whole Temple Mount area is holy to Moslems, not only the Al-Aksa Mosque, and this fact has long been recognized, including by the Zionist movement and by Israel.").

[188] A waqf is an inalienable and perpetual religious endowment in Islamic law. The plural form of waqf is awqaf.

[189] Two of the most prominent examples include the outbreak of the second Palestinian intifada on September 28, 2000, following Ariel Sharon's visit to the Compound, and recent violent clashes in the latter half of 2015, which seem motivated in part by actual or rumored changes to the status quo at the Compound.

[190] Commentary, GC (IV) art. 27.

[191] Enrico Molinaro, The Holy Places of Jerusalem in Middle East Peace Agreements: The Conflict Between Global and State Identities (2009) 110-111.

[192] Hague Regulations, supra n. 42, art. 43.

[193] See Zander, "Truce on the Temple Mount," supra n. 187.

[194] Molinaro, The Holy Places of Jerusalem, supra n. 191, at 102, citing Shlomo Slonim, Jerusalem in America's Foreign Policy (1998) 221.

[195] Zander, "Truce on the Temple Mount, supra n. 187; Molinaro, The Holy Places of Jerusalem, supra n. 191, at 102, citing Shlomo Slonim, Jerusalem in America's Foreign Policy (1998) 221.

[196] Molinaro, The Holy Places of Jerusalem, supra n. 191, at 120.

[197] Molinaro, The Holy Places of Jerusalem, supra n. 191, at 111-112.

[198] Shmuel Berkovitz, "Proposals for a Political Status of the Holy Places within the Context of a Peace Treaty," in Jerusalem: Legal Aspects 7 (1983) xi.

[199] Basic Law: The Government, 22 LSI 257 (1969), sec. 1 (declaring that "the Government is the executive authority of the State.")

[200] SC Res. 801, para. 5, UN Doc. S/RES/801 (May 29, 1948) (emphasis added).

[201] GA Res. 194(III), supra n. 157, para. 7 (emphasis added).

[202] Molinaro, supra n. 191, at 89, citing Israeli Ministry of Foreign Affairs, Israel's Foreign Relations, Vol. 1, Selected Documents, 1947-1974 (Meron Medzini, ed., 1976), at 223.

[203] See ILC Guiding Principles Applicable to Unilateral Declarations of States Capable of Creating Legal Obligations, supra n. 39, art. 3 ("To determine the legal

effects of such declarations, it is necessary to take account of their content, of all the factual circumstances in which they were made, and of the reactions to which they gave rise"), citing, e.g., Nuclear Test Case (Australia and New Zealand v. France), 1974 ICJ 253, para. 43-50.

[204] Report of the Commission Appointed by His Majesty's Government in the United Kingdom of Great Britain and Northern Ireland, with the Approval of the Council of the League of Nations, to Determine the Rights and Claims of Moslems and Jews in connection with the Western or Wailing Wall at Jerusalem (1930). The findings of the Report were brought into force through the Palestine (Western Wall) Order in Council, 1931.

[205] Legality of the Threat or Use of Nuclear Weapons, Advisory Opinion, 1996 ICJ 266, para. 26; see generally Harvard University, Program on Humanitarian Policy and Conflict Research, "From Legal Theory to Policy Tools: International Humanitarian Law and International Human Rights Law in the Occupied Palestinian Territory" (2007) 7-12, http://www.hpcrresearch.org/sites/default/files/publications/IHRLbrief.pdf.

[206] See "Debate on Israel's sovereignty over Temple Mount held in Knesset Plenum" (Feb. 26, 2014), Knesset, Press Releases, https://www.knesset.gov.il/spokesman/eng/PR_eng.asp?PRID=11172.

[207] Molinaro, The Holy Places of Jerusalem, supra n. 191, at 101-102; see also "Summary of a Report of the Commission of Inquiry into the Events on Temple Mount" (Oct. 26, 2000), Chapter 3 ("the internal administration of matters relating to the Temple Mount, including the mosques thereon, has been given to the authority of the Moslem Wakf.") (available from Israeli MFA website); Ruth Lapidoth, "A Recent Agreement on the Holy Places in Jerusalem," Israel Journal of Foreign Affairs VII: 3, 61-70 (2013), http://www.israelcfr.com/documents/7-3/7-3-5-RuthLapidoth.pdf ("Israel, back in 1967, entrusted to the Muslim Waqf the custodianship of the Muslim Holy Places on the Temple Mount in all matters except for external security.").

[208] Jordan-Israel Treaty of Peace (Oct. 26, 1994), art. 9(2), http://www.kinghussein.gov.jo/peacetreaty.html. See generally Moshe Hirsh et al., Wither Jerusalem?: Proposals and Positions Concerning the Future of Jerusalem (1995) 135-140 (discussing Jordanian final-status position on Jerusalem).

[209] See Menachem Klein, Jerusalem: The Contested City (2001) 176-182; International Crisis Group, "The Status of the Status Quo at the Holy Esplanade" (June 30, 2015), http://www.crisisgroup.org/en/regions/middle-east-north-africa/israel-palestine/159-the-status-of-the-status-quo-at-jerusalem-s-holy-esplanade.aspx, at 7 and n. 27.

[210] Jordanian-Palestinian Agreement to Jointly Defend al-Masjid al-Aqsa (March 31, 2013), unofficial English translation at

http://jordanembassyus.org/news/jordanian-palestinian-agreement-jointly-defend-al-masjid-al-aqsa; see also Lapidoth, "A Recent Agreement on the Holy Places in Jerusalem," supra n. 207, at 62 (concluding that the Agreement was intended to be legally binding).

[211] Jordanian-Palestinian Agreement to Jointly Defend al-Masjid al-Aqsa, supra n. 210, at art. 2.1(D)-(E).

[212] Knesset, "Debate on Israel's sovereignty over Temple Mount," supra n. 206.

[213] See generally Hassan Barari, Jordan and Israel: A Troubled Relationship in a Volatile Region (2014).

[214] Molinaro, The Holy Places of Jerusalem, supra n. 191, at 138, annex IV (discussion the different meanings of the term 'sovereignty' as used in relation to the Holy Places).

[215] Orna Ben-Naftali, Aeyal M. Gross, and Keren Michaeli, Illegal Occupation: Framing the Occupied Palestinian Territory, 23 Berkeley J. Int'l L. 551, 570-574 (2005).

[216] In the aftermath the 1948 War, the newly-declared State of Israel asserted sovereignty over West Jerusalem while Jordan asserted sovereignty over East Jerusalem, defined as a 6.5 km² area covering the Old City and its surrounding neighborhoods. Following the 1967 War, the Israeli government enacted a series of measures which authorized the expansion of Jerusalem's municipal boundaries to include not only Jordanian-defined East Jerusalem but 28 surrounding Palestinian villages, thereby increasing its area from 6.5 km² to 71 km²; and the application of Israeli law, jurisdiction and administration to East Jerusalem. See generally Ruth Lapidoth, Jerusalem – Some Jurisprudential Aspects, 45 Cath. U. L. Rev. 661 (1996).

While these measures were widely seen as de facto annexation, Israel officially represented to the UN that "the term 'annexation' is out of place. The measures adopted related to the integration of Jerusalem in the administrative and municipal spheres and furnish a legal basis for the protection of the Holy Places." See Letter from Israel's Foreign Minister, Abba Eban, to the UN Secretary-General, July 10, 1967, UN GAOR, 5th Emergency Special Session, UN Doc. A/6753-S/8052 (1967). Indeed, "there has never been an official act that has declared expanded East Jerusalem as having been annexed by the State of Israel." Ian Lustick, Has Israel Annexed Jerusalem?, 5 Middle East Policy 34, 44 (1997).

The Basic Law: Jerusalem, adopted in 1980, declares "complete and united" Jerusalem as the capital of Israel and was widely condemned as a confirmation of Israel's annexation of East Jerusalem. However, "the consensus of legal scholars is that this action added nothing to the legal or administrative circumstance of the city." (Lustick, supra, at 40.) Nor, by the same logic, does a 2000 amendment to the Basic Law: Jerusalem references the city's municipal boundaries and prohibits the transfer of authority over any part of the municipality to a "foreign body" except by a Basic Law passed by a majority of the Knesset. Nevertheless, UNSC Resolution 478 declares that the Basic Law: Jerusalem violates international law and does not affect the applicability of Geneva Convention (IV) to East Jerusalem. (SC Res. 478, UN Doc. S/RES/478 (Aug. 20, 1980), art. 2.) The resolution further "determines that all legislative and administrative measures and actions taken by Israel, the occupying Power, which have altered or purport to alter the character and status of the Holy City of Jerusalem, and in particular the recent 'basic law' on Jerusalem, are null and void and must be rescinded forthwith." (Id., art. 3.) Even before Resolution 478, the Security Council had adopted numerous resolutions declaring that any attempt by Israel to change the status of occupied East Jerusalem is null and void. (See, e.g., UNSC Res. 252 (1968); Res. 267 (1969): Res. 298 (1971); Res. 476 (1980).)

Lustick notes that "[d]espite its official position" that East Jerusalem has not been annexed, "successive governments in Israel have tried, in their policies and propaganda, to create the impression that the fate of Jerusalem has been sealed-that politically and legally and in every other respect the portions of the municipality over the Green Line are as much a part of the country as any other district." Lustick, supra, at 39-40.

[217] The annexation of East Jerusalem would violate article 2(4) of the United Nations Charter, which forbids the acquisition and aggrandizement of territory by force.

[218] League of Nations, Mandate for Palestine (1922), art. 13.

[219] L.G.A. Cust, The Status Quo in the Holy Places (His Majesty's Stationery Office, 1930). Israeli law recognizes the Cust Memorandum as a binding legal document and admissible evidence to prove Status Quo rights in the Christian Holy Places. See HCJ 222/68 National Circles v. Minister of Police, PD 24(2) 141; HCJ 109/70 Orthodox Coptic Patriarch of Jerusalem v. Minister of Police, PD 25(1) 134.

[220] Shmuel Berkovitz, The Temple Mount and the Western Wall in Israeli Law (2001) 83.

[221] Zander, "Truce on the Temple Mount," supra n. 187.

[222] ICG, "Status of the Status Quo," supra n. 209, at 4.

[223] Molinaro, The Holy Places of Jerusalem, supra n. 191, at 94.

[224] Molinaro, The Holy Places of Jerusalem, supra n. 191, at 97-98 and n. 633.

[225] Shmuel Berkovitz, "The Temple Mount and the Western Wall," supra n. 220, at 44 (discussing order of August 20, 1967).

[226] ICG, "The Status of the Status Quo," supra n. 209, at 4.

227 Israel's Chief Rabbis jointly reiterated this ban in December 2013. During the unrest of the summer of 2014, Chief Sephardic Rabbi Yitzhak Yosef condemned the "B-rate rabbis" who encourage Jews to pray at the Compound for "adding fuel to the fire." Yair Ettinger, "Jews forbidden from going to Temple Mount, says chief Sephardi rabbi," Haaretz (Nov. 7, 2014), http://www.haaretz.com/news/national/1.625233.

228 ICG, "Status of the Status Quo," supra n. 209, at 5.

229 HCJ 222/68 National Circles v. Minister of Police, PD 24(2) 141.

230 Protection of Holy Places Law, 1967, 21 LSI 76 (1966-67), sec. 1. In March 2015, the Jerusalem Magistrate Court ordered the state to pay NIS 500,000 ($126,000) in damages to a right-wing Jewish activist, Yehuda Glick, for prohibiting him from praying at the Mosque Compound between 2011 and 2013, which the court found to violate the Law. See Jeremy Sharon, "Jerusalem Court Upholds Jewish Prayer on Temple Mount," Jerusalem Post (Mar. 3, 2015), http://www.jpost.com/Israel-News/Jerusalem-court-upholds-Jewish-prayer-on-Temple-Mount-392744.

231 HCJ 99/76 Cohen v. Minister of Police, PD 30(2) 505; HCJ 4354/92 Temple Mount and Eretz Israel Loyalists Movement v Prime Minister, PD 47(1) 37; HCJ 3358/95 Hoffman v. Prime Minister's Office, P.D. 54(2) 345.

232 Berkovitz, "The Temple Mount and the Western Wall," supra n. 220, at 47-49.

233 See "Sharon Touches a Nerve, and Jerusalem Explodes," N.Y. Times, Sept. 28, 2000, http://www.nytimes.com/2000/09/29/world/29ISRA.html. Among the politicians who accompanied Sharon is current Israeli president Reuven Rivlin. According to Sharon's former spokesman, Ra'anan Gissin, the visit was a show of Jewish sovereignty over the Compound intended to solidify Sharon's leadership of the Likud in anticipation of an expected leadership contest with Benjamin Netanyahu. See Gil Hoffman, "Gissin talks Sharon's Temple Mount visit 10 years later," Jerusalem Post, Sept. 29, 2010, http://www.jpost.com/Israel/Gissin-talks-Sharons-Temple-Mount-visit-10-years-later%20.

234 Ir Amim and Keshev, Dangerous Liaison: The Dynamics of the Rise of the Temple Movements and Their Implications (2013) 61 (noting that a ban was in effect at the time of publication).

235 Tova Zimuki and Akiva Novick, "AG mulls barring Knesset members from Temple Mount," Ynet News, Nov. 27, 2014, http://www.ynetnews.com/articles/0,7340,L-4596532,00.html (quoting Danino as saying on Nov. 25, 2014, "We have seen and identified, since the last election, radical right-wing elements which have made a priority out of changing the status quo on the Temple Mount. To them we say – stay away from the Temple Mount.")

236 Dangerous Liaison, supra n. 234, at 62.

237 Ben-Ari, an acknowledged follower of Rabbi Meir Kahane and a former member of the banned Kach party, was denied a visa to the United States in 2009 for membership in a terrorist organization.

238 Sarah Posner, "Advocacy groups woo US lawmakers amid fervor over prayer at Temple Mount," Al-Jazeera America, June 12, 2014, http://america.aljazeera.com/articles/2014/6/12/politicians-jerusalemprayer.html..

239 Gil Hoffman, "Pro-Israel congressional caucus to meet Knesset Christian Allies Caucus," Jerusalem Post, Feb. 19, 2014, http://www.jpost.com/Diplomacy-and-Politics/Pro-Israel-congressional-caucus-to-meet-Knesset-Christian-Allies-Caucus-341864. In addition to the visit to the Compound, the Israel Allies Foundation delegation agenda reportedly includes meetings with representatives of Ariel University in the West Bank settlement of Ariel. Id.

240 Jake Wallis Simons, "The rabbi, the lost ark and the future of Temple Mount," The Independent, Sept. 12, 2013, http://www.telegraph.co.uk/news/worldnews/10287615/The-rabbi-the-lost-ark-and-the-future-of-Temple-Mount.html.

241 See, e.g., Jack Khoury et al., "Jordan Asks Israel for Clarifications Over Temple Mount Bill," Haaretz, Oct. 21, 2014, http://www.haaretz.com/news/diplomacy-defense/.premium-1.622031; Nir Hasson, "Israeli Right Increasingly Critical of Limited Jewish Access to Temple Mount," Haaretz, Oct. 14, 2014, http://www.haaretz.com/news/israel/.premium-1.620685. One of the bill's co-sponsors, Labor MK Hilik Bar, withdrew his support one week after the bill was introduced.

242 ICG, "The Status of the Status Quo," supra n. 209, at 20.

243 Dangerous Liaison, supra n. 234, at 28.

244 Dangerous Liaison, supra n. 234, at 28.

245 See generally Micah Goodman, "Three Paradoxes of Religious Zionism," Haaretz (Sept. 11, 2015), http://www.haaretz.com/israel-news/.premium-1.675538 (discussing the doctrinal differences and relationship between secular and religious Zionist movements).

246 Dangerous Liaison, supra n. 234, at 14-15 (in 2013, estimating a yearly average of 10,000-15,000 visits to the Compound by Jewish Israelis, including "serial" visitors.)

247 See Peter Beaumont, "Israel closes Al-Aqsa mosque compound to all visitors," The Guardian, Oct. 30, 2014, http://www.theguardian.com/world/2014/oct/30/israel-closure-al-aqsa-mosque-temple-mount-mahmoud-abbas-war.

[248] Dangerous Liaison, supra n. 234, at 33.

[249] Dangerous Liaison, supra n. 234, at 11.

[250] Dangerous Liaison, supra n. 234, at 70, and sources cited therein.

[251] Video available at http://www.kikar.co.il/%D7%94%D7%A8-%D7%94%D7%91%D7%99%D7%AA-4.html.

[252] Dangerous Liaison, supra n. 234, at 70, and sources cited therein.

[253] For a list of notable past attempts by Jewish extremists to destroy the Muslim Holy Places at the Compound and the relationship between their perpetrators and contemporary Temple movements, see Dangerous Liaison, supra n. 234, at 68.

[254] 16th Knesset, 160th session (July 28, 2004), cited in Dangerous Liaison, supra n. 234, at 29.

[255] Letter from Attorney-General Meir Shamgar (Nov. 24, 1971) (Hebrew), reproduced and quoted in translation in Dangerous Liaison, supra n. 234, at 53-54.

[256] Dangerous Liaison, supra n. 234, at 53-54. For a full list and overview of registered and unregistered Temple movements, see id. at 33-51.

[257] Dangerous Liaison, supra n. 234, at 58-59.

[258] See UN Human Rights Council, Report of the detailed findings of the independent commission of inquiry established pursuant to Human Rights Council resolution S-21/1, UN Doc. A/HRC/29/CRP.4 (June 24, 2015), para. 533 (noting UN finding that 14 of the 27 Palestinians killed in the West Bank between 12 June and 26 August 2014 "were incurred in clashes that erupted following protests against the hostilities in Gaza and restrictions on access to Al Aqsa Mosque").

[259] Institute for Middle East Understanding, "Discrimination and Hate Crimes Against Christian Palestinians in the Holy Land" (May 19, 2014), available at http://imeu.org/article/discrimination-hate-crimes-against-christian-palestinians-in-the-holy-land.

[260] ICCPR art. 18(1).

[261] ICCPR art. 2(1), 18(1), 27.

[262] Biblical Centre of the Chuvash Republic v. Russia, 2014 ECHR 606, para. 53.

[263] Biblical Centre of the Chuvash Republic, supra n. 262, para. 54.

[264] See, e.g. Jehovah's Witnesses of Moscow v. Russia, App No. 302/02 (Decision, June 10, 2010), para. 70.

[265] Jehovah's Witnesses of Moscow, supra n. 264, at para. 24.

[266] Jehovah's Witnesses of Moscow, supra n. 264, at para. 54; see also Association Rhino and others v. Switzerland, App. No. 48848/07 (Oct. 11, 2011) para. 62 (Swiss government's liquidation of squatters' community was a disproportionate response to the protection of landowners' rights and thus violated freedom of association under article 11 ECHR).

[267] Biblical Centre of the Chuvash Republic, supra n. 262, at para. 58.

[268] Krupko and Others v. Russia, App. No. 6587/07, 2014 ECHR 802 (dispersal by armed riot police of Jehovah's Witnesses religious meeting held without requisite permit was disproportionate to the aim of protecting public order).

[269] 2015 USCIRF Report.

[270] 2015 USCIRF Report; 2013 State Department Religious Freedom Report.

[271] 2015 USCIRF Report.

[272] 2015 USCIRF Report.

[273] Protection of Holy Places Law, 1967, supra n. 230, sec. 1.

[274] Protection of Holy Places Law, 1967, supra n. 230, sec. 2(a)-(b).

[275] 2009 State Department Religious Freedom Report.

[276] Adalah, "Supreme Court Rejects Adalah's Petition Demanding the Protection of Muslim Holy Sites in Israel Claiming that the Definition of Specific Sites as Muslim is a 'Sensitive Matter,'" (Mar. 16, 2009), http://www.adalah.org/en/content/view/7038.

[277] 2011 State Department Religious Freedom Report.

[278] "Israeli police demolish mosque," Al-Jazeera, Nov. 7, 2010, http://www.aljazeera.com/news/middleeast/2010/11/201011716263863880.html.

[279] 2011 State Department Religious Freedom Report.

[280] Id.; See also Ben White, "Be'er Sheva's Mosquerade," Al-Jazeera, Sep. 4, 2012, http://www.aljazeera.com/indepth/opinion/2012/09/20129475526951177.html; Nasser Rego, "Dispute over wine festival Be'er Sheva mosque: 'Muslim Rage' or Israeli hypocrisy?," +972 Magazine (Sept. 12, 2012), http://972mag.com/dispute-over-wine-festival-in-beer-sheva-mosque-muslim-rage-or-israeli-hypocrisy/56075/.

[281] GA Res. 194, supra n. 157, para. 8; GA Res. 181, part I(A), para. 3, UN Doc. A/RES/181(II) (Nov. 29, 1947) ("Independent Arab and Jewish States and the Special International Regime for the City of Jerusalem ... shall come into existence in Palestine two months after the evacuation of the armed forces of the mandatory Power has been completed but in any case not later than 1 October 1948.")

[282] ICCPR art. 18(1). The relevant language of article 18 UDHR is virtually identical: "to manifest [one's] religion or belief in teaching, practice, worship and observance." Universal Declaration of Human Rights, adopted by GA Res. 217, UN Doc. A/RES/3/217A (Dec. 10, 1948).

[283] HRC General Comment 22, art. 18 (1993), para. 4.

[284] See, e.g., Perry v. Latvia, App. No. 30273/03 (Decision, Nov. 8, 2007).

[285] ICCPR art. 18(3).

[286] HRC General Comment 22, art. 18 (1993), para. 8.

[287] See generally Council of Europe, Freedom of Thought, Conscience and Religion: A Guide to the Implementation of Article 9 of the European Convention on Human Rights (2007) 38-43 (reviewing ECtHR jurisprudence on article 9).

[288] In General Comment 23, the HRC distinguished the collective right of self-determination under article 1 ICCPR from the individual rights of minority under article 27. See HRC General Comment 23, art. 27 (1994), para. 3.1.

[289] HRC General Comment 23, para. 5.1-5.2.

[290] HRC General Comment 23, para. 6.1, 6.2, 9.

[291] HRC General Comment 23, para. 6.2, 8.

[292] Moscow Branch of the Salvation Army v. Russia, App. No. 72881/01, 2006 ECHR 828.

[293] Id.

[294] Cyprus v. Turkey, supra n. 47, paras. 47, 241-47.

[295] Perry v. Latvia, supra n. 284.

[296] USCIRF, "Russia: Concern about growing influence of undemocratic forces." (May 30, 2003), http://www.uscirf.gov/advising-government/government-correspondence/russia-concern-about-growing-influence-undemocratic.

[297] 2015 USCIRF Report.

[298] 2015 USCIRF Report.

[299] Entry Into Israel Law, 1952, 6 LSI 159 (1951-52), sec. 2-3.

[300] See Israel Consulate General to the Midwest, Chicago, "Visa Applications," http://embassies.gov.il/chicago/ConsularServices/Pages/Visa-Applications.aspx.

[301] 2003 State Department Religious Freedom Report.

[302] 2013 State Department Religious Freedom Report.

303 At an August 2010 meeting hosted by the Greek Orthodox Patriarchate, officials from the Ministry of Interior and Ministry of Religious Affairs told the heads of the main Christian communities that Israel no longer conducted security investigations on A/3 visa applicants, including those from Arab states. See "Meeting concerning visas for the religious people [sic]," Latin Patriarchate of Jerusalem, Aug. 10, 2010, http://en.lpj.org/2010/08/10/reunion-concernant-les-visas-pour-les-religieux/.

304 2013 State Department Religious Freedom Report.

305 Fundamental Agreement Between the Holy See and the State of Israel (Dec. 30, 1993), 33 ILM 153 (1994) [hereinafter "Fundamental Agreement"].

306 See generally Marshall J. Breger, The Fundamental Agreement Between the Holy See and the State of Israel: A Symposium, 47 Cath. U. L. Rev. 369 (1998).

307 Fundamental Agreement, supra n. 305, art. 3(2).

308 Fundamental Agreement, supra n. 305, art. 4(4), 6, 9.

309 Report of the Ad Hoc Committee charged with examining the problem of Catholic religious personnel whose visas have been requested from the Ministry of the Interior of Israel but have not yet been granted, (March 22, 2003), http://hcef.org/1063-denial-of-freedom-of-religion-as-guaranteed-by-the-fundamental-agreement-between-the-holy-see-and-th/.

310. See "Archbishop rebukes Israel over visas for clergy," Ekklesia, http://www.ekklesia.co.uk/content/news_syndication/article_04044visas.shtml.

311 UN Human Rights Committee, CCPR General Comment No. 22: Article 18 (Freedom of Thought, Conscience or Religion), UN Doc. CCPR/C/21/Rev.1/Add.4 (July 30, 1993) [hereinafter "HRC General Comment No. 22"], para. 4.

312 1981 UN Declaration, supra n. 37, art 6(b), (e), (g), (i).

313 ICCPR art 18(3).

314 ICCPR art 4(1), (2).

315 Legal Consequences of the Construction of a Wall, supra n. 16, para. 105-106.

316 Legality of the Threat or Use of Nuclear Weapons, Advisory Opinion (July 8, 1996), 1996 ICJ Rep. 66, para. 25; see also UN Human Rights Committee, CCPR General Comment No. 29: Article 4: Derogations during a State of Emergency, UN Doc. CCPR/C/21/Rev.1/Add.11 (Aug. 31, 2001), para. 4.

317 2013 USCIRF Annual Report.

318 USCIRF, "Prisoner of Belief: Individuals Jailed under Blasphemy Laws" (March 2014), 2.

319 Applied Research Institute-Jerusalem (ARIJ), "The Strangulation of Beit Jala" (2006),
http://www.arij.org/files/admin/2006/2006%20The%20strangulation%20of%20 Beit%20Jala.pdf

320 Fundamental Agreement, supra n. 305, art. 3(2).

321 HCJ 5163/13 Beit Jala Municipality et al. v. Ministry of Defense et al. (Decision, Apr. 2, 2015), English translation at www.saintyves.org/uploads/files/Cremisan%20Final%20Ruling.pdf.

322 Letter of the Latin Patriarch of Jerusalem (Aug. 13, 2015), reproduced in Society of St. Yves, "The Last Nail in Bethlehem's Coffin: The Annexation Wall in Cremisan" (Aug. 2015),
http://www.saintyves.org/downloads/reports/20150902063619.pdf.

323 See Israel Consulate General to the Midwest, Chicago, "Visa Applications," supra n. 300 (noting that "a clergyman who goes to Israel for a visit and requires an entry visa will receive the regular B/2 visa.")

324 Entry into Israel Law, 1952, supra n. 299, sections 10-12 (permitting denial of entry and deportation on various grounds, including noncompliance with the terms of a visa previously issued).

325 The PA issues ID cards to residents of the West Bank and the Gaza Strip in accordance with the Interim Agreement on the West Bank and the Gaza Strip. (See Interim Agreement, supra n. __, annex III, article 10.) While the Interim Agreement provides for the Palestinian side to maintain the population registry with regard to existing residents, in practice, the Israeli version of the population registry remains authoritative (see discussion at section __, supra) and determines eligibility for a PA-issued ID card. Most Syrians living in the Israeli-occupied Golan Heights, like Palestinian residents of East Jerusalem, have Israeli permanent residency pursuant to the Golan Heights Law, 1981. See Abdel Monem Said Aly, Shai Feldman, Khalil Shikaki, Arabs and Israelis: Conflict and Peacemaking in the Middle East (2013) 206.

326 UN Human Rights Council, Report of the Special Rapporteur on Freedom of Religion or Belief, Asma Jahangir, UN Doc. A/HRC/10/8 (January 12, 2009) [hereinafter A/HRC/10/8"], ¶ 22.

327 2012 State Department Human Rights Report.

328 Sinan Işik v. Turkey, App No 21924/05 (Decision, Feb. 2, 2010), para. 41; see also Press Release, Sinan Isik v. Turkey: Indication of Religion on Identity Cards was in Breach of Convention, Feb. 2, 2010, http://hudoc.echr.coe.int/eng-press?i=003-3013376-3325600.

329 Sinan Işik v. Turkey, supra n. 328, at para. 49-51.

330 Sinan Işik v. Turkey, supra n. 328, at para. 49.

331 Sinan Işik v. Turkey, supra n. 328, at para. 51.

332 Sinan Işik v. Turkey, supra n. 328, at para. 51.

333 Sinan Işik v. Turkey, supra n. 328, at paras. 40, 43 (noting the "frequent use" of ID cards for "school registration, identity checks, military service," etc.).

334 Sinan Işik v. Turkey, supra n. 328, at para. 51.at para. 50.

335 Report of the Special Rapporteur on Religious Freedom, supra n. 326, ¶ 42.

336 Report of the Special Rapporteur on Religious Freedom, supra n. 326, ¶ 42.

337 2013 USCIRF Report (noting that some Baha'i can decline to indicate their religion on their ID cards).

338 2014 USCIRF Report.

339 See generally Lina Kassim, The Construction of Druze Ethnicity: Druze in Israel Between State Policy and Palestinian Arab Nationalism (2005).

340 See "An Interior Minister in Contempt," Haaretz (July 3, 2002) http://www.haaretz.com/print-edition/opinion/an-interior-minister-in-contempt-1.51067.

341 See Kobi Nahshoni, "Yishai reinstates nationality in ID cards," Ynet (June 21, 2011) http://www.ynetnews.com/articles/0,7340,L-4084936,00.html.

342 English language sources are unclear as to when Jewish Israelis were given the right to change the format of their birth dates from the Hebrew to the Gregorian calendar. While the State Department's religious freedom reports state that the Knesset passed legislation in 2007 which made this legally possible, the 2013 Freedom House Report on Israel 2013 states that this right was recognized by judicial decision in 2011.

343 Freedom House, Freedom in the World: Israel (2015), www.freedomhouse.org/report/freedom-world/2015/israel.

344 UN Human Rights Council, Report of the Special Rapporteur on Freedom of Religion or Belief, Asma Jahangir – Addendum - Mission to Israel and the Occupied Palestinian Territory, UN Doc. A/HRC/10/8/Add.2 (January 12, 2009), [hereinafter "A/HRC/10/8/Add.2"], ¶¶ 40-43.

345 Cooperative Societies Ordinance (Amendment) (No. 8), 2011 ("Admissions Committee Law"), English translation at http://www.adalah.org/uploads/oldfiles/Public/files/Discriminatory-Laws-Database/English/12-Admissions-Committees-Law-2011.pdf.

[346] See Adalah, "Israeli Supreme Court upholds 'Admissions Committees Law' that allows Israeli Jewish communities to exclude Palestinian Arab citizens," (Sept. 17, 2014) http://www.adalah.org/en/content/view/8327 (reporting a chilling effect on the number of minority applicants to join these communities, thereby exacerbating divisions along religious and ethnic lines within Israeli society).

[347] Id. See also Bethan Staton, "Apartheid Housing: Israeli Court Upholds 'Discriminatory' Laws," Global Research Centre, Sept. 26, 2014, http://www.globalresearch.ca/apartheid-housing-israeli-court-upholds-discriminatory-laws/5404611 (noting that the communities to which the Admissions Committee Law applies are heavily concentrated in the Galilee and the Naqab (Negev), areas with the high concentrations of Palestinian citizens of Israel).

[348] See Adalah, "Adalah and ACRI call to cancel discriminatory land swap agreement between Israeli government and the JNF," Jan. 7, 2016, http://www.adalah.org/en/content/view/8724; HCJ 2504/11, *Adalah v. The Knesset* (upholding Admissions Committee Law); CA 3094/11, *Ibrahim Farhood Abu al-Qi'an, et al. v. State of Israel* (Decision, May 5, 2015) (dismissing petition by residents of Umm al-Hiran against their removal and the demolition of their community); Civil Further Hearing No. 3959/15, *Ibrahim Farhood Abu al-Qi'an, et al. v. State of Israel* (Decision, Jan 17, 2016) (denying Umm al-Hiran residents' motion for reconsideration).

[349] Human Rights Watch, "Israel: Grant Status Long Denied to Arab Village in Central Israel: Discriminatory Planning Procedures Prevent Access to Basic Services; Court to Rule on Demolition Orders," Oct. 8, 2010, http://www.hrw.org/news/2010/10/08/israel-grant-status-long-denied-arab-village-central-israel.

[350] See Sergio DellaPergola, John F. May, and Allyson C. Lynch, "Israel's Demography Has a Unique History" (2014), http://www.prb.org/Publications/Articles/2014/israel-demography.aspx; see also Pew Research Center, "The Future of the Global Muslim Population," pp. 19, 95 (2011), http://www.pewforum.org/files/2011/01/FutureGlobalMuslimPopulation-WebPDF-Feb10.pdf_(stating that Muslim population of Israel (comprised almost entirety of Palestinians) has doubled in past 20 years).

[351] Adalah, "Deliberate Obstacles, Not Failures: Adalah's response to the State Comptroller's Report on the subject of the housing crisis in Israel," April 2015, http://www.adalah.org/uploads/Response-to-Comptroller-Housing-Report-27-Apr-2015.pdf (describing the tenets of a state policy which creates administrative obstacles for Arab municipalities and for minorities seeking housing, resulting in an acute housing crisis facing Arab Palestinian citizens).

[352] Committee on Economic, Social and Cultural Rights, Concluding Observations: Israel, 2011, supra n. 135, ¶ 25 (noting the lack of availability of affordable housing

and lack of regulation of the private rental market), and ¶¶ 26-27, 37 (criticizing ongoing and planned home demolitions in Jerusalem, Bedouin towns in the Naqab (Negev), and the West Bank, and urging Israel to provide recognition and adequate services to unrecognized towns in the Naqab).

[353] Committee on Economic, Social and Cultural Rights, Concluding Observations: Israel, 2011, supra n. 135, ¶¶ 30-31.

[354] See generally Zama Coursen-Neff, Discrimination Against Palestinian Arab Children in the Israeli Educational System, 36 NYU J. Int'l L. & Pol. 749 (2004) (detailing institutionalized discriminatory practices against Palestinian Arab students in Israel's education system, in violation of its international legal obligations) ("Although the Israeli government has previously acknowledged that Arab schools generally receive less funding than Jewish schools, it does not officially release data on how much it spends total per Palestinian Arab child compared to how much it spends per Jewish child. There are no separate lines in the budget for Arab education, and the Ministry of Education takes the position that it is not possible to determine the amount spent on Arab education.")

[355] Committee on Economic, Social and Cultural Rights, Concluding Observations: Israel, 2011, supra n. 135, ¶ 33 (noting the serious shortage of classrooms available to Arab Palestinian children, and calling on Israel to (i) ensure that children in East Jerusalem can access adequate education; and (ii) take measures to reduce the dropout rate for Arab Palestinian children, including Bedouin). See also Mossawa Center, "Position Paper: The Israeli State Budget and the Government Decision for Economic Development in the Arab Community for the Years 2016-2020," (Feb. 2, 2016), http://www.mossawa.org/uploads/Position%20Paper%20Budget%202016-2020.pdf (noting that while the five-year development plan for the Arab sector, approved by the Israeli government on Dec. 30, 2015, allocates a reported NIS 10-15 billion to close gaps between Jewish and Arab Palestinian citizens in the areas of education, public services, health, culture, and housing, "the education funding in the government decision only addressed extra curricular activates to fight violence among youth.")

[356] Committee on Economic, Social and Cultural Rights, Concluding Observations: Israel, 2011, supra n. 135, ¶¶ 9, 14.

[357] Human Rights Watch, "Israel: Grant Status Long Denied to Arab Village in Central Israel" (Oct. 2010), http://www.hrw.org/news/2010/10/08/israel-grant-status-long-denied-arab-village-central-israel.

[358] Rami Younes, "High Court to rule over fate of unrecognized Palestinian village," +972 Magazine (Mar. 13, 2015), http://972mag.com/high-court-to-rule-over-fate-of-unrecognized-palestinian-village/104194/.

[359] 2013 State Department Religious Freedom Report.

[360] A/HRC/10/8/Add.2, supra n. 344.

[361] A/HRC/10/8/Add.2, supra n. 344, §46.

[362] HRC General Comment No. 22, supra n. 311, para. 2.

[363] CCPR/C/21/Rev.1/Add.4, p.2, §5.

[364] ICCPR art. 18.

[365] ICCPR art. 23.

[366] ICCPR art. 23, Reservation by State of Israel ("'With reference to Article 23 of the Covenant, and any other provision thereof to which the present reservation may be relevant, matters of personal status are governed in Israel by the religious law of the parties concerned. To the extent that such law is inconsistent with its obligations under the Covenant, Israel reserves the right to apply that law.")

[367] UN Human Rights Committee, CCPR General Comment No. 24: Issues Relating to Reservations Made upon Ratification or Accession to the Covenant or the Optional Protocols thereto, or in Relation to Declarations under Article 41 of the Covenant, UN Doc. CCPR/C/21/Rev.1/Add.6 (Nov. 4, 1994) [hereinafter "General Comment 24 on Reservations and Declarations"], §6(3).

[368] General Comment 24 on Reservations and Declarations, supra n. __, §§7-8.

[369] General Comment 24 on Reservations and Declarations, supra n. __, §8.

[370] General Comment 24 on Reservations and Declarations, supra n. __, §9.

[371] General Comment 24 on Reservations and Declarations, supra n. __, §9.

[372] UN Human Rights Committee, CCPR General Comment No. 28: Article 3 (The Equality of Rights Between Men and Women), UN Doc. CCPR/C/21/Rev.1/Add.10 (Mar. 29, 2000), §5.

[373] General Comment 24 on Reservations and Declarations, supra n. __; see also Elena A. Baylis, General Comment 24: Confronting the Problem of Reservations to Human Rights Treaties, 17 Berkeley J. Int'l L. 311 (1999).

[374] UN Human Rights Committee, Concluding Observations: Israel, 2014, supra n. __, para. 5(c).

[375] Convention on the Elimination of All Forms of Discrimination Against Women, Dec. 18, 1979, 1249 UNTS 13 [hereinafter "CEDAW"] art. 2(a), (2)f.

[376] CEDAW art. 5.

[377] CEDAW art. 7(a)-(c).

[378] CEDAW art. 7(a).

379 CEDAW art. 7(f) (under halakha, the wife's property acquired prior to the marriage is managed by her husband during the marriage).

380 CEDAW art. 16, Reservation by the State of Israel, para. 2 ("The State of Israel hereby expresses its reservation with regard to article 16 of the Convention, to the extent that the laws on personal status which are binding on the various religious communities in Israel do not conform with the provisions of that article.")

381 UN Committee on the Elimination of Discrimination Against Women (CEDAW), Concluding observations: Israel, UN Doc. CEDAW/C/ISR/CO/5 (Dec. 16, 2011), §9, §10, §11, p.3 and §49, p.12.

382 CEDAW/C/ISR/CO/5, supra n. 381, §8.

383 CEDAW/C/ISR/CO/5, supra n. 381, §49.

384 2014 USCIRF Report; 2013 USCIRF Report.

385 2014 USCIRF Report; 2013 USCIRF Report.

386 2014 USCIRF Report; 2013 USCIRF Report.

387 2015 USCIRF Report; 2014 USCIRF Report; 2013 USCIRF Report.

388 USCIRF, International Human Rights Standards: Selected Provisions on Freedom of Thought, Conscience, and Religion or Belief, http://www.uscirf.gov/reports-briefs/human-rights-documents/international-human-rights-standards-selected-provisions.

389 2015 USCIRF Report.

390 2015 USCIRF Report.

391 Cumhuriyetçi Eğitim Ve Kültür Merkezi Vakfi v. Turkey, ECtHR App No. 32093/10 (Decision, Dec. 2, 2014).

392 USCIRF, International Human Rights Standards, supra n. 388.

393 USCIRF, International Human Rights Standards, supra n. 388 (emphasis added).

394 USCIRF, International Human Rights Standards, supra n. 388.

395 USCIRF, International Human Rights Standards, supra n. 388 (emphasis added).

396 2015 USCIRF Report.

397 2015 USCIRF Report..

398 USCIRF, "Burma: Religious Freedom and Related Human Rights Violations are Hindering Broader Reforms" (Nov. 2014) 9, http://www.uscirf.gov/sites/default/files/BurmaReport.ReligiousFreedomAndHumanRightsViolations.pdf.

[399] 2015 USCIRF Report.

[400] 2015 USCIRF Report.

[401] 2015 USCIRF Report.

[402] 2015 USCIRF Report.

[403] ICCPR art 18.

[404] Letter from Jewish Agency to Executive Committee of Agudat Yisrael, dated June 19, 1947 [hereinafter "Status Quo Agreement"], reprinted in Israel in the Middle East: Documents and Readings on Society, Politics, and Foreign Relations, Pre-1948 to the Present (2008) 57; see also Ruth Lichtenstein, "The History of the 'Status Quo' Agreement," Hamodia (Dec. 31, 2013), http://hamodia.com/2013/12/31/history-status-quo-agreement/.

[405] See Daphne Barak-Erez, Law and Religion Under the Status Quo Model: Between Past Compromises and Constant Changes, 30 Cardozo L. Rev. 2495, 2499 (2009).

[406] See, e.g., Moshe Avarick, "The True Source of Religious-Secular Tension in Israel: The Arrogance of Ben-Gurion (and now Naftali Bennett)," Algemeiner (Mar. 12, 2013), http://www.algemeiner.com/2013/03/12/the-true-source-of-religious-secular-tension-in-israel-the-arrogance-of-ben-gurion-and-now-naftali-bennett/; Stuart Schoffman, "Raw Deal," Tablet Magazine (Oct. 28, 2011), http://www.tabletmag.com/jewish-news-and-politics/81660/raw-deal; Rich Westhead, "Forget Hamas and Iran. This may be Israel's most pressing problem," Toronto Star (Dec. 1, 2012), http://www.thestar.com/news/world/2012/12/01/forget_hamas_and_iran_this_may_be_israels_most_pressing_problem.html.

[407] Ruth Levush, "Israeli Conscription Laws for Ultra-Orthodox Jews," Library of Congress (2014), http://blogs.loc.gov/law/2014/04/israeli-conscription-laws-for-ultra-orthodox-jews/, at 2, quoting Michael Corinaldi, Status, Family and Succession: Law Between State and Religion (2004) 235 (Hebrew).

[408] See generally Gal Levy, "Secularism, Religion and the Status Quo," in Religion and the State: A Comparative Sociology (2011) 95-122.

[409] Israel Democracy Institute, A Portrait of Israeli Jews: Beliefs, Observance, and Values of Israeli Jews, 2009 (2012) at 30, http://en.idi.org.il/media/1351622/GuttmanAviChaiReport2012_EngFinal.pdf; see also Jodi Rudoren, "The Fight Over Who Fights in Israel," New York Times (May 19, 2012), http://www.nytimes.com/2012/05/20/sunday-review/the-fight-over-who-fights-in-israel.html (estimating that Haredim comprise 9 percent of Israel's population).

[410] Tamar Hermann and Chanan Cohen, "Reform and Conservative Jews in Israel: A Profile and Attitudes" (June 30, 2013), http://en.idi.org.il/analysis/articles/the-reform-and-conservative-movements-in-israel-a-profile-and-attitudes/.

[411] Israel Democracy Institute, A Portrait of Israeli Jews, supra n. 409, at 17.

[412] Karaite Jews (Karaim) are authorized to register marriages of its members. The Supreme Court has upheld this right, reasoning that membership in the Karaite community is by birth while affiliation with Reform Judaism is by personal belief. See Shimon Shetreet, "The Model of State and Church Relations and Its Impact on the Protection of Freedom and Conscience and Religion," in Religion in the Public Sphere: A Comparative Analysis of German, Israeli, American and International Law (2007) 87, 149-150.

[413] Netanel Fisher, "A Jewish State? Controversial Conversions and the Dispute Over Israel's Jewish Character," 33 Contemporary Jewry 217, 220 (2013); Yüksel Sezgin, Human Rights under State Enforced Religious Family Laws in Israel, Egypt and India (2013) 80-83; Gideon Sapir and Daniel Statman, Minority Religions in Israel, 30 Journal of Law & Religion 65, 75-76 (2015); Margit Cohn, "Women, Religious Laws and Religious Courts in Israel – The Jewish Case," 107 Retfaerd (Scandinavian Journal of Social Sciences) 57, 62 (2004).

[414] Martin Eidelman, "A Portion of Animosity: The Politic of the Disestablishment of Religion in Israel" 5 Israel Studies 204, 210 (2000); Ruth Halperin-Kaddari, 'Women, Religion and Multiculturalism in Israel' 5 UCLA J. Int'l L. & Foreign Affairs 339, 348 (2000); 2013 State Department Religious Freedom Report.

[415] 2013 State Department Religious Freedom Report.

[416] HCJ 47/82 Movement for Reform Judaism Fund in Israel v. Minister of Religious Affairs, 43(2) PD 661 (denying Reform rabbis marriage licensing authority). See also Israel Religious Action Center, "Marriage in Israel," http://www.irac.org/IssuePapers.aspx.

[417] A/HRC/10/8/Add.2, supra n. 344.

[418] 2013 State Department Religious Freedom Report; Halperin-Kaddari, Women, Religion and Multiculturalism in Israel, supra n. 414, at 348.

[419] Maintenance here entails the alimony or spousal support to be paid to the wife or husband after a divorce or support in the form of chalitza (obligation of the brother in law of a wife come widow to pay alimony or maintenance), see Rabbinical Court Jurisdiction (Marriage and Divorce) Law, 1953, 7 Laws of the State of Israel 139 (1952/53), http://www.knesset.gov.il/review/data/eng/law/kns2_rabbiniccourts_eng.pdf.

[420] A/HRC/10/8/Add.2, supra n. 344, §§ 22, 44; 2013 State Department Religious Freedom Report.

[421] Yüksel Sezgin, The Israeli Millet System: Examining Legal Pluralism through Lenses of Nation-Building and Human Rights, 43 Israeli L. Rev. 631, 631-632 (2010); Gideon Sapir and Daniel Statman, Minority Religions in Israel, 30 Journal of Law and Religion 65, 75-76 (2015).

[422] A/HRC/10/8/Add.2, supra n. 344, § 22.

[423] 2013 State Department Religious Freedom Report. Under the Matters of Dissolution of Marriage (Jurisdiction in Special Cases) Law, 1969, as amended, family courts have jurisdiction to adjudicate divorces involving spouses belonging to different religious communities or belonging to a religious community not recognized in Israel.

[424] Sezgin, The Israeli Millet System, supra n. 421, at 631-632. Israel has recognized three additional religious communities: the Druze Community (1957), the Evangelical Episcopal Church (1970), and the Bahai Community (1971).

[425] Haim H. Cohn, "Religious Freedom and Religious Coercion in the State of Israel," in Israel Among the Nations: International and Comparative Law Perspectives on Israel's 50th Anniversary (1998) 93. Cohen notes: "curiously enough...[t]he Jews who did opt out were only the ultra-orthodox, for whom the rabbinical courts were not orthodox enough, or were infected by Zionism." See also Michael Weiss, "The Other Civil Union," Tablet Magazine (July 1, 2009), http://www.tabletmag.com/jewish-news-and-politics/8651/the-other-civil-union.

[426] Cohn, supra n. 425, at 93. See generally Netanel Fisher, 'A Jewish State? Controversial Conversions and the Dispute Over Israel's Jewish Character' 33 Contemporary Jewry 217, 220 (2013); Sezgin, Human Rights under State Enforced Religious Family Laws in Israel, Egypt and India, supra n. 421, at 80-83; Sapir and Statman, Minority Religions in Israel, supra n. 421, at 75-76 ; Margit Cohn, 'Women, Religious Laws and Religious Courts in Israel, supra n. 413, at 62; Sezgin, The Israeli Millet System, supra n. 424, at 631-632.

[427] Rabbinical Court Jurisdiction (Marriage and Divorce) Law, 1953, supra n. __; see also HCJ 47/82 Movement for Reform Judaism Fund in Israel v. Minister of Religious Affairs, 43(2) PD 661.

[428] Fisher, A Jewish State?, supra n. 426, at 220; see also A/HRC/10/8/Add.2, supra n. 344, §50: "Non-Orthodox Jewish institutions do not have official status and consequently their rabbis cannot officiate at marriages in Israel."

[429] Debra Nussbaum Cohen, "Diverse U.S. Jewish coalition seeks to Challenge Israel's Chief Rabbinate's monopoly", Haaretz, November 27, 2014, http://www.haaretz.com/jewish-world/.premium-1.628700.

[430] A/HRC/10/8/Add.2, supra n. 344, §§ 44-48.

[431] Levush, "Israel: Spousal Agreements for Couples Not Belonging to Any Religion--A Civil Marriage Option?" (2015) 3.

[432] On marriages between Karaites and Orthodox Jews, see Ariel Finguerman and Elana Shap, "Karaites Flourish in Israel," Jewish Telegraphic Agency, Sept. 4, 2003, http://www.jta.org/2003/09/14/life-religion/features/karaites-flourish-in-israel>; Gershom Schocken, "The Curse of Ezra," Haaretz, Dec. 22, 2010, http://www.haaretz.com/print-edition/features/the-curse-of-ezra-1.331931.

[433] Judy Maltz, "Why bother with non-Orthodox Conversion in Israel?" Haaretz, December 11, 2013, http://www.haaretz.com/jewish-world/the-israeli-reformation/1.561961.

[434] ICCPR art. 18(2); A/HRC/10/8/Add.2, supra n. 344, § 46.

[435] Levush, Spousal Agreements for Couples Not Belonging to Any Religion, supra n. 431, at 12, citing [Draft] Law on Spousal Agreements for Persons without a Religion, 2009, Government Bill No. 445, p. 748, http://www.knesset.gov.il/Laws/Data/BillGoverment/445/445.pdf (Hebrew) (explanatory notes to Knesset bill, which sets number at 300,000); A/HRC/10/8/Add.2, supra n. 344, § 45 (setting number at 250,000).

[436] A/HRC/10/8/Add.2, supra n. 344, § 46.

[437] Law on Spousal Agreements for Persons without a Religion, 2010, SH 5770 No. 2235 p. 428 (in Hebrew), English translation at https://www.knesset.gov.il/review/data/eng/law/kns18_CivilUnion_eng.pdf. While the Knesset's translation refers to the legislation as the "Civil Union Law for Citizens with no Religious Affiliation," insofar as the law expressly provides that it does not "harm the laws of marriage and divorce and the jurisdiction of the religious courts," it "clearly does not offer a civil marriage option for religious marriages in Israel." Levush, Spousal Agreements for Couples Not Belonging to Any Religion, supra n. 431, at 13.

[438]Law on Spousal Agreements for Persons without a Religion, supra n. 437, sec. 6-8 (creating "procedures for verification of nonaffiliation with any recognized religious community in Israel," wherein the registrar of the spousal agreements registry must make an announcement of the proposed spousal agreement registration to the public and all the recognized religious communities. A religious community may block the registration by objecting that one of the applicants belongs to the religious community within the jurisdiction of its religious courts.); see also Levush, Spousal Agreements for Couples Not Belonging to Any Religion, supra n. 431, at 12 (quoting MK Dov Khenin as saying, "the law is terrible; it harms the status quo and provides superior authorities to the religious courts. A legal creature is thereby created which harms human dignity and freedoms.").

[439] Levush, Spousal Agreements for Couples Not Belonging to Any Religion, supra n. 431, at 12.

[440] CEDAW/C/ISR/CO/5, p.12 §48 & §49; Cohn, 'Women, Religious Laws and Religious Courts in Israel, supra n. 413, at 57.

[441] CEDAW/C/ISR/CO/5, supra n. 381, §§48-49.

[442] CEDAW/C/ISR/CO/5, supra n. 381, §§48-49; Ruth Levush, "Israel: Wanted: Husbands Who Disappear Without Divorcing Their Wives," Library of Congress, May 14, 2013,
http://www.loc.gov/lawweb/servlet/lloc_news?disp3_l205403521_text.

[443] Ruth Levush, Wanted: Husbands Who Disappear, supra n. 442; Shahar Lifshitz, "Who is Responsible for Finding a Solution to the Plight of Mesoravot Get?," Israel Democracy Institute, March 16, 2014,
http://en.idi.org.il/analysis/articles/who-is-responsible-for-finding-a-solution-to-the-plight-of-mesoravot-get/.

[444] Lifshitz, Plight of Mesoravot Get, supra n. 443.

[445] CEDAW/C/ISR/CO/5, supra n. 381, §§48-49.

[446] Cohn, Women, Religious Laws and Religious Courts in Israel, supra n. __, at 66-67.

[447] Cohn, Women, Religious Laws and Religious Courts in Israel, supra n. __, at 66-67.

[448] Israel Ministry of Foreign Affairs, "Consular Services,"
http://mfa.gov.il/MFA/ConsularServices/Pages/Ministry_Interior.aspx.

[449] Rabbinical Court Jurisdiction (Marriage and Divorce) Law, 1953, supra n. __.

[450] Ruth Levush, Wanted: Husbands Who Disappear, supra n. 442; Human Rights Watch, World Report 2015, http://www.hrw.org/world-report/2015/country-chapters/israel-and-palestine?page=3.

[451] Shachar Lifshitz, The External Rights of Cohabitating Couples in Israel, 37 Israel L. Rev. 346 (2004).

[452] See Menashe Shava, The Property Rights of Spouses Cohabiting Without Marriage in Israel - A Comparative Commentary, 13 Georgia J. Int'l. & Comp. L 465, 468 (1983) ("Israel has witnessed, since the State's establishment, the legislature's increasing recognition of the institution of the reputed spouse, with particular reference to the extension of various social rights and benefits.")

[453] Lifshitz, supra n. 443, at 417; see also Zvi Triger, "Freedom from Religion in Israel: Civil Marriages and Cohabitation of Jews Enter the Rabbinical Courts," Israel Studies Review, Volume 27, Issue 2, Winter 2012: 1–17.

[454] Triger, Freedom from Religion in Israel, supra n. 453, at 13.

[455] Lifshitz, supra n. 443, at 417.

[456] Lifshitz, supra n. 443, at 417.

[457] Lifshitz, supra n. 443, at 418.

[458] New Family, "Domestic Union Cards," http://www.newfamily.org.il/en/.

[459] Women in Israel are exempted from mandatory military service if they are married, pregnant, have children or are religiously observant or from a religious background. See Ministry of Aliyah and Immigrant Absorption, "Military Service" (2014) 12, http://www.moia.gov.il/Publications/idf_en.pdf.

[460] New Family, "Common-Law Marriages," http://www.newfamily.org.il/en/common-law-marriage/.

[461] Cohen, Diverse U.S. Jewish Coalition Seeks to Challenge Israeli Chief Rabbinate's Monopoly, supra n. 429; Martin Edelman, "A Portion of Animosity: The Politics of the Disestablishment of Religion in Israel," 5 Israel Studies 204-227 (2000).

[462]See, e.g., Rabbi Julie Schonfeld, "Ma Nishtana? Why is this night a night to think about religious pluralism in Israel?" Jewish Religious Equality Coalition (2015), http://www.ajc.org/atf/cf/%7Bf56f4495-cf69-45cb-a2d7-f8eca17198ee%7D/J-REC-PESACH-MESSAGING-V2.PDF.

[463] A/HRC/10/8/Add.2, supra n. 344, §51: "In 1995, [the Israeli Supreme Court] decided that the Ministry of Interior had no authority to refuse to recognize non-Orthodox conversions to Judaism performed inside Israel for purposes of recognition under the Law of Return. In another decision of 2005, it held that non-Jews living legally in Israel would be able to convert to Judaism by Reform and Conservative religious courts abroad and that State authorities would register their conversion."

[464] 2013 State Department Religious Freedom Report; A/HRC/10/8/Add.2, supra n. 344, §51.

[465] Yair Sheleg, "Conversion – Implications for Jewish Culture and Peoplehood," Israel Democracy Institute, 10 August 2009, http://en.idi.org.il/analysis/articles/conversion-%E2%80%93-implications-for-jewish-culture-and-peoplehood/; Eli Ashkenazy, "Shortage of non-religious cemeteries burdens families," Haaretz, July 18, 2008, http://www.haaretz.com/print-edition/news/shortage-of-non-religious-cemeteries-burdens-families-1.249975; Edelman, A Portion of Animosity, supra n. 461, at 218.

[466] Fisher, A Jewish State?, supra n. 426, at 233; Sheleg, Conversions: Implications for Jewish Culture and Peoplehood, supra n. 465.

[467] HCJ 1031/93 Pessaro (Goldstein) et al. v. Minister of the Interior [1995] IsrSC 49(4) 661; Edelman, A Portion of Animosity, supra n. 461; Yedidia Z. Stern, "Conversion in Israel: From Bethlehem to Chelm to Sodom," Israel Democracy Institute (2013), http://en.idi.org.il/analysis/articles/conversion-in-israel-from-.

468 Center for Women's Justice, "Supreme Court Rebukes Rabbinic Court Revocation of Druckman Conversions," April 22, 2012, http://www.cwj.org.il/en/news/supreme-court-rebukes-rabbinic-court-revocation-druckman-conversions; Yair Ettinger, "Israel's High Court affirms that thousands of Jewish conversions are kosher," Haaretz, April 27, 2012, http://www.haaretz.com/news/israel/israel-s-high-court-affirms-that-thousands-of-jewish-conversions-are-kosher-1.426770; Nathan Jeffay, "Rabbinical Court Puts Thousands of Converts in Legal Limbo," Forward, May 8 2008, http://forward.com/news/13347/rabbinical-court-puts-thousands-of-converts-in-leg-01823/.

469 Maltz, Why bother with non-Orthodox Conversion in Israel? supra n. __.

470 Isabel Kershner, "Israeli Cabinet Rejects Measure to Ease Jewish Conversions," New York Times, July 5, 2015, www.nytimes.com/2015/07/06/world/middleeast/israeli-cabinet-rejects-measure-to-ease-conversions.html.

471 Kershner, Israeli Cabinet Rejects Measure to Ease Jewish Conversions, supra n. 470.

472 A/HRC/10/8/Add.2, supra n. 344, §50; Laurence Wolff, "The Reform Movement in Israel: Past, Present, Future," Institute for Israel Studies, University of Maryland (2015) 1, http://www.israelstudies.umd.edu/Larry%20Wolff%20Research%20Paper%20-%20January%202015.pdf.

473 A/HRC/10/8/Add.2, supra n. 344, §50; Wolff, "The Reform Movement in Israel, supra n. 472.

474 Shmuel Rosner, "The Ultimate Conversion," New York Times (July 9, 2013), http://latitude.blogs.nytimes.com/2013/07/09/the-ultimate-conversion; John Daniszewski, "Burial Rules Compound Family's Tragedy," Los Angeles Times (Aug. 5, 1997) http://articles.latimes.com/1997/aug/05/news/mn-19613.

475 A/HRC/10/8/Add.2, supra n. 344, §50.

476 2013 State Department Religious Freedom Report; Yair Ettinger, "For first time, Israel to recognize Reform and Conservative rabbis," Haaretz, 29 May 2012, http://www.haaretz.com/jewish-world/jewish-world-news/for-first-time-israel-to-recognize-reform-and-conservative-rabbis-1.433171.

477 2013 State Department Religious Freedom Report.; Ettinger, "Israel to recognize Reform and Conservative rabbis," supra n. 476.

478 Wolff, The Reform Movement in Israel, supra n. 472, at 6-7; Judy Maltz, "Who's funding non-Orthodoxy in Israel? Not who you think...," Haaretz, Dec. 11, 2013, http://www.haaretz.com/jewish-world/the-israeli-reformation/1.561847.

[479] Universal Karaite Judaism, http://www.karaite.org.il/node/469.

[480] "Who's a Jew?," The Economist, May 18, 2013, http://www.economist.com/news/middle-east-and-africa/21578098-old-religious-argument-once-again-rears-its-angry-head-whos-jew.

[481] UN Human Rights Committee, Addendum to the Initial Report of States Parties Due in 1993, Israel, UN Doc. CCPR/C/81/Add. 13 (June 2, 2000), para. 532.

[482] The term "proselytism" is used consistently throughout this section in lieu of "proselytization." For a short history of the generally-pejorative use of the term "proselytism", see Lawrence Uzzell, "Don't Call It Proselytism," First Things, October 2004, http://www.firstthings.com/article/2004/10/dont-call-it-proselytism.

[483] Tad Stahnke, Proselytism and the Freedom to Change Religion in International Human Rights Law, BYU L. Rev. 251, 255 (1999). See also Tad Stahnke, "Proselytism," in Routledge Handbook of Law and Religion (2015) 395-414. Stahnke was the Commission's Deputy Executive Director for Policy from 2000 to 2007.

[484] IRFA sec. 3(13)(A)(iii)-(iv).

[485] UDHR art. 18(1) (using identical language but rearranging the words to read "teaching, practice, worship, and observance"); 1981 UN Declaration, supra n. 37, art. 1(1) (identical formulation to art. 18(1) ICCPR).

[486] UN Commission on Human Rights, Report of the Working Party on an International Convention on Human Rights, E/CN.4/56 (Dec. 11, 1947), art. 15(2), http://www.un.org/en/ga/search/view_doc.asp?symbol=E/CN.4/56; see also Stahnke, Proselytism and the Freedom to Change Religion, supra n. 483, at 275 n. 66.

[487] Stahnke, Proselytism and the Freedom to Change Religion, supra n. 483, at 275.

[488] American Convention on Human Rights, art. 12(1) (guaranteeing the right to "disseminate one's religion or beliefs").

[489] Moshe Hirsch, The Freedom of Proselytism Under the Fundamental Agreement and International Law, 47 Cath. U. L. Rev. 407, 417 (1998) ("In light of these international [human rights] agreements, it is clear that where proselytism is part of 'manifesting a religion with others,' proselytism is prima facie included with the freedom of religion.")

[490] Arcot Krishnaswami, Study of Discrimination in the Matter of Religious Rights and Practices, UN Doc. E/CN.4/Sub. 2/200/Rev. 1 (1960) 39, http://www1.umn.edu/humanrts/Krishnaswami_1959.pdf.

[491] HRC General Comment No. 22, supra n. 311, para. 2.

[492] ICCPR art. 18(3).

[493] HRC General Comment No. 22, supra n. 311, at para. 8.

[494] Interim report of the Special Rapporteur on freedom of religion or belief, Heiner Bielefeldt, UN Doc. A/67/303 (Aug. 13, 2012), para. 46.

[495] ICCPR art. 20(1)-(2); HRC General Comment No. 22, supra n. 311, para. 7.

[496] HRC General Comment No. 22, supra n. 311, at para. 7; see also UN Human Rights Committee, CCPR General Comment No. 11: Article 20 Prohibition of Propaganda for War and Inciting National, Racial or Religious Hatred (July 29, 1983).

[497] Stahnke, Proselytism and the Freedom to Change Religion, supra n. 483, at 287.

[498] ICCPR art. 18(1).

[499] HRC General Comment No. 22, supra n. 311, at para. 5.

[500] See Hirsch, Freedom of Proselytism Under the Fundamental Agreement, supra n. 489, at 411-413.

[501] UDHR art. 18; ECHR art. 9(2); American Convention, art. 12(1).

[502] See Stahnke, Proselytism and the Freedom to Change Religion, supra n. 483, at 284-285.

[503] Kokkinakis v. Greece, App. No. 14307/88 [1993] ECHR 20, para. 31.

[504] Report of Special Rapporteur on freedom of religion or belief, Heiner Bielefeldt, UN Doc. A/HRC/22/51 (Dec. 24, 2012), para. 66.

[505] HRC General Comment No. 22, supra n. 311, at para. 5.

[506] ICCPR art. 18(2). For a discussion of the tension between proselytism and privacy in the U.S. context, see Richard Garnett, Changing Minds: Proselytism, Freedom, and the First Amendment, 2 U. St. Thomas L. J. 453 (2005).

[507] Kokkinakis v. Greece, supra n. 503, para. 21.

[508] Kokkinakis v. Greece, supra n. 503, para. 21.

[509] Stahnke, Proselytism and the Freedom to Change Religion, supra n. 483, at 289.

[510] UN Commission on Human Rights, Report of the Special Rapporteur on the promotion and protection of the right to freedom of opinion and expression, Abid Hussain, UN Doc. E/CN.4/1995/32 (Dec. 14, 1994), para. 53 (emphasis added).

[511] Stahnke, Proselytism and the Freedom to Change Religion, supra n. 483, at 286.

[512] See Martin v. City of Struthers, 319 U.S. 141, 143 (1943); Lovell v. Griffin, 303 U.S. 444 (1938) (vacating conviction of Jehovah's Witness for failure to obtain a

permit for distributing literature, as required by a Georgia municipal ordinance, on the basis that the ordinance allowed the city manager to impose a prior restraint on protected religious speech); see generally Howard Hunter and Polly Price, Regulation of Religious Proselytism in the United States, 2001 BYU L. Rev. 537 (2001) (reviewing U.S. Supreme Court jurisprudence treating proselytism as protected speech).

513 See, e.g., Good News Club v. Milford School, 533 U.S. 98, 121 (2001) (Scalia, J., concurring) ("What is at play here is not coercion, but the compulsion of ideas - and the private right to exert and receive that compulsion … is protected by the Free Speech and Free Exercise Clauses….")

514 See Employment Div. v. Smith., 494 U.S. 872, 881 (1990) ("The only decisions in which we have held that the First Amendment bars application of a neutral, generally applicable law to religiously motivated action have involved not the Free Exercise Clause alone, but the Free Exercise Clause in conjunction with other constitutional protections, such as freedom of speech and of the press.").

515 Stahnke, Proselytism and the Freedom to Change Religion, supra n. 483, at 286.

516 HRC General Comment No. 22, supra n. 311, at para. 8 ("The Committee observes that paragraph 3 of article 18 is to be strictly interpreted: restrictions are not allowed on grounds not specified there, even if they would be allowed as restrictions to other rights protected in the Covenant, such as national security."); see also Stahnke, supra n. 483, at 279.

517 Wingrove v. United Kingdom, App. No. 17439/90, 24 Eur. H.R. Rep. 1 (1996), para. 30.

518 Wingrove v. United Kingdom, supra n. 517 (upholding application of British blasphemy law to block the distribution of an artist's video depiction of the ecstatic visions of Jesus Christ, where the law's coverage was not limited to the expression of views offensive only to Christians); Otto-Preminger-Institut v. Austria, App. No. 13470/87, 295 Eur. Ct. H.R. 1 (1994) (upholding, as necessary to preserve public order, the seizure of a film under an Austrian law making it an offense to disparage a person or object of "veneration," a dogma, a lawful custom, or a lawful institution of a church or religious community).

519 2014 USCIRF Report. All citations in this section are to the 2013-2015 USCIRF annual reports.

520 2013 USCIRF Report.

521 See 2013 USCIRF Report (noting deportation of Jehovah's Witness of Uzbek nationality who had been arrested and beaten while in detention).

522 2013 State Department Religious Freedom Report.

[523] Penal Law Amendment (Enticement to Change Religion), 1977, 32 LSI 62 (1977-1978).

[524] Ruth Lapidoth, Freedom of Religion and of Conscience in Israel, 47 Cath. U. L. Rev. 441, 461 (1998).

[525] Lapidoth, Freedom of Religion and of Conscience in Israel, supra n. 524, at 461; see also Walter Rodgers, "Proposed Israeli law would ban Christian missionaries," CNN (July 8, 1997), http://www.cnn.com/WORLD/9707/08/israel.missionaries/index.html?eref=site search.

[526] Lapidoth, Freedom of Religion and of Conscience in Israel, supra n. 524, at 459.

[527] Lapidoth, Freedom of Religion and of Conscience in Israel, supra n. 524, at 459-460; see also HCJ 1031/93 Goldstein v. Minister of Interior, 51(4) P.D. 661 (requirement of consent of new religious community relevant only to the jurisdiction of its religious tribunals).

[528] Penal Law, 1977, article 144A, English translation in Suzi Navot, Constitutional Law of Israel (2007) 240-242.

[529] See Crim. App. 2831/95 Elba v. State of Israel, 50(5) P.D. 221 (announcing this standard in upholding the conviction of Rabbi Ido Elba for publication of article entitled, "Clarification of the laws concerning the killing of a non-Jew," which argued that killing of Arabs was permitted and justified); see generally Raphael Cohen-Almagor, The Scope of Tolerance: Studies on the Costs of Free Expression and Freedom of the Press (2006) 144-146 (discussing Elba case and standard for incitement under Israeli law).

[530] 2011 State Department Religious Freedom Report.

[531] 2013 State Department Religious Freedom Report.

[532] 2013 State Department Religious Freedom Report; Lapidoth, Freedom of Religion and of Conscience in Israel, supra n. 524, at 462 (listing unrecognized religious communities).

[533] Yohai Hakak, "Battling against interfaith relations in Israel: religion, therapy and social services," 42 Journal of Marital and Family Therapy 45-57 (2015); Schocken, The Curse of Ezra, supra n. 432.

[534] Videos at: https://www.youtube.com/watch?v=JAkXBULjUCk ("Christmas"); https://www.youtube.com/watch?v=KfuUa_yNz9s ("Daddy"); https://www.youtube.com/watch?v=RwXpkYQZHlo ("Boyfriend")

[535] See Jeffrey Goldberg, "Netanyahu Government Suggests Israelis Avoid Marrying American Jews," The Atlantic (Nov. 30, 2011), http://www.theatlantic.com/international/archive/2011/11/netanyahu-government-suggests-israelis-avoid-marrying-american-jews/249166/.

536 Moria Ben Yosef, "Tel Aviv: City launches program to prevent relationships between Jewish girls and minorities," Maariv (Feb. 23, 2010) (Hebrew), http://www.nrg.co.il/online/54/ART2/066/580.html?hp=54&loc=4&tmp=7464, English translation at http://coteret.com/2010/02/24/tel-aviv-presents-municipal-program-to-prevent-arab-boys-from-dating-jewish-girls/.

537 Ben Yosef, "Tel Aviv: City launches program to prevent relationships between Jewish girls and minorities," supra n. 536.

538 Uri Blau and Shai Greenberg, "A Strange Kind of Mercy," Haaretz (May 27, 2011), http://www.haaretz.com/israel-news/a-strange-kind-of-mercy-1.364417.

539 Blau and Greenberg, "A Strange Kind of Mercy," supra n. 538.

540 HRC General Comment No. 22, supra n. 311, para. 7; accord ICERD art. 4; UN Committee on the Elimination of Racial Discrimination, General Recommendation XV on article 4 of the Convention (Mar. 17, 1993), para. 3-4.

541 2013 State Department Religious Freedom Report.

542 Messianic Jewish Alliance of America, "Messianic Judaism," http://www.mjaa.org/site/PageServer?pagename=rd_messianicmovement_messianic_judaism.

543 See Sarah Posner, "Kosher Jesus: Messianic Jews in the Holy Land," The Atlantic, Nov. 9, 2012, http://www.theatlantic.com/international/archive/2012/11/kosher-jesus-messianic-jews-in-the-holy land/265670.htm (estimating number at 10,000-20,000); Tim McGirk/Ariel, "Israel's Messianic Jews Under Attack," Time, June 6, 2008, http://content.time.com/time/world/article/0,8599,1812430,00.html (estimating number at 6,000-15,000).

544 Yuval Azoulay, "Suspected Jewish Terrorist Admits to Anti-Missionary Activities," Haaretz, 10 February 2010, http://www.haaretz.com/print-edition/news/suspected-jewish-terrorist-admits-to-anti-missionary-activities-1.263044.

545 Yad L'Achim, "Background," http://yadlachim.org/?CategoryID=188.

546 2011 State Department Religious Freedom Report; see also https://www.youtube.com/watch?v=zrSJLPfJkRU&feature=related (HOT TV segment regarding Jews for Jesus proselytism and Yad L'Achim anti-missionary work [Hebrew]).

547 See https://donate.yadlachim.org/ (noting tax-deductible donations); https://www.charitynavigator.org/index.cfm?bay=search.irs&ein=237126417 (Charity Navigator listing for Yad L'Achim Peyle Israel).

548 2011 State Department Religious Freedom Report.

[549] Ilan Lior, "Israeli Town Council Cancels Jehovah's Witnesses Event," Haaretz (Apr. 19, 2015), http://www.haaretz.com/news/israel/.premium-1.652440.

[550] Zafrir Rinat, "Court Lets Jehovah's Witnesses Hold Event in Israeli Town," Haaretz (May 1, 2015), http://www.haaretz.com/news/israel/.premium-1.654450

[551] Rinat, Court Lets Jehovah's Witnesses Hold Event in Israeli Town, supra n. 550.

[552] 2010 State Department Religious Freedom Report.

[553] 2010 State Department Religious Freedom Report.

[554] 2011 State Department Religious Freedom Report.

[555] 2013 State Department Religious Freedom Report.

[556] Posner, Kosher Jesus, supra n. 543; "Orthodox Jews Burn New Testaments in Or Yehuda," Haaretz, May 20, 2008, http://www.haaretz.com/news/orthodox-jewish-youths-burn-new-testaments-in-or-yehuda-1.246153.

[557] Seth Freedman, "Israel's vile anti-miscegenation squads," The Guardian (Sept. 29, 2009), http://www.theguardian.com/commentisfree/2009/sep/29/israel-jewish-arab-couples; Sheera Frenkel, "Israeli vigilantes target young Arab-Jewish couples," The Times of London (Sept. 28, 2009), http://www.timesonline.co.uk/tol/news/world/middle_east/article6851624.ece.

[558] See generally Vered Lee, "Love in the Time of Racism: The New, Dangerous Low in the Campaign to Stop Interracial Relationships," Haaretz, Apr. 25, 2013, http://www.haaretz.com/weekend/magazine/love-in-the-time-of-racism-the-new-dangerous-low-in-the-campaign-to-stop-interracial-relationships.premium-1.517545.

[559] Blau and Greenberg, "A Strange Kind of Mercy," supra n. 538.

[560] Gili Cohen, "No Grounds for Outlawing Racist Group, Concludes Israeli Security Agency," Haaretz (Aug. 4, 2015), http://www.haaretz.com/israel-news/.premium-1.669424. The State Department's 2014 IRF report notes Gopstein's arrest but fails to mention his release without charge three days later. See 2014 State Dept. IRF Report, http://www.state.gov/j/drl/rls/irf/2014/nea/238458.htm.

[561] Five suspects in the arson attack, all Jewish Israelis, were arrested in July 2015. Two of the suspects were indicted. See Mitch Ginsburg, "Two indicted for Church of Multiplication arson," Times of Israel (July 29, 2015) http://www.timesofisrael.com/two-indicted-for-church-of-multiplication-arson/. The Israeli Security Agency (Shin Bet) has identified Ettinger as the leader of the Revolt extremist group. See Isabel Kershner, "Israel Faces New Brand of Terrorism, This Time From Young Settlers," New York Times (Jan. 11, 2016), http://www.nytimes.com/2016/01/12/world/middleeast/revolt-network-foments-new-brand-of-jewish-terror-in-israel.html. Members of the Revolt have

also been indicted for the July 31, 2015 arson attack on a Palestinian home in the West Bank village of Duma that killed an 18-month-old infant and his parents and left another child badly injured. See Isabel Kerschner, "Israel Continues Crackdown on Jewish Extremist Network in West Bank," New York Times, Aug. 9, 2015, http://www.nytimes.com/2015/08/10/world/middleeast/israel-crackdown-revolt-jewish-extremist-network-duma-arson.html; "Two Israelis charged over West Bank arson attack," Al-Jazeera, Jan. 3, 2016, http://www.aljazeera.com/news/2016/01/israelis-charged-deadly-west-bank-arson-attack-160103090836011.html

562 Institute for Middle East Understanding, "Lehava: State-Sponsored Incitement" (Sept. 10, 2012) http://imeu.org/article/lehava-state-sponsored-incitement.

563Renee Ghert-Zand, "Will arrest of Lehava leader extinguish anti-assimilation activists' fervor?," Times of Israel (Dec. 16, 2014), http://www.timesofisrael.com/will-arrest-of-lehava-leader-extinguish-anti-assimilation-activists-fervor/.

564Michele Chabin, "Vatican: Jewish Extremist Poses Threat To Holy Land Christians," Huffington Post (Aug. 10, 2015), http://www.huffingtonpost.com/entry/vatican-benzi-gopstein_55c92903e4b0f1cbf1e61874.

565 Gili Cohen, "No Grounds for Outlawing Racist Group, Concludes Israeli Security Agency," Haaretz (Aug. 4, 2015), http://www.haaretz.com/israel-news/.premium-1.669424.

566 Neil Rubin, "In Christian version of AIPAC conference, CUFI draws 5,600 to Washington for pro-Israel lobbying," Jewish Telegraphic Agency (July 17, 2012), http://www.jta.org/2012/07/17/news-opinion/politics/in-christian-version-of-aipac-conference-cufi-draws-5600-to-washington-for-pro-israel-lobbying.

567 Brigham Young University, "A History of the Department of Continuing Education" at 270, http://intranet.ce.byu.edu/sites/intranet.ce.byu.edu/files/chapter16.pdf.

568 Blair Van Dyke, "The Mormon University on the Mount of Olives: A Case Study in LDS Public Relations," Journal of Media and Religion, Vol. 12, Issue 4 (2013).

569 Yair Rosenberg, "The Mormons on Mount Scopus," Tablet Magazine (May 15, 2015), http://www.tabletmag.com/jewish-life-and-religion/190863/byu-jerusalem-campus.

570 Van Dyke, "The Mormon University on the Mount of Olives," supra n. 568.

571 Brigham Young University, "A History of the Department of Continuing Education," supra n. 567, at 270.

572 BYU Jerusalem Center Non-Proselyting Agreement, available at
http://jerusalemcenter.ce.byu.edu/sites/jerusalemcenter.ce.byu.edu/files/non-proselytizingagreement.pdf.

573 Yair Rosenberg, "The Mormons on Mount Scopus," supra n. 569.

574 Jewish Telegraphic Agency, "No Legal Way to Halt Mormon School" (Aug. 12, 1986) http://www.jta.org/1986/08/12/archive/no-legal-way-to-halt-mormon-school.

575 Yair Rosenberg, "The Mormons on Mount Scopus," supra n. 569.

576 Sephardic Jews – understood in the sense of all non-Ashkenazi "eastern" or "oriental" Jews, rather than strictly those of Iberian origin – actually comprise a majority (an estimated 52-55 percent) of Israel's Jewish population. (See Centre for Israel and Jewish Affairs, "Demographics of Israel," http://www.cija.ca/resource/israel-the-basics/demographics-of-israel/.) However, Ashkenazi Jews comprise over 75 percent of the world's Jewish population, and Sephardic Jews comprise up to 20 percent. (See Georgetown University, Berkeley Center for Religion, Peace, and World Affairs, "Demographics of Judaism," http://berkleycenter.georgetown.edu/essays/demographics-of-judaism.) Sephardic Jews have suffered political, socioeconomic, and educational discrimination since the State's establishment and have struggled to maintain their cultural identity while challenging Ashkenazi dominance. (See generally Bryan K. Roby, The Mizrahi Era of Rebellion: Israel's Forgotten Civil Rights Struggle, 1948-1966 (2015); Ella Shohat, "Sephardim in Israel: Zionism from the Standpoint of Its Jewish Victims," Social Text (1988), pp. 1-35.)

577 Mizrahi is here used to connote Jews whose historic communities were in Arab- or Muslim-majority states.

578 As of 2011, 15 percent of Israelis (all members of the Jewish le'om) spoke Russian as a first language. (Israeli Central Bureau of Statistics, "Selected Data from the 2011 Social Survey on Mastery of the Hebrew Language and Usage of Languages" (Jan. 21, 2013), http://www1.cbs.gov.il/reader/newhodaot/hodaa_template.html?hodaa=2013190 17.) Israel's Ethiopian population was 125,500 (as of 2011), 65 percent of whom was born in Ethiopia and presumably speak Amharic as a first language. ((Israeli Central Bureau of Statistics, "The Ethiopian Community in Israel" (Nov. 12, 2012), http://www.cbs.gov.il/reader/newhodaot/hodaa_template_eng.html?hodaa=2012 11307.)

579 UN Human Rights Committee, CCPR General Comment No. 23: Article 27 (Rights of Minorities), UN Doc. CCPR/C/21/Rev.1/Add.5 (Apr. 8, 1994) [hereinafter "General Comment No. 23"], para. 6.1.

580 United Nations Declaration on the Rights of Indigenous Peoples, adopted by UNGA Res. 61/295, UN Doc. A/RES/61/295 (Sept. 13, 2007), articles 4, 5.

[581] General Comment No. 23, supra n. 579, para. 5.2.

[582] General Comment No. 23, supra n. 579, para. 6.2.

[583] General Comment No. 23, supra n. 579, para. 6.2.

[584] UN Human Rights Council, Report of the Independent Expert on minority issues, Rita Izsák, UN Doc. A/HRC/22/49 (Dec. 31, 2012), para. 79.

[585] UN Declaration on the Rights of Persons Belonging to National or Ethnic, Religious and Linguistic Minorities, adopted by UNGA Res. 47/135 (Dec. 18, 1992) [hereinafter "UN Declaration on Minorities"], article 4.3.

[586] Don Handelman, "Contradictions between Citizenship and Nationality: Their Consequences for Ethnicity and Inequality in Israel," 7(3) International Journal of Politics, Culture, and Society, 441, 444 (1994).

[587] CA 630/70 Tamarin v. State of Israel, 26(1) PD 197, reprinted at 2 Isr. Y.B. Human Rights 327 (1972).

[588] Tamarin, supra n. 587, 2 Isr. YB Human Rights at 328.

[589] CA 8573/08 Ornan v. State of Israel (Decision, Oct. 2, 2013), para. 3, partial translation at http://web.law.columbia.edu/sites/default/files/microsites/gender-sexuality/ornan_v_state_of_israel_summary.pdf/.

[590] Ornan, supra n. 589, para. 3.

[591] Ornan, supra n. 589, para. 19.

[592] Ornan, supra n. 589, para. 25.

[593] Ornan, supra n. 589, para. 25.

[594] Ornan, supra n. 589, concurring opinion of Meltzer, J., para. 1(c).

[595] Ornan, supra n. 589, concurring opinion of Meltzer, J., para. 7.

[596] Ornan, supra n. 589, concurring opinion of Meltzer, J., para. 12(a).

[597] See Francesco Capotorti, Study On The Rights Of Persons Belonging To Ethnic, Religious, And Linguistic Minorities, U.N. Doc. E/CN.4/Sub.2/384/Rev.1 (1991) at 15.

[598] Tamarin, supra n. 587, 2 Isr. YB Human Rights at 330.

[599] Jonathan Lis, "Arab MKs Blast Likud Bill, Say It Sets Country's Christians Against Muslims," Haaretz (Feb. 6, 2014), http://www.haaretz.com/news/israel/.premium-1.572713 (quoting Likud MK Yariv Levin, co-sponsor of the February 2014 Christian nationality bill, as saying that "Christians "are our natural allies, a counter-balance against the Muslims who want to destroy the state from within."")

[600] A/HRC/10/8/Add.2, supra n. 344, § 22.

[601] See generally Dugard & Reynolds, Apartheid, International Law, and the oPt, supra n. 34.

[602] Jonathan Lis, "Israel Recognizes Aramean Minority in Israel as Separate Nationality," Haaretz (Sept. 17, 2014), http://www.haaretz.com/news/israel/1.616299.

[603] Lori Lowenthal Marcus, "Israel Officially Recognizes Nationality of 'Aramean,'" Jewish Press (Sept. 17, 2014), http://www.jewishpress.com/news/breaking-news/israel-officially-recognizes-nationality-of-aramean/2014/09/17/.

[604] Tilde Romer, "Contesting Christian Identity in Israel: Arab, Aramean, Palestinian or Other?," New Middle East Blog (Oct. 21, 2014) https://newmeast.wordpress.com/2014/10/21/contesting-christian-identity-in-israel-arab-aramean-palestinian-or-other/.

[605] "Israeli Christians Officially Recognized as Arameans, Not Arabs," Israel Today (Sept. 18, 2014), http://www.israeltoday.co.il/NewsItem/tabid/178/nid/24936/Default.aspx.

[606] United Nations Office of the High Commissioner for Human Rights, "Minorities under international law: Who are minorities under international law?," http://www.ohchr.org/EN/Issues/Minorities/Pages/internationallaw.aspx.

[607] E/CN.4/Sub.2/384/Rev.1, supra n. 597, para. 568.

[608] Tamarin, supra n. 587, at 329.

[609] Tamarin, supra n. 587, at 331.

[610] Yaron Druckman, "CBS: 161,000 Christians live in Israel," Jerusalem Post (Dec. 24, 2013), http://www.ynetnews.com/articles/0,7340,L-4469209,00.html (citing Israeli Central Bureau of Statistics).

[611] Jacky Hugi, "Aramaic Language Project in Israel Furthers Maronite Minority," Al-Monitor (Mar. 15, 2013) (quoting Halul as saying, "I am a Maronite; the language of my ancestors is Aramaic … and I want to resurrect it. Rather than telling others to do it, I decided to revive the language in my own home.")

[612] Justice and Peace Commission of the Assembly of the Catholic Ordinaries of the Holy Land, Recognition of the "Arameans": an attempt to divide Palestinian Christians?, Latin Patriarchate of Jerusalem (Sept. 16, 2014), http://en.lpj.org/2014/09/19/recognition-of-the-arameans-an-attempt-to-divide-palestinian-christians/.

[613] Judi Maltz, "Israeli Christian Community, neither Arab nor Palestinian, are fighting to save identity," Haaretz (Sept. 3, 2014), http://www.haaretz.com/news/israel/.premium-1.613727.

614 Declaration on the Rights of Indigenous Peoples, supra n. 580, art. 8(1).

615 Declaration on the Rights of Indigenous Peoples, supra n. 580, art. 8(2)(a).

616 John Quigley, The Case For Palestine (2005) 131 et seq.; see also Michal Vexler, Visualizing Occupation: Divide and Conquer, +972 Magazine (Jul. 21, 2012) http://972mag.com/visualizing-occupation-divide-and-conquer/51479/.

617 See, e.g., Jonathan Cook, "Israel's Christians Need All The Support They Can Get" (May 25, 2014), http://www.jonathan-cook.net/2014-05-25/israels-christians-need-all-the-support-they-can-get/>; Jonathan Cook, "Israel: Divide-and-conquer in Nazareth?" Al-Jazeera (Jan. 17, 2014), http://www.aljazeera.com/indepth/features/2014/01/israel-divide-conquer-nazareth-201411273429333378.html; Sharif Nashshibi, "Divide and conquer: Israel seeks to split Palestinians," Al-Arabiya (May 19, 2014), http://english.alarabiya.net/en/views/news/middle-east/2014/05/19/Israel-seeks-to-create-Palestinian-religious-divisions.html.

618 Jonathan Cook, Christians Object to Serve in Israel's Army (Jun. 5, 2014), http://www.jonathan-cook.net/2014-06-05/christians-object-to-serving-in-israels-army/.

619 Ariel Ben Solomon, "Christian Knesset candidate: Arab parties do not represent me," Jerusalem Post (Jan. 2, 2015), http://www.jpost.com/Israel-Elections/Israeli-Arab-Christian-candidate-for-Yisrael-Beyetenu-Arab-parties-do-not-represent-me-389649.

620 Jonathan Lis, "Netanyahu Announces New Forum to Encourage Christian Arabs to Serve in Military," Haaretz (Aug. 6, 2013), http://www.haaretz.com/news/israel/.premium-1.539957.

621 Uri Perednik, "Fighting for the Right to Serve: Israeli Christians Brave Arab Opposition to Enlist," Mida Magazine (Mar. 12, 2014), http://mida.org.il/2014/03/12/fighting-for-the-right-to-serve-israeli-christians-brave-arab-opposition-to-enlist-in-the-idf/.

622 Israel Defense Forces, "IDF to Begin New Outreach Program with Christians Eligible for Draft" (Apr. 22, 2014), https://www.idfblog.com/blog/2014/04/22/idf-begin-new-outreach-program-christians-eligible-draft/.

623 Gili Cohen, "Israel to Send 'Voluntary Draft Notices' to Christian Arabs," Haaretz (Apr. 22, 2014), http://www.haaretz.com/news/diplomacy-defense/.premium-1.586678; Jonathan Cook, "Israel Wants Its Arab Christian – But Not Muslim – Citizens to Join Military," Global Research (Nov. 26, 2013), http://www.globalresearch.ca/israel-wants-its-arab-christian-but-not-muslim-citizens-to-join-military/5359511; Siham Nuseibeh, "Divide and Conquer:

Palestinian Christians for the IDF," Muftah (Apr. 23, 2014), http://muftah.org/divide-conquer-palestinian-christians-idf/.

[624] Ma'an News Agency, "Christian leaders tell youth to 'tear up' Israel army forms" (Apr. 25, 2014), http://www.maannews.com/Content.aspx?id=692816.

[625] Ariel Ben Solomon, "Arab sector turnout for recent elections reached 63.5%, polling data shows," Jerusalem Post (Mar. 24, 2015), http://www.jpost.com/Israel-Elections/Arab-sector-turnout-for-recent-elections-reached-635-percent-polling-data-shows-394878.

[626] Communist Party of Israel (MAKI), "The Political Platform of the 'Joint List': Our Answer to Racism" (Feb. 26, 2015), http://maki.org.il/en/?p=3827. The Joint List is a political alliance of four Arab-majority political parties: Hadash (Democratic Front for Peace and Equality, Communist Party of Israel), the Islamic Movement, Balad (National Democratic Assembly), and Ta'al (Arab Movement for Change). It was formed in response to March 2014 enactment of the Governance Law, which raised the electoral threshold from representation in the Knesset from 2.0% to 3.25%. The Joint List received 10.61% of the popular vote in the 2015 elections and took 13 seats, making it the third-largest party in the Knesset. (See Israeli Central Elections Committee, "Results of the 20th Knesset Elections," http://www.votes20.gov.il/ (Hebrew)).

[627] Adalah, "Arab citizen placed under five days house arrest for Facebook post against recruitment of Christian Arabs into the Israeli army" (May 2, 2014), http://www.adalah.org/en/content/view/8275; Edo Konrad, Palestinian activist given house arrest for a Facebook status, +972 Magazine (Apr. 29, 2014), http://972mag.com/palestinian-activist-given-house-arrest-for-a-facebook-status/90226/.

[628] Declaration on the Rights of Indigenous Peoples, supra n. 580, art. 19.

[629] National Coalition of Christian Organizations in Palestine, Attempts to mobilize Christians into the Israeli military – The case of Christian Arab citizens of Israel, http://d3n8a8pro7vhmx.cloudfront.net/globalministries/legacy_url/10239/NCCOP-Case-of-Christian-Arab-Citizens-of-Israel-Feb-2014.pdf?1419972682.

[630] Quoted in Ben White, "In the fight against apartheid, Christian Palestinians defy Israel's propaganda," Middle East Monitor (Dec. 20, 2014), https://www.middleeastmonitor.com/articles/debate/15914-in-the-fight-against-apartheid-christian-palestinians-defy-israels-propaganda.

[631] Latin Patriarchate of Jerusalem, "For peace in the Middle East listen to the voice of the Church" (Sept. 9, 2014), http://en.lpj.org/2014/09/09/for-peace-in-the-middle-east-listen-to-the-voice-of-the-church/.

[632] Address made at an academic conference held January 19-20, 2015 at the Hebrew University of Jerusalem regarding "New Trends of Research on Palestinian

Christian Identity in Israel," reported in Zenit, "Emeritus Patriarch of Jerusalem Considers Palestinian Christian Identity in Mideast" (Jan. 21, 2015), http://www.zenit.org/en/articles/emeritus-patriarch-of-jerusalem-considers-palestinian-christian-identity-in-mideast.

[633] General Comment No. 22, supra n. 311, para 11. For a complete overview of international legal standards and jurisprudence on conscientious objection, see UN Office of the High Commissioner for Human Rights, "Conscientious Objection to Military Service" (2012), http://www.ohchr.org/Documents/Publications/ConscientiousObjection_en.pdf.

[634] UN Human Rights Council Resolution 20/2, UN Doc. A/HRC/20/2 (July 5, 2012), http://www.ohchr.org/Documents/HRBodies/HRCouncil/RegularSession/Session20/A-HRC-20-2_en.pdf.

[635] UN Commission on Human Rights, Conscientious objection to military service, UN Doc. E/CN.4/RES/1998/77 (Apr. 22, 1998), http://www.refworld.org/docid/3b00f0be10.html.

[636] Bayatyan v Armenia, ECtHR App. No. 23459/03, 54 EHRR 15 (2012), para. 110; see also Petr Munzy, "Bayatan v. Armenia: The Grand Chamber Renders a Grand Judgment," 12 Human Rights Law Review 135-147 (2012).

[637] Bayatyan v Armenia, supra n. 636, para. 124.

[638] Savda v Turkey, ECtHR App. No. 42730/05 (Judgment, June 12, 2012), para. 107-111; see also Press Release: Savda v. Turkey http://hudoc.echr.coe.int/eng?i=003-3980699-4625431.

[639] UNGA Res. 33/165 (Dec. 20, 1978), para. 1. The resolution further calls upon member states to offer asylum or safe transit to conscientious objectors fleeing compulsory service in such circumstances.

[640] See n. 35, supra.

[641] 2015 USCIRF Report.

[642] 2015 USCIRF Report.

[643] USCIRF, "Did you know…South Korea," http://www.uscirf.gov/reports-briefs/spotlight/did-you-knowsouth-korea.

[644] Amnesty International, "Israel and the Occupied Territories: Druze Conscientious Objectors to Military Service" (Nov. 1991), at 7, https://www.amnesty.org/download/Documents/196000/mde150551991en.pdf.

[645] See Etta Bick, "Institutional layering, displacement, and policy change: The evolution of civic service in Israel," Public Policy & Administration (Jan. 14, 2016), at 6 ("with this patriotic republican regard for army service, Israel has never offered

an alternative track of civic service to conscientious objectors as did many countries in Europe.")

[646] Defense Service Law (Consolidated Version) 1986, 40 LSI 112 (1985-86), §§ 1, 13, 15, http://www.mfa.gov.il/mfa/mfa-archive/1980-1989/pages/defence%20service%20law%20-consolidated%20version--%205746-1.aspx.

[647] Defense Service Law, §5(c) (medical deferral/exemption), §39(a)-(c) (categories of exemptions for women).

[648] The Defense Minister has traditionally invoked this discretion to exempt Arab Palestinian and Haredi Jewish citizens from military service. See Shachar, Whose Republic?, supra n. 76, at 415 and n. 167.

[649] Defense Service Law, supra n. 646, § 36; see also HCJ 7622/02 Zonshein v. Judge-Advocate General, 57(1) P.D. 726, English translation at 36 Israel L. Rev. 1 (2002), para. 7 (recognizing that section 36 of the Law grants the defense minister discretion to exempt a male conscript who "objects to the framework of military service as a matter of principle.").

[650] Zonshein, supra n. 649, at para. 12; see also HCJ 1380/02 Ben Artzi v. Minister of Defense, IsrSC 56(4) 476.

[651] Defense Service Law, supra n. 646, § 39(c).

[652] HCJ 2383/04 Milo v. Minister of Defence [2004] IsrSC 59(1) 66. For a critical analysis of the Milo decision, see Amir Paz-Fuchs, Objectionable Work in Israel, 31 Comp. Lab. L. & Pol'y J. 471, 473 (2009).

[653] Barak Medina, Political Disobedience in the IDF: The Scope of the Legal Right of Soldiers to Be Excused from Taking Part in Military Activities in the Occupied Territories, 36 Israel L. Rev. 73, 78 (2002).

[654] See Medina, Political Disobedience, supra n. 653, at 76.

[655] See Medina, Political Disobedience, supra n. 653, at 78.

[656] HCJ 470/80 Algazi v. Minister of Defense (unpublished), quoted in Medina, Political Disobedience, supra n. 653, at 78 n. 20.

[657] Leora Bilsky, Uniforms and Veils: What Difference Does a Difference Make?, 30 Cardozo L. Rev. 2715, 2725 n. 20 (2009).

[658] Bradley Burston, "When Israelis Say, 'Hell No, We Won't Go,'" Haaretz (Feb. 4, 2004), http://www.haaretz.com/news/background-when-israelis-say-hell-no-we-won-t-go-1.113027.

659 Amnesty International, "Israel: Conscience Behind Bars" (Dec. 18, 2008), http://www.amnesty.ie/news/israel-conscience-behind-bars-youths-jailed-refusing-serve-army.

660 Concluding observations on the fourth periodic report of Israel, supra n. 133.

661 For a contemporary Druze narrative, see, e.g., Kais Firro, The Druzes in the Jewish State: A Brief History (1999); Jonathan Oppenheimer, "The Druze in Israel as Arabs and Non-Arabs: Manipulation of Categories of Identity in a Non-Civil State," in Studies in Israeli Ethnicity: After the Ingathering (Weingrod, ed., 1985) p. 264; see also Michael Dumper, "Book Review: The Druze in the Jewish State: A Brief History, by Kais M. Firro," in Shofar: An Interdisciplinary Journal of Jewish Studies, Vol. 20, No. 2 (2002) 138-140 ("Firro can be placed in the new revisionist school of Israeli historiography.") The "new revisionist school" is a reference to Israel's "New Historians," who, relying on newly-declassified government materials, challenge "official" Israeli history on matters including the British role in Israel's establishment, the events of the Palestinian Nakba and responsibility for the Palestinian refugee crisis, the acts and attitudes of Arab states towards the Zionist movement, and responsibility for the failure to achieve Middle East peace. For the traditional Israeli narrative of the Zionist's movement's natural partnership with the Druze of Mandatory Palestine, see, e.g., Gabriel Ben-Dor, The Druzes in Israel: A Political Study (1979).

662 Lisa Hajjar, "Israel's Interventions Among the Druze," in Middle East Report, Vol. 26 (2000), available at http://www.merip.org/mer/mer200/israels-interventions-among-druze.

663 Rhoda Kanaaneh, Surrounded: Palestinian Soldiers in the Israeli Military (2008) 10-11.

664 Kanaaneh, Surrounded, supra n. 663, at 11. Druze work in the security field in disproportionately high numbers, with over 30 percent of employed Druze working in the security services, particularly the Border Patrol and Prison Service. Hajjar, "Israel's Interventions Among the Druze," supra n. 662, at n. 10.

665 See 2013 State Department Religious Freedom Report; Jacob Landau, The Arabs in Israel: A Political Study (1969).

666 American Friends Service Committee, "The Druze Initiative Committee," https://afsc.org/resource/druze-initiative-committee.

667 In 2007, Nafaa led a group of nearly 300 Druze clerics on a 2007 trip to Syria, during which he met a representative of a Palestinian political party, Popular Front for the Liberation of Palestine-General Command (PLFP-GC), that is banned as a terrorist organization in Israel. He was stripped of his parliamentary immunity, tried, convicted, and sentenced to prison under an Israeli law that bans visits to enemy states. The Supreme Court affirmed his conviction and sentence in August 2015. CrimA 6833/14 Said Nafa v. State of Israel (Decision of Aug. 31, 2015); see

also Library of Congress, Law Library, "Israel: Conviction of Former Arab-Israeli Parliamentarian for Visiting Syria Upheld" (Sept. 11, 2015), http://www.loc.gov/lawweb/servlet/lloc_news?disp3_l205404599_text (summarizing Supreme Court's ruling); see also Elhanan Miller, "Headed to prison for Syria visit, ex-lawmaker vows to fight travel ban," Times of Israel (Sept. 30, 2015), http://www.timesofisrael.com/headed-to-prison-for-syria-visit-ex-lawmaker-vows-to-fight-travel-ban/.

[668] Swarthmore College, "Golan Druze resistance to Israeli forced citizenship, 1981-1982," Global Nonviolent Action Database (June 17, 2009), http://nvdatabase.swarthmore.edu/content/golan-druze-resistance-israeli-forced-citizenship-1981-1982.

[669] Hajjar, "Israel's Interventions Among the Druze," supra n. 662.

[670] Hajjar, "Israel's Interventions Among the Druze," supra n. 662; see also Hassan Abu Libdeh et al., A Survey of the Syrian Population in the Occupied Golan Heights: Demography and Health (1994) 51-53.

[671] Elhanon Miller, "From Israel's most loyal minority, draft objectors emerge," Times of Israel (May 15, 2014), http://www.timesofisrael.com/from-israels-most-loyal-minority-draft-objectors-emerge/ (citing IDF data showing Druze enlistment rate of 82 percent and national average of 75 percent).

[672] Creede Newton, "Palestinian-Israeli conscientious objector awarded scholarship for refusal," Middle East Eye, Sept. 22, 2014, http://www.middleeasteye.net/in-depth/features/palestinian-israeli-conscientious-objector-awarded-scholarship-refusal-99993376.

[673] Amnesty International, Druze Conscientious Objectors, supra n. 644, at 2.

[674] Miller, "From Israel's most loyal minority, draft objectors emerge," supra n. 671.

[675] Amnesty International, Druze Conscientious Objectors, supra n. 644, at 2-6.

[676] Amnesty International, "Annual Report: Israel and the Occupied Palestinian Territories 2015/2016," https://www.amnesty.org/en/countries/middle-east-and-north-africa/israel-and-occupied-palestinian-territories/report-israel-and-occupied-palestinian-territories/.

[677] Report of the Special Rapporteur on the situation of human rights in the Palestinian territories occupied since 1967, Richard Falk, supra n. 35, at para. 75, http://www.ohchr.org/EN/HRBodies/HRC/RegularSessions/Session25/Documents/A-HRC-25-67_en.doc, quoting Saad's letter open letter to the prison warden, translated and reproduced at http://www.newprofile.org/english/node/440.

[678] Report of the Special Rapporteur on the situation of human rights in the Palestinian territories occupied since 1967, Richard Falk, supra n. 35, at para. 75.

679 This framework of this accommodation was established in Status Quo Agreement between the Jewish Agency and the Agudat Israel, supra n. 404.

680 Medina, Political Disobedience, supra n. 653, at 91.

681 In 1998, the Supreme Court of Israel ruled that the government lacked legal authorization to grant deferrals or exemptions en masse to Haredi Jews. In 2002, the Knesset enacted the Tal Law, which formally recognized the exclusion of Haredi Jews from military service while seeking to encourage their voluntary enlistment.681 In 2012, the Israeli Supreme Court declared that the Tal Law was inconsistent with the Basic Law: Human Dignity and Liberty (from which the Court inferred a right to equality, since equal protection is not expressly guaranteed in Israeli constitutional law) and could not be extended in its present form beyond that year.681

682 The 2015 Israel Religion & State Index, produced by the trans-denominational Israeli NGO Hiddush, found that 86 percent of the Israeli Jewish public supports requiring Orthodox yeshiva students to do military or national service. The level of support for compulsory service for yeshiva students has consistently stood at 80% or higher since the Index was established in 2009. (See Hiddush, 2015 Israel Religion and State Index (Sept. 16, 2015), at 33, http://hiddush.org/article-15754-0-2015_Religion__State_Index__support_for_religious_freedom_rises.aspx.)

683 Ruth Levush, "Israeli Conscription laws for Ultra-Orthodox Jews," Library of Congress (Apr. 17, 2014), http://blogs.loc.gov/law/2014/04/israeli-conscription-laws-for-ultra-orthodox-jews/. A 2014 poll found that 61 percent of Israeli Jews believed that the Haredi conscription law would not succeed in drafting a significant amount of yeshiva students. See http://hiddush.org/article-6662-0-Hiddush_Releases_2014_Israel_Religion_and_State_Index;_Strong_desire_for_inv olvement_of_world_Jewry_in_efforts_for_freedom_of_marriage.aspx.

684 Naomi Zeveloff, "Ultra-Orthodox Celebrate Rollback of Israel Draft Law," Forward (May 6, 2015), http://forward.com/news/israel/307624/orthodox-draft-laws/.

685 Arik Bender, Jeremy Sharon, and Lahav Harkov "Israeli Parliament Approves Law Exempting Ultra-Orthodox From Army Service," Jerusalem Post (Nov. 24, 2015), http://www.jpost.com/israel-news/politics-and-diplomacy/israeli-parliament-approves-law-exempting-ultra-orthodox-from-army-service-435147.

686 According to the Israeli NGO Hiddush, the number of Haredi recruits dropped by 40 percent in the first half of 2014, immediately before and after the Law's enactment, compared with the second half of 2013. See http://hiddush.org/article-6656-0-Hiddush_report_exposes_Israeli_governments_misleading_claims_about_ultraOrt hodox_enlistment_to_the_IDF.aspx.

687 General Comment No. 23, supra n. 579, para. 6.2.

[688] 2015 USCIRF Report: Russia. All subsequent quotations in Russia paragraph from this report.

[689] 2015 USCIRF Report: Turkey.

[690] 2013 USCIRF Report: Turkey.

www.ingramcontent.com/pod-product-compliance
Lightning Source LLC
Chambersburg PA
CBHW070925210326
41520CB00021B/6806